AFRICAN TEARS

THE ZIMBABWE LAND INVASIONS

AFRICAN TEARS

The Zimbabwe Land Invasions

Catherine Buckle

COVOS DAY

Johannesburg & London

By the same author:
Pookie, the monkey that came to town
The Animals of the Shashani
Rusty Velvet
The Litany Bird

Published by Covos Day Books, 2001
Oak Tree House, Tamarisk Avenue,
P.O. Box 6996, Weltevredenpark 1715, South Africa
Email: covos@global.co.za

Copyright © Catherine Buckle 2001

Cover design by JANT Design
Design and origination by JANT Design
Email: j.design@mweb.co.za

Printed and bound by United Litho

All rights reserved. No part of this publication may be reproduced, stored,
manipulated in any retrieval system, or transmitted in any mechanical, electronic
or digital form or by any other means, without the prior written authority of the
publishers. Any person who engages in any unauthorized activity in relation to this
publication shall be liable to criminal prosecution and claims for civil and criminal
damages.

ISBN 1-919874-27-5

Dedication

African Tears is dedicated to all Zimbabweans who suffered in the year 2000. To those who were beaten, burnt, tortured, raped, lost their homes, or were caught up in any way in the wave of political violence that has engulfed our land.

And, to all those, named and unnamed who died, I dedicate this book:

Mr Banda
Wilhelm Botha
Takundwa Chapunza
Nicholas Chatitama
Zeke Chigagwa
Constable Tinashe Chikwenya
Tichaona Chiminya
Mr Chinyere
Laban Chirwa
Sergeant Alex Chisasa
Alan Dunn
Henry Elsworth
Edwin Gomo
Luckson Kanyurira
Peter Kariza
Messiah Kufandiedza
Talent Mabika

Doreen Marufu
Mationa Mashaya
Onias Mashaya
Samson Mbewe
Rogers Murirawanhu
Musoni Robert
Mandishona Mutandya
Patrick Nabanyama
Mr Ndebele
Tony Oates
Martin Olds
Matthew Pfebve
Thadeus Runukuni
Mr Simudananhu
David Stevens
John Weeks
Finos Zhou

The only thing we have to fear is fear itself

Author's notes and acknowledgements

African Tears tells how a group of strange men arrived at our farm gate, claimed that they were war veterans and that our land was now theirs. It tells how these men moved onto our farm and terrorized me, my family and all the men, women and children who lived on the farm. It tells of a police force that refused to protect our rights. It tells of a government that gave its blessing to the rape of her citizens—a government that described Zimbabwe's land invasions as "a peaceful demonstration by land-hungry peasants".

African Tears tells of my struggle to hang on to a farm that I had run almost completely alone for a decade. A farm whose purchase in 1990 was sanctioned by a government Certificate of No Interest. It was the financial sacrifice we made, which forced my husband Ian to work away from home in order to pay the 46% interest on the purchase loan. Ian too had no choice but to watch as our lives and livelihood were destroyed. I cannot even begin to contemplate his pain. I cannot describe how he felt when he could not protect his land, his home or even his wife and son. That must be Ian's story and I weep for his anguish too.

I wrote *African Tears* because I wanted all Zimbabweans, of all colours, to know what it was like on the other side of the farm fence. I wanted the world to know what this "peaceful demonstration" was really all about, to see beyond the colour of my skin. I wanted to tell the other side of the story. Mostly though, I wrote *African Tears* because I love my country and all the people in it and I want this to stop.

It is with sincere humility that I have decided to donate ten percent of my royalties from the sale of *African Tears* to the family of Patrick Nabanyama. Patrick Nabanyama was abducted at 4pm on 19th June 2000 by a gang of known war veterans. These men were eventually arrested and appeared in court. Most are now free men having benefited from the Presidential Amnesty. Patrick Nabanyama has never been found and is now presumed dead. He leaves behind his wife Patricia (44) and their children: Melinda (2), Melusi (6), Abraham (9) and Mtabisi (14). And Patrick and Patricia's children from previous marriages: Nonsikelelo, Nomathemba, Sithembile and Nomakosi.

The views expressed in this book are my own and do not represent those of any union or organization. Thanking all the people who held out the hand of friendship is almost impossible. I have tried to remember you all.

For your overwhelming love and support, your daily phone calls and the endless conversations. For putting your lives on hold and always being there for us. For taking us in when we were at our wits' end and for helping us to keep our sanity, I thank you: Elizabeth Bishop, Micky and Myrtle Buswell, Bill and Ann Glover, Pauline Henson.

For never giving up. For bombarding us with calls and emails. For offering to take us in. For answering every question and encouraging us to continue. For teaching me more about myself, I thank you: Brenda Burrell, Bev Clarke, Di and Peter Charsley, Pat and John Deary, Suzie Garnett, Kara and Paul Pearce, Margie Rees, Simon Spooner, Lucy Tarr, Anne and Steve Wellsted.

For your loyalty and dedication. For protecting us and for suffering far more than I will ever know, I thank you: Anna, Arthur, Clemence, Emmanuel, George, Isaya, Jane and Wilfred.

For finding words of hope and encouragement. For never forgetting our plight and for your caring and sharing. For your compassion and for allowing me to use your words, I thank you: Ann Anderson, Tony Ballinger, Hayley Balmer, John and Chris Barron, Andrew Bishop, Dr Alex Bishop, Dr David Bishop, Dr Peter Bishop, Dr Nick Bishop, Rob and Sue Braxton, Rob and Mandy Buckle, Karen Collins, Dave and Jenny Coltart, Rich and Lynette Conlon, Eddie Cross, Keith and Kirsten Davel, Malcolm Davidson, Francis Deary, Pat and Helen Doherty, Alan Doyle, Patrick Dube, David Easley, Joan Edridge, Sian Ellis, Mark Everest, Pat Everest, Peter Everest, Debbie Graham, Pam Graves, Ann Harben, Margaret Haslem Jones, Norman Henry, Clifford Gerry Herroth, Colin and Jean Hilligan, Dennis and Jean Hogben, Nigel Hogben, Rockie and Wadzi Katsande, Jill Lambert, Mac and Trish Macdonald, Rob Mandy, David Mills, Barry and Val Morgan, Bessie Muchanyuka-Wilson, Verity Mundy, Ray and Louise Munro, Trevor Ncube, Debbie Nicholl, Michael and Caroline Norton, Ndai Nyamakura, Marty Pereira, Bob and Estelle Pieters, Steve Pratt, John Redfern, James and Marina Reilly, Jonathan Renouf, Charles Riddle, Gayle Rix, Diana Ryan, Bill Saidi, Claudia Senekal, Hellen Silverman, Mark and Shirley Swannack, Heather Tarr, Julian Taylor, Brigitte Theuma, Ray and Caren Tiemstra, David Wheeler, Karl Wright.

For all the people who, like Trevor Ncube, felt betrayed when I finally gave up the struggle, I apologize. I know I had become your hope, but I am only human and could endure it no more.

For all the farmers who are stronger than I, who continue to try, continue to struggle. For all of you who continue to put your lives on the line and grow food for us, I thank you.

Cathy Buckle
January 2001

Contents

Foreword

I will never be able to erase from my mind the BBC Television images of a farm going up in flames, farm workers running for dear life with axe and knobkerrie-wielding Zanu PF youths in hot pursuit on a farm in Domboshawa outside Harare. Tears welled up in my eyes as I watched the footage of the youths torching the farm workers' dwellings and meagre possessions. One of them descended on a dog in its kennel with bricks, stones and sticks killing it mercilessly.

It was a Friday and I had come home slightly early to take a break from a rather traumatic week in Zimbabwe's political life. What was my country coming to? I wondered. The BBC Television crew interviewed the leader of this marauding gang. He said they were destroying the workers' quarters because they were the hideout of the opposition Movement for Democratic Change. I thought how sad it was that political differences in this once peace-loving nation were now legitimate grounds for beating, arson, murder and savagery.

"How was all this possible?" is a recurring question in Cathy's book. Like Cathy I asked myself this question repeatedly during this troubled time.

Cathy is white and I am black. But we have a lot in common. We belong to the same human race and ascribe to the basic norms that have made this race different from animals. The most basic of these is the respect for other human beings and their right to hold and impart views different from our own. We share the same commitment to a constitutional democracy buttressed by the rule of law. But perhaps most important of all in the context of this book is that we are all Zimbabweans in a country we love and cherish dearly. Unfortunately the norms and values we share as Zimbabweans are threatened by Mugabe's naked lust for power.

It is for this reason that when Cathy asked me to write the Foreword to her book I didn't hesitate. Interesting isn't it, that as I write the Foreword I have never set eyes on Cathy. But thanks to the Internet and email I have come to know her as if I had met her in person. I got to know Cathy via her weekly email briefing to the world and city folks like me on what was happening on largely white-owned commercial farms. Cathy used the email to publicize her ordeal, which mirrored the situation on the majority of commercial farms in Zimbabwe. Every week I looked forward to receiving my instalment from Cathy.

"Hour after hour, day after day I sat at my computer sending out hundreds of emails, determined that Zimbabweans and the world would hear the true story", Cathy says in this book. She succeeded in her mission to keep the world informed about Zimbabwe's ordeal. This book will go a long way to ensure that that story is immortalized. As far as I know it is the first book on the effects of the land invasions in Zimbabwe under the pretext of giving land to the people.

There were times when Cathy's email did not arrive and I thought that the worst had happened. But Cathy would soon come through explaining that either her email had been down or the pressure from the thugs occupying her farm had become unbearable. While I heaved a sigh of relief that she was alive, the contents of her email soon brought me back to mother earth with a loud thud. In the comfort of our suburban homes it was so easy to forget the difficulties that those in the rural areas and on commercial farms were going through.

Life was far from normal for Cathy. She and her family lived in terror. Who wouldn't under these circumstances? They were imprisoned in their own home by strangers claiming that the land Cathy and her husband Ian had bought long after Independence in 1980 was theirs. What must have made things even worse was the chilling thought that the government, particularly the head of state who had a duty to afford them protection, had declared white commercial farmers "enemies of the state" and threatened them with death. There was nobody to protect Cathy and her family and the other commercial farmers throughout the country. They were on their own. The police had been told not to interfere as this was a political issue. Court rulings ordering the land invasions be halted had been ignored with impunity by those who had taken an oath to uphold the law. The courts of the land had been rendered impotent.

In many ways Cathy gives the world a unique window into the chaos and mayhem that was unleashed by Zimbabwe's ruling Zanu PF. Her family's ordeal told via the email and now captured in this book adds a human dimension to Robert Mugabe's desperate quest to win the June 2000 general election at any cost. In an attempt to win public support for a crude and openly racist political campaign, Mugabe clothed his ambitions under the garb of redistributing land to the millions of landless black peasant farmers in Zimbabwe. He openly prostituted the people's legitimate cause for land reform to advance his own short-term political agenda. Thus according to Mugabe's propaganda, it was people such as Cathy and her family who were the stumbling blocks to equitable land redistribution in Zimbabwe.

And yet if the truth be told, Mugabe's own government could not escape blame for failing to embark on a land reform programme during the 20 years we have been an independent nation. If anything, Mugabe's regime had made land available to the ruling elite and not the people that he now claimed to be so passionately fighting for. And as Mugabe set out to grab more land from the white farmers, his government was sitting on vast estates acquired in the 1980s that it had failed to redistribute, except to the president's cronies.

Mugabe clearly wanted to project his political campaign as a land reform crusade and as a war between blacks and recalcitrant whites. And yet it wasn't. And many Zimbabweans saw it for what it was, namely Mugabe's frantic attempt to hold onto political power. For the first time since his ruling party was swept into office in 1980, Mugabe faced the real prospect of losing power to an opposition party. The Movement for Democratic Change, formed with the help of the Zimbabwe Congress of Trade Unions and backed by a wide cross-section of society, clearly captured the public mood that it was time up for Mugabe and his cronies.

But it must be said that many whites share with Mugabe and his government the burden of blame for the failure to attend to the land issue. While Mugabe failed to provide the political leadership needed to give direction to a just and properly planned land reform programme over 20 years, the majority of the whites were largely content with the status quo. Their century-old access to land provided them with a firm foundation for economic success. The overcrowded rural areas on their doorstep, overstocked and overpopulated, failed to prick their collective conscience. They were prepared to do nothing that would radically alter their access to this critical means of production. Their failure to be proactive as far as land reform was concerned gave a hostage to fortune.

Zimbabwe has been sadly lacking in both statesmanship and vision in its post-Independence experience. But the ordeal of the past year has brought to the fore men and women of goodwill and purpose who are beginning to refashion our society. Mugabe's hired bands may hold sway in remote parts of the country. But across the country there is a palpable mood of resistance and a confident anticipation of liberation from the tyranny Mugabe has spawned. Ask the youth!

Cathy's emails and now this book tell the story of one family's struggle against state-sponsored terror. A torrent of emotions is what I experienced as I read Cathy's emails. I would become angry as she related the gory events of the previous week. And then my spirits would be lifted by her dogged determination to remain on the farm and fight this evil. But above all, I would be emboldened and encouraged by her call for Zimbabweans not to give in to tyranny. When she couldn't take it any more and lacked the financial resources to stay on the farm, and succumbed to Mugabe's primitive and crude tactics, I must admit to feeling betrayed.

I felt betrayed every time I heard that a white farmer or businessman had decided to leave the country. I felt betrayed when I saw white farmers on television chanting slogans at Zanu PF rallies when they and their workers were not allowed to attend opposition meetings. I felt very betrayed when many whites left the country just before the election in June arguing that they feared that the level of political violence would escalate during this period. I felt betrayed when my own black brothers and sisters succumbed to intimidation and attended Mugabe's rallies against their will. What would it take for Zimbabweans to make sacrifices for the things that they strongly believed in?

Nobody in their normal senses, either black or white, would disagree with the urgent need for land reform to bring the majority of black people into the mainstream economy. Such a land reform exercise could be done in an orderly manner, transparently and based on Zimbabwe's laws. Its main goal and purpose would be to increase agricultural output and contribute to economic growth. I have always believed that not every black person deserves a piece of land and that not every white person is inherently a good farmer.

The colonial racially-skewed land distribution legacy could not be justified. Almost everybody who did not benefit from Zanu PF's patronage system disagreed with the abuse of the legitimate land hunger within the black community in Zimbabwe by the Mugabe regime.

I have never believed that two wrongs make a right. The fact that whites had forcibly removed blacks from their land at the turn of the 20th century did not in any way justify what Mugabe was doing. Are we not supposed to be civilized human beings living in the 21st century and not half-naked savages bent on revenge?

Having watched the country being destroyed in the run-up to the election, I comforted myself by telling myself—and anybody who cared to listen—that after the election Zanu PF would leave us alone to get on with the job of picking up the pieces and rebuilding this country. I honestly believed that after the election, life would revert to some normality. I reasoned that Mugabe's party would win the election but that the opposition would win a significant number of seats to be a factor in parliament.

Realizing that a significant proportion of the electorate had voted against him, I was convinced Mugabe would work towards winning them back by attending to their concerns, namely rampant corruption, an under-performing economy, the breakdown of law and order and withdrawal of our troops from the Democratic Republic of Congo. Indeed I was convinced that the mayhem and the political madness would end with the election.

But I was way off the mark. Mugabe emerged from the June parliamentary poll angry and wounded. He was determined to teach those that had voted against him, namely the commercial farmers and the urban population, a lesson they would never forget. Mugabe would soon after the parliamentary election intensify the onslaught against the white commercial farmers and the urban voters using the army and the ruling party's rent-a-mob. He was in fact already preparing the groundwork for the presidential election in 2002. The main strategy for this political campaign was the systematic use of violence and intimidation to force people to vote for him.

Reading Cathy's book was like reliving those traumatic days in the life of our young nation.

Like Jane, Cathy's storekeeper, many Zimbabweans, black and white, walk around with physical scars bearing testimony to this political madness. Some lost life or limb and many more are psychologically scarred. What for? Did it have to happen?

People were not going to vote for the ruling party because of two decades of economic mismanagement, corruption, cronyism and downright political arrogance. In the past 20 years Zimbabweans had seen their standards of living decline as the politicians and their hangers on grew more opulent. Zanu PF had no record upon which to sell itself to the electorate. To have any chance of remaining in power it had to intimidate and beat up those who did not support it.

Cathy's story is one of courage, of Zimbabweans black and white in the towns and across the countryside in the face of the worst form of provocation, intimidation and psychological torment that this peace-loving country has ever been subjected to.

There are hundreds of farmers who endured similar humiliation and suffering at the hands of the so-called war veterans who could write their own stories on Zimbabwe's botched land redistribution exercise. Indeed, many more black Zimbabweans in the cities and the countryside without a piece of land to call their own have shocking stories to tell about what they endured during those months of horror.

Their only crime was supporting the opposition and in many instances the mere suspicion of being an MDC supporter was good reason to invite trouble of the worst sort. All, to prove that this was not about land at all but about one man's fear of losing political power. About one man's obsession with revenge. And about one man's racial bigotry. Zimbabwe's land invasions were not about land but about Robert Mugabe's desperate bid to leave behind a legacy at whatever cost.

Sadly more people will go through this as Mugabe launches his campaign for the 2002 presidential election. More farmers will be thrown off the land and more people maimed and killed to satisfy Mugabe's insatiable appetite for raw political power.

Yet another dimension to this national drama was the impact of the world's television cameras. With the benefit of hindsight, we must ask the question: Did the television images hinder, aggravate or aid the cause of the larger public in Zimbabwe? Certainly they brought home to the rest of the world the horror Mugabe's followers were prepared to inflict to keep their master in power.

"Peaceful demonstrations", Mugabe called the farm invasions. Nothing could have been less so. For many farmers, years of backbreaking work and investment went up in a puff of smoke. In many instances farm labourers, subjected to abductions, beatings, and "re-education" camps, suffered a worse fate than that of their employers.

But when it came to the polls, both in the February referendum and the June election Zimbabweans voted as one. At the end of the count in June more Zimbabweans had voted against Mugabe's party than for it, a statistic that is rarely mentioned! That unanimity is surely the conclusion Cathy would welcome to her story.

But it is not over yet. Despite such solidarity Mugabe shows no sign of letting go. Zimbabweans will need every scrap of resourcefulness, stamina and goodwill to defeat the evil that stalks our land. It would appear that more African tears and blood will have to flow before Zimbabweans get a government of their choice.

Trevor Ncube
Harare, Zimbabwe
January 2001

ONE..

HONDO

O n Wednesday 1ˢᵗ March 2000 I heard through the very convoluted grapevine, so typical of Africa, that our farm was about to be invaded by war veterans and squatters. I was not the first farmer in Zimbabwe to be overrun by veterans of the 1970s War of Independence. Perhaps it was because I was not the first, that the thought was even more terrifying. In the previous fortnight, dozens of other farms had been invaded and there had been no shortage of film footage on the local and international television stations. Scenes of huge crowds of hostile-looking men and women wielding axes, pangas and hefty sticks and shouting, singing and demanding they be given land, had been making front page news and I could not believe that this was about to happen to me. I was alone on the farm with Richard, my seven-year-old son, my husband Ian being out of the country on business, and I had no idea of what to do, whom to turn to for help or advice. My initial reaction was to get out, evacuate the farm, hide somewhere, run away from the confrontation that so many others had already encountered. How could I do this though? How do you make the decision to walk out on your life, your home, your belongings, everything you have worked so hard for, all the people and animals that depend on you? I didn't know how to start, so decided it was perhaps easier to try to get through it.

Sitting in the living room of a neighbour's house, I didn't really listen to what anyone was saying. Everyone was giving me conflicting advice about the impending invasion. No one could agree on what I should do and as the talk went round and round, I sat hugging my knees, shivering, a deafening roaring in my ears, desperate for someone to shake me awake from this bad dream. But no one did and try as I might, I could not stop the tears. Shaking and sobbing, I couldn't bear another second of it and stumbled blindly out to my truck. Struggling with my hands that had taken on a life of their own, I finally managed to fit my key in the ignition, couldn't thank anyone, couldn't even say goodbye and leaving in a cloud of dust, drove home in a blur. The moment I arrived home I closed myself in my study and made two phone calls, one to my husband and the second to my mother. Both of them asked what I was going to do and what they could do to help. I didn't have any answers to their questions. I didn't know what I was going to do, or what they could do. My mother immediately dropped everything, put her life on hold and came to stay; my husband put plans in place to return home within days. Eventually I managed to calm down enough to be able to face the workers and called a meeting. Ours is a small farm so it didn't take long for the group of seven to gather outside the gate. Because I knew almost nothing, it took only a couple of minutes for me to tell them that we were going to be invaded. Their united reaction was one first of shock and then disbelief.

'They won't come here!' George, the foreman said.

'Aah, it's just talking,' Emmanuel said. 'There's nothing here for them.'

'But we're not designated!' Isaya said, looking to me for acknowledgement. Our farm had never been on any list for government acquisition and I hoped their doubts were right. Certainly there was nothing on our little farm that was of much interest but still we had to be prepared for an invasion and the first priority was to tighten up the security.

We changed every padlock on every gate, of which farms seem to have a large number, and spent all our time repairing holes in the three main security fences and preparing for the unknown. We cleared every blade of grass from underneath the bottom strand of the electric fence surrounding the house so that nothing except a genuine intruder would set off the alarm. All tools, wheelbarrows and any things that could be used as weapons against us, were locked up. We cut all the lower branches of the young trees behind the house and maniacally slashed all the grass around the buildings so that when the invaders came, at least we'd be able to see them. I'd been told that the war veterans were set to come on Saturday morning. At least I had notice; I thought, at least I'd be prepared.

On Thursday morning I held Richard's hand as we walked up the long tree-lined driveway to wait for his lift to school. This was a walk that I usually loved, quality time with my son when we looked at tracks in the dust of creatures that had passed in the night, stopped to pick up pretty stones, inspected dew-laden spider webs and investigated strange animal droppings on the road. Now, for me, the walk was filled with fear. I scanned all around for people hiding in trees, jumped at every rustle in the dry leaves and cocked my head to listen for singing or shouting in the wind. Halfway up the drive I heard someone shouting and calling my name and turned to see Anna, the woman who works in our house, come running through the trees.

'They're coming today,' she called out. 'It's not Saturday, it's today!' Anna's son had seen a notice up outside one of the little shops in the nearby growth point. The notice had said that anyone wanting land should meet at the gates to Stow Farm at 8am on Thursday morning and to bring an axe, panga and their identity cards. Bending down, I took Richard's suitcase from his hand.

'Run home Rich, go on run home to Gogo.' (His name for my mother, Shona for grandmother).

'Why? What's wrong Mum? What about school?' His questions came tripping out and I did not have any answers. I hadn't told him anything yet, not knowing how you explain to a seven-year-old that a bunch of crazed men is going to try to force you out of your house and off your land.

'Just go home Rich, please,' I begged. 'I'll tell you all about it in a minute. You go home and get changed; you can have a day off school today.' Richard turned and started trudging back down the driveway towards the house, looking back over his shoulder every couple of seconds, totally confused. I didn't dare send him to school because I didn't know which way this invasion might go. I might be forcibly evicted, I might be barricaded in, as had happened to other farmers, and then be unable to collect him from school in the afternoon.

The rest of Thursday was a nightmare. All day we waited, to hear shouting and singing, to see crowds of people outside the gate but nothing happened. The anticipation, and not knowing what to expect, was more stressful than anything I'd ever encountered before. Just as hard was trying to explain to Richard what was going on. 'There are some people that want a farm,' I told him. 'But because they haven't got one of their own, they've decided they want our farm.'

'So,' he said, 'we'll just tell the police!' Oh God, don't I wish, I thought, knowing that the police had long since been instructed not to interfere. This was a political issue, they said.

'Yes Rich we will. But when these people come they might make a lot of noise, you know shout and sing and stuff, but we'll just ignore them, okay?'

'Okay,' he said turning back to his Lego, effectively finishing the conversation. Thursday had been a good practice false alarm for me. I had a chance to discover all the things I'd forgotten. Like turning the car round, ready for a hasty exit; like making sure I had all the keys in one place; like getting a change of clothing packed for Richard and me. I also packed a small duffle bag with Richard's most treasured toys and teddies—God forbid he lost or left behind his beloved bedtime friends. It also gave all the workers a chance to prepare. Suddenly dishes and things normally left in the sun outside their houses were put under lock and key; their children were told not to wander out of sight; washing did not hang on the line for very long and they all filled buckets with water, which they kept indoors in case I was unable to run the borehole that supplied their housing complex with fresh water.

By Friday I was sure I was ready. I sent Richard to school and spent the rest of the day packing our most treasured belongings. I chose one room—my small study—where I felt I would be safe in the event that the war veterans got into the house, and locked everything into that room. In there was my computer with its email, my lifeline to the world. I threaded the telephone wires under the door and into my study, moved the kettle and tea things in and enough cigarettes to last me a few days. Now I really was ready.

Saturday morning arrived and, exhausted, with nerves strained to the limit, I let Mum out of the gates. She had urgent business in Marondera and since we didn't know when, or even if, the invasion was going to happen, I told her to leave me, sure that I'd be all right for a couple of hours. I packed Richard's little suitcases and treasures into my sister's car. He was off to have an exciting weekend with her, something I had decided days before, not wanting to have to worry about him, not wanting him to experience whatever terrors lay ahead. The buckets of milk arrived from the dairy and the two workers on duty locked all the gates and left as we had planned. I waved a very tearful goodbye to my son and my sister Wiz, and then everything happened so fast that I was almost caught unprepared.

As my sister's car bumped down the driveway, Jane, our storekeeper, came running through the gum trees from our little trading store. 'They're coming, they're coming,' she screamed. 'Hide yourself, they're coming.'

On her head Jane had a plastic crate with three dozen loaves of bread in it from the store. She had managed to recruit someone to come with her and this woman carried ten dozen sweet buns. So now with all these things to carry, four dogs to coax into the house and the gates to lock, I reached the edge of hysteria.

'Run,' Jane said, 'I'll wait for you. Run!' I ran to the house carrying the large box of bread and buns, dogs sniffing eagerly at all the food, dumped it inside and ran back out to lock the gates.

'Thank you Jane, thank you,' I said, now completely overcome with emotion, crying and sniffing. Jane had seen the people gathering outside our store, she had seen them all with their axes and pangas, had heard others being called to come and join the invasion. She thought there were about 40 of them. Someone had organized them into the spirit of things and they were singing war songs. It was moments away now and my hands were shaking so badly that it seemed to take me forever to clip the padlock onto its chain around the gates. Jane left, running, and now I was completely alone.

I ran to the house, with the dogs more excited every minute by all the activity. Snatching a big box of dog biscuits from the shelf, I finally managed to persuade them all inside, locked two dogs on the front verandah, one in my bedroom and the last in my study. Hurriedly I phoned my Mum on her cell phone but was so terrified and traumatized that all I could say was: 'Don't come home Mum, please don't try to come back.' I didn't want to think of what might happen to her if she arrived back at the gate and was surrounded by an angry mob. I closed and locked the kitchen door, switched on the electric fence, closed all the curtains in the house and waited.

The next five minutes were eternity. It was quiet, so quiet I couldn't even hear the birds outside. All I could hear was my heart pounding and the blood hitting my eardrums. And then it started: whistling, very loud whistling, and one voice shouting clearly, "Hondo, hondo, hondo" (Shona for "war").

When the shouting stopped, the singing began and by then the dogs were going crazy, scratching on the doors to get out, whining, barking and howling. From one window in the pantry I could just see the gate through the thick Hibiscus hedge and could see seven or eight people. They all looked to be men, all wearing dark blue overalls and hats. I knew that they couldn't see me but they were very persistent and kept on singing and then shouting and whistling—calling me to come out. I saw one of them lob a brick at the gate and watched the read-out on the control box of the electric fence suddenly turn from green to red, knowing that the alarm was about to go off. The noise was not something I could deal with, an extremely loud siren that would send the dogs wild and probably the men at the gate too. Hurriedly I switched the alarm off before it could ring and, leaving the fence charged, retreated into my study. I locked myself in and sat down on the floor with my hands over my head.

About ten minutes later all went quiet. The dogs stopped barking and howling and that was perhaps more frightening than the shouting and whistling. I didn't know where they were, where they'd gone. Didn't know if they'd managed to find a way through the security fence and were moments away from smashing the doors down. I picked up the phone and called three of my neighbours, asking if they could try to drive past and see what was happening. I phoned our local farmers' union and told them what was going on and then phoned the police. The minutes dragged by and still nothing happened and at last I pulled myself together and let myself out of my study. It was now 11.30 and I poured myself a stiff drink and sat on a stool by the phone, which was ringing incessantly. Every time I put it down it would ring again—concerned neighbours and friends trying to find out what was happening. Whilst one neighbour walked all around my security fence, another relayed to me what he was saying on his radio—there was no one to be seen. It seemed they had given up and I had managed to avoid the confrontation at the gate.

Some time later the dogs on the front verandah started barking again and I peeped through the curtains. Swarming across the fields below our house were 30 or 40 people, all carrying axes. I couldn't see what they were doing but could hear their singing drifting up belatedly on the wind. I watched with mounting anger as gates were left open and people dispersed in all directions, thanking God that we'd left all the cattle and sheep in their night paddocks close to the house. About half an hour later I saw people starting to go back across the fields and out onto the main road that marks the farm boundary. I let the dogs out and again made all the phone calls, telling everyone that for now it seemed to be over and telling Mum it was safe to come home.

By three in the afternoon my neighbour, Roy, who'd been scouting around in the bush for over three hours, confirmed that they'd all gone. He told me that they'd forced their way onto the farm by cutting off the chain and padlock on the gate of the boundary fence where we cross the road with the cattle for dipping every week.

The whole thing lasted only four hours but they were the longest four hours in my life. I've been chased by elephants, charged by rhinos, ran for my life from bush fires but never been as terrified as I was during those four hours. With little bits and pieces of information from all directions, I managed to piece the events together into some semblance of order. When Jane, the storekeeper, had come running down to the house there had been about 40 people gathered outside the store. They had marched the few metres to our gate on the road and there had stopped and waited while eight men came down the long driveway and tried to roust me from the house. When the men eventually gave up, they returned up the road, picked up the crowd and after marching around the corner cut off the padlock and chain, trashed the gate and were instructed to go onto the fields and peg the land. These pegs, short wooden truncheons hacked from our trees, were hammered into the ground, marking out people's plots, indicating their ownership of the land. A worker of one of my neighbours, unable to suppress his curiosity, had joined in the mêlée and later helped piece another part of the story together. All the gathered people had been told that the whites were going to be forced off the farms and anyone who wanted land should register with our local war veteran, and they would be allocated a plot on our farm. This was after all, they were told, the land of their ancestors and had been stolen from them by the whites. They were further told that the president of the country was going to amend the constitution (by way of invoking his presidential powers) and just take the land from the whites so there was nothing to worry about. This was apparently going to happen in thirty days' time and when it did everyone could come and claim their new plots of land.

As the sun dropped in the sky that evening, I sat quietly with my mother, still in shock about the events of the day. Poor Mum, how hard it was for her to listen to what her child had been forced to endure. When everything had been told, retold and retold again, I made up my mind. I didn't want to stay here any more, not after today. In the last few years the situation had become more and more desperate. With the economy on the brink of collapse, interest rates at over 55 percent and inflation at more than 60 percent, it had become almost impossible to make a living. With our farm on the boundary of a communal land, we were in the front lines of an increasing amount of lawlessness. Almost all the wild game animals that had been resident on the farm for the last decade—reedbuck, kudu, duiker, steenbok and grysbok—had been poached out of existence. Trespassers, woodcutters and firewood gatherers were the order of the day and if we tried to apprehend them, even to warn them, we had to pay the price. Three times in the last year, after stopping people from cutting trees, mysterious fires had sprung up on the farm in the middle of the night. Fishing in our three little dams by a handful of children a decade ago had now reached outrageous proportions and we regularly removed very large nets strung from one side of the dam to the other. We had to spend an increasing amount of time and money securing our fences. Poles were regularly pulled out of the ground, droppers snipped off the fence and wire removed. On one particularly outrageous occasion, three or four men had been poaching and had the audacity to take their kill under a tree in full view of our farm road where they proceeded to skin their civet cats, guinea fowl and mongoose. The police not once came to our assistance, always saying that these were minor incursions. So, the arrival of the squatters and war veterans had put the lid on things for me. I'd had enough.

Idly I picked up the weekly newspaper Mum had brought home. Too depressed to read the front page and my mind too confused to concentrate, I flipped the paper over and read the back page headlines: "Chris and Cath are, or should be, our cue". Shocked to see my name, I read on. Responding to a letter I'd written to a weekly newspaper a fortnight before, the columnist had picked up on my pleas for the government to let us farm in peace. He'd applauded both my sentiments and compared my hard work with that of a young black Zimbabwean farmer.

Suddenly I felt ashamed of my earlier thoughts of defeat. Here I was, along with others, being held up as an example to the country. How could I give up now? What hope was there for my country of birth if I couldn't take more pressure, hold up just a little bit longer while the electioneering ran its course? Doing something I'd never done before, I wrote to the columnist and concluded my letter with: "Thank you, I think, for encouraging me to give it another go".

Later that evening I sat and thought about everything that had happened. In retrospect, perhaps it wasn't so bad. I had survived the "hondo" at the gate, the people had come and pegged out their plots and had left. There wasn't actually anyone living on our farm that night; they hadn't actually forced me off the property or out of the house.

Sleep was a long, long time coming. Every creak and groan of the tin roof was a war veteran, every hoot of our resident barn owls was someone at the gate. I couldn't get out of my mind the horrific pictures in a recent daily newspaper. Pictures of a farm that had been invaded, of the farm house that had been "liberated", of the war veterans sitting in the farmers' lounge, watching his television, playing with his computer. I tossed and turned until almost dawn and finally fell asleep knowing that right would prevail, that this would be over soon. That there were still 30 days before the constitution was to be amended and that was a long time. Something was bound to happen between now and then; someone was bound to put a stop to these invasions; the police were sure to begin doing their jobs; the world would never allow this to continue; the courts were bound to force the powers that be to stop this violation of our human and constitutional rights.

How wrong I was. About everything!

THE RAPE OF THE LAND

The morning after the initial invasion of our farm, I felt devastated. Stress, fear and exhaustion were already taking their toll and I ached from top to bottom. The phone started ringing at six in the morning and my first visitors arrived shortly after seven. Bill and Ann and their two teenage children had decided that they were going to do a complete sweep of the farm for me and had left Harare early. It was silly but as soon as they got out of the car I started crying as we embraced. Having been friends for over 25 years, they knew everything about our struggle to build up the farm and were as shocked as I was. For a moment we all laughed at the only evidence I had of yesterday's furore at the gate—a couple of half bricks and three or four branches from our fig tree that lay strewn on the driveway. Leaving Bill and the teenagers, Nina and Daniel, to go on their marathon search of the 1,000-acre farm, Ann and I did what we always do, drank tea and tried to make sense of what was happening to our beloved country.

Barely a fortnight before, a referendum had been held questioning the adoption of a new constitution. Bombarded with propaganda on both local radio and television and with probably as much as three quarters of the population not having even seen the proposed new constitution, the people of Zimbabwe voted against its adoption. This was undoubtedly where and why the farm invasions had started. The new constitution had covered a wide range of changes and one of them had been the seizure or compulsory acquisition of white-owned farms without payment of compensation for the land itself. Since 1977 the government had been trying to take, in the first instance, over 1,400 white-owned farms. A list had been published in the local press of the farms the government was going to seize and there had begun a series of appeals and legal wranglings to try to put the land question in Zimbabwe into perspective. The real problem was that of the 1,400 farms the government had listed for compulsory acquisition, the large majority were highly productive properties, growing huge hectarages of wheat and maize, producing highly valuable foreign currency crops such as tobacco, export quality flowers and vegetables.

As farmers we were all to blame for the position we now found ourselves in as our lands were invaded. When the list came out in 1997, we all made a lot of noise, offered alternatives and suggestions, but left it up to someone else to sort out. We assumed that somewhere along the line someone would step in and do this thing properly. We believed that specialists would be called in, experts consulted and mediators appointed who would handle the highly emotive issue diplomatically and to the satisfaction of all. We assumed that this was in fact happening. (Perhaps it was).

When Ian and I bought our farm in 1990, before we could even begin the process of finding the funding and obtaining the title deeds, we had to apply for government permission to purchase this particular piece of land. This process had been in place for some time. As every farm went on the market, the property had to be offered first to the government. If they were not interested in it, they would give a Certificate of No Current Interest. For our little farm in Marondera, bought ten years after Independence, we had the certificate, knew this land wasn't wanted by the country, was not on "The List", and started to try to build the property up, thinking it was ours forever.

'But,' said Ann, as we drank our fourth, or was it fifth, cup of tea, 'we all know this isn't about land.'

'No, it isn't,' I said. 'It's about politics. But it doesn't mean that, as farmers, we were right to sit here all these years thinking that this land thing would go away or sort itself out. I just wish we'd done more Ann, much more, so that the government couldn't play the land card again to win another election.'

'I know, it's just vote buying. Let's face it, they got a real shock when they lost the referendum. I think they didn't realize how disenchanted the people are. You know, inflation at over 60 percent, unemployment at over 56 percent. Times are really hard and people have had enough of corruption and bad governance.'

'Yes but land is an issue; we all know it is. And Ann, I'm just so angry. Angry at myself for every meeting I didn't go to, every letter I didn't write, every debate I didn't take part in. We should never have let it get to this stage.'

'I'll put the kettle on again,' Ann said as we saw the weary foot soldiers trudging back up from the fields after their search.

Hours of tramping across the fields through tall, dew-laden grass, had exhausted my guests who were covered in blackjacks, mud, burrs and scratches and were gasping for tea. They hadn't found much aside from the pegs that the invaders had planted. Bill laughed as he explained that the pegs were half-metre-long sticks hammered into the mud and stones, sticks that would probably fall over in the wind, certainly would not stand up to the heavy hooves of our breeding herd of cattle. Aside from that there wasn't much to see. Every now and again there were scrapes in the ground where someone had marked out the boundaries of their future plot and some of the fences were damaged where the invaders had pushed their way through. Bill had carefully closed all the gates that had been left open the previous day and we all laughed at the lack of visible proof that I had to justify my terror of Saturday, 1st March.

As Bill and Ann left, our next-door neighbours arrived. Myrtle would not take no for an answer and had brought lunch with her. She and Micky were determined that I needed cheering up and before long we all sat with gin and tonics in hand and the whole story had to be told all over again. Later still, Roy, the neighbour who had helped out so much during the fracas at the gate, also arrived and presented me with a memo from our local farmers' union entitled "Guidelines in the event of a squatter invasion". I giggled a bit as the gin took effect. It was rather late now to be telling me what to do but as I read the list of points, I felt afraid again. Perhaps this wasn't over; perhaps it was in fact just beginning.

1   Lock all security gates.
2   Do not negotiate with the squatters. You are wasting time and putting yourself at risk.
3   Do not provide them with accommodation, food or water.
4   Stay calm, do not panic and do not be intimidated.
5   Report all crime ie wood-cutting and theft to the police.

There were a further eight points but for now I'd seen enough. Perhaps my invasion had been the exception rather than the rule. "My" lot had come, seen and gone. Where or when did all these other things come from: accommodation, food, water, theft? As I felt an icy chill sweeping over me, I filled my glass again and tried not to think further than just that day. In my naïve way I was still convinced that it was all going to blow over, just go away. Only two days previously, a High Court Order had been issued instructing squatters and war veterans to vacate all commercial farms that they had invaded. Admittedly nothing had happened yet but, after all, this was a weekend. I was sure that by the next morning reports would start coming in of police evicting people from farms across the country. As my seven-year-old son had so innocently said a few days before, 'We'll just tell the police.'

By the end of the weekend, life had returned to some sort of normality. Richard had come home after a wonderful weekend with his aunt, spoilt rotten and full of himself.

'So,' he demanded, hands on hips, 'did they come?'

'They came Rich and sort of shouted and stuff and then they wandered around the farm for a bit, but they've gone now.'

For now my explanation sufficed but that night when Richard went to bed, he took all his teddies under the blankets with him, instead of the normal one. This was the first warning sign that I didn't really pay attention to—that Richard was already under stress because of the disruption to his routine and our lives.

The following morning the state-run *Herald* screamed front-page headlines: "State gives notice to amend constitution". The government, oblivious to the fact that 60 percent of the population had rejected the proposed draft constitution, had decided to go ahead and make an amendment to the existing law of the land. The Amendment Bill would, within a month, bring into law the issue of taking land without paying compensation for it and, in a move that would herald the beginning of a war of words between Britain and Zimbabwe, a part of the Bill read: "The former colonial power has an obligation to pay compensation for agricultural land compulsorily acquired for resettlement". It continued that if Britain would not provide the money for land that government acquired, then the Zimbabwean government was under no obligation to pay compensation. In the weekly *Financial Gazette*, the commissioner of police, when asked what the police were going to do about enforcing the High Court Order, was quoted as saying: "It's a political issue. What do you expect the police to do?" This did not augur well for the land crisis, the invasions or the confidence of the farmers and left us feeling not only angry and alone, but really frightened about our legal rights as citizens of this beautiful country.

As was to be the case so many times in the following weeks and months, a tiny shred of hope came then in a pronouncement by the Home Affairs minister when he ordered war veterans to vacate the farms they had occupied. But, on the same day, the president directly contradicted his minister and in a television interview stated: 'No, we are not going to put a stop to the invasions that are demonstrations, peaceful demonstrations and lawful demonstrations by the ex-combatants.' At this statement I felt a combination of nausea and hysteria and was more than a little tempted to rattle the gates of State House, push a few pegs into the lush lawns and see how my peaceful demonstration would be taken. Clearly there was conflict within government itself that could only be resolved there or perhaps through the ballot boxes in the pending elections. For now though, we farmers were alone and would have to manage as best we could.

As the days passed there were more and more invasions of farms all over the country and with a feeling of desperation and powerlessness, I wrote an appealing letter to a weekly newspaper asking Zimbabweans if they were going to sit by and watch the agro-based economy of Zimbabwe collapse completely. Having described the weekend's events at the gate, I wrote: "Are you okay about this? Can you empathize at all with the people supplying the food you are eating, the clothes you are wearing, the cigarettes you are smoking, the foreign currency that is allowing you to live the way you are living? Are you going to continue sitting in your living rooms watching your DStv while this goes on?" I ended with a series of questions that no one was able to answer but which I hoped would make people think: "Now must I wait the thirty days and go through it all again? What would you do? Do you think we farmers are made of the same stones that pave my farm? Do you really think we are a bunch of racist Rhodies who should leave?"

Perhaps it was my letter published in the *Independent* or perhaps it was coincidence, but the war veterans returned to our farm within days and this time they came to stay.

Exactly a week and a day after the first bunch of war veterans came to the gate of our farm, they returned but this time didn't announce their presence; they simply cut the wire on our boundary fence and moved into the field about 100 metres below the house. By now Ian was home and it was an enormous relief not to have to deal with this violation on my own. Again we had evacuated Richard to my sister's house so that he wouldn't have to see what was going on, stupidly thinking that what he didn't see wouldn't hurt him. At mid-morning there were about 30 people in the field, sitting peacefully and patiently in the grass listening as someone addressed them. All day there were people on the land—some would leave and others would arrive. At times there were upward of 100 people there and nothing we could do about it. As evening approached most of the people dispersed and the leaders, clearly unsure about what to do, spent the night around a campfire on the verge of the road, just outside our boundary fence. The next morning though, they had obviously made up their minds and in our field, further down from where they'd held their meetings, under a big old Msasa tree, was a blue tent. Through binoculars we could see the smoke of a campfire and five or six people huddled around it. On Monday morning I phoned the Marondera police, reported the incident and they said that "until someone gets hurt" there was nothing they could do. That was a great comfort, I thought—until someone gets hurt. By this time over 300 farms around the country had been invaded and the police, still without orders or direction, clearly had all the answers worked out perfectly.

As the week wore on there was no indication at all that our campers were going to move. If anything they were settling in. Regularly we saw them tramping backwards and forwards carrying buckets, blankets, pots and pans and heavy bags obviously filled with food. One morning as Ian and I headed out of the driveway, we were waved down by a man who came running over to the truck. I was driving and Ian told me to stop so that we could talk to him. I was hesitant but stopped, leaving the car in gear, ready to roar off if need be.

'Hello Mr and Mrs Buckle,' the man said, 'I am Edward. I am the war veteran of this area and I wanted to let you know that I am the one sleeping here on your farm.'

I was temporarily struck dumb and with my foot hovering on the throttle, let Ian do the talking.

'Oh,' Ian said, 'we don't want any trouble, Edward.'

'Aah, there's no trouble here,' Edward said. 'We are just sitting here until we get further orders from the Party.'

Edward then proceeded to pull out of his pocket a very dog-eared page from a newspaper dated 17th December 1979 and asked Ian for directions to another farm in the area. This page that Edward had was a supplement to a newspaper that had a list of farms that had been designated by government three years before. Ian and I grinned at each other. This takes the cake, I thought; he's asking us for directions to a property he wants to invade. Edward rambled on, showing Ian the list and explaining that the ones with blue ticks next to them were the ones they "had hit" and eventually asked us if we could give him a lift into Marondera town. He said he had to draw money to pay his men, the men who were helping him squat on our property. Politely Ian said we weren't going into town and started to wind his window up, the signal I had been waiting for and we left fairly rapidly. Later— unannounced and unexpected—we had a contingent of police arrive at the gate. They were passing by and had called in to see what the situation was. They were only interested in what physical damage had been done and what the loss of revenue was to the farm. We told them everything and they left saying they were going down to the tent to talk to the men there and that was the last we saw of them. That night was a very bad one for us. Edward had obviously been successful in getting his money and there was a beer drink going on down at the tent. It was a full moon and the dogs barked incessantly as the raucous laughter and shouts of drunken men filled the still night air and seemed to go on until almost dawn.

When we woke up the next morning we saw immediately the response of our squatters to the visit from the police. The blue tent had moved and was now much closer to us, about 100 metres below our house, standing under a big old Muhacha tree. A Zimbabwean flag had been erected atop a very long bamboo pole that had been planted in the open field. Now there was no way of avoiding them and it seemed as if they were always watching us. There was almost nowhere we could go now without them watching us. They watched as we went to switch on the borehole three times a day. They watched when I went out to feed the chickens. They watched as I weeded and watered my little vegetable garden. They watched when we checked the cattle and the sheep. They watched me going up to the store. They watched as we walked in our own garden. They watched every time we drove out of the gate. This was almost intolerable and at night I felt sure they were patrolling outside our security fence and watching which lights went on and off and where. This was a desperate situation and I spent hours writing dozens of letters to human rights organizations begging for help, for intervention. Not even one of them answered so I resorted again to a letter, this time to the weekly farming newspaper.

"For God's sake what's happening? We've had enough!" I said in my letter and begged the farmers to take action—anything to put a stop to this. I suggested a boycott of perishable produce. I knew this was pretty radical but the situation was getting out of hand and perhaps the time had come for drastic action. It had been going on for a month, there were over 500 affected farms and nothing was being done. Nothing could be done though. The farmers despaired of help. Union officials were fearful of taking any action that could be seen as antagonistic. Dr Grant, a senior official with the Commercial Farmers' Union was interviewed by the *Financial Gazette* and said: 'We have given up hope. The whole commercial farming sector is just going to grind to a standstill since the invasions are now a free-for-all.'

Pressure was beginning to mount though as the European leaders urged an end to the farm invasions and a restoration of law and order. By now it had become blatantly clear though, that it was a highly charged political manoeuvre and was not going to be easy to stop. It became even more frightening when a senior official from the War Veterans' Association played the next card of what was appearing to be a master plan. The first card had been land, the second was race. Whites, farmers in particular, were accused of attempting to return the country to its previous status of being a colony. On the front page of the *Daily News*, the War Veterans' official said that members of his association would go to any lengths to prevent any party except the ruling party from controlling the country. He further said that the former fighters had arms caches hidden all over the country and would go back to war if necessary. When asked if he thought the weapons would still be functional after 20 years, the official said: 'We will get arms from the government armouries ... we will invade military camps just as we have gone to the farms.'

Threat or promise? It was hard to tell and perhaps even harder to tell who was now pulling the strings, who was actually at the helm.

In the third week of March, another High Court Order, upholding the first one, was granted in favour of farmers, ordering war veterans and squatters off all farms within 24 hours. Eagerly we watched the response of the men in their little blue tent in our field. The days passed and nothing happened; in fact, if anything, the situation actually became worse.

As Saturday approached, the rumours drifting down to the house were that something big was going to happen at the weekend and again we braced for trouble; again we evacuated Richard to his aunt for the weekend. At 10 o'clock on Saturday morning, the nonsense began. Fifty head of cattle from the neighbouring communal land were pushed through what was now known as the "liberated gate" and into our land. In a truly rustic setting with the tent, the flag fluttering in the wind and a campfire burning, people began arriving from all directions. Some walked in, others came on their bicycles and then more started coming in pickup trucks. Soon there were cars parked on the verge, two small trucks parked at the tent itself and when a seven tonner arrived, there must have been almost 200 people in our field below the house. I began to feel really frightened! That was a lot of people and although they were down in the fields, it was a frightening build-up from the usual half dozen men who lived in the tent. Thank God I'd evacuated Richard, I thought, as I felt the nausea of panic flooding my system. Ian and I watched through binoculars and soon a red car arrived bringing a very portly and well-dressed man. He was obviously the guest speaker and almost immediately everyone sat down in the grass. From our hiding place, we could see 200 arms with clenched fists being raised, again and again; we could very clearly hear the shouts, 'Pamberi, pamberi.' With each passing minute my fear increased, knowing only too well how the hypnotic effect of slogan chanting can lead to action. I left Ian watching and ran to the house and with shaking hands phoned the police.

'Please, please,' I begged, 'can you send someone out here?'

The officer I was speaking to informed me that they were unable to help with any "rural" reports over the weekend.

Incensed I slammed the phone down and phoned everyone I could think of, asking each one please to call the police on my behalf. Perhaps if they were bombarded with calls they would do something. Sure enough, half an hour later a police Land Rover arrived at our gate. Three policemen, unarmed, had come to deal with over 200 chanting, shouting people. They looked visibly uncomfortable when I told them what was going on. They had not yet been given any orders, they said. They could do nothing.

'But what about the Court Order?' I asked.

'We are not allowed to act on instructions from the media,' one answered. Although they all knew about the High Court ruling as it had been splashed all over the newspapers, they had not been given direct, verbal orders by the commanding officer and so could do nothing.

'Oh please, this is ridiculous!' I said. 'Can't you at least find out what's going on down there? There're a lot of people and we are really scared of what may happen. Can't you at least tell them not to move the tent any closer to the house and to remove all their cattle?'

Finally, perhaps shamed by a terrified white woman, the three policemen agreed, promising to return and tell me what they had found.

Intrigued to see what would happen, I relocked the gate and raced back to where George, Emmanuel and Ian were hiding. Ian had gone through the bush with his video camera and I huddled in next to my workers who were clearly as frightened as I was.

'What's happening?' George asked.

'Watch!' I grinned and pointed to the road where we could see the police Land Rover stopping on the verge. A large body of people got up instantly and started across the field, whether to go towards the police or to escape from them was unclear and I shuddered, glad I wasn't in that vehicle.

'Look,' Emmanuel said and we passed the binoculars from hand to hand as the police got back into their vehicle and for one dreadful moment I thought they were going to do a U-turn and leave. Instead they bumped across the field and headed directly for the tent. The three got out and stood close together as one man came out of the crowd and spoke to them. For 20 minutes the police stayed in the field and although I was never to discover what had really been discussed, I did feel slightly comforted by both their presence and their courage in confronting such a large crowd of people. They came back to the house chuckling and giggling, like nervous schoolboys who have narrowly escaped being caught by the headmaster. They said that I shouldn't worry, nothing was going to happen to us, it was all right, it was just some sort of a meeting.

Later when Ian arrived home and we watched the video footage I could only sit and cry with my hands over my mouth. I'd had enough.

The next day I did the only thing that I seemed to be good at. I wrote another letter to the newspaper titled *When is enough, enough?* I related the story of the previous week's events and began to understand as I wrote, the full impact of this invasion of our land.

"...Two small earth dams are now in "liberated land" and I can no longer water my livestock. I have had to move all my cattle and probably only have enough grazing for another three or four weeks. The liberated land now sports 50 head of communal cattle—pushed in to graze my fields every morning. The liberated land also includes two plantations, each of 10,000 gum trees we grew to provide poles and paper for Zimbabwe".

"Today, 24 hours after the eviction deadline, my new neighbours hacked down 30 gum trees to build their houses—gum trees that I have nurtured for six years. They stripped bark off nearby Msasa trees to strap their shelters together. I too feel completely stripped now, of all my human rights".

"When is enough, enough? When will the outside world stop blaming me for being a white landowner and see this for what it really is? When will I again be able to sleep at night secure in the knowledge that no one is watching me? When will I be allowed to get on with the business of growing food for Zimbabwean stomachs?"

"Will it be enough when all the farm-dependent towns like Marondera are gone? Will it be enough when Zimbabweans have to import all the food on their tables? Can any of us, town and country alike, ever feel safe again when the police refuse to act? I don't know about you, but I'm ashamed to be a Zimbabwean at the moment".

THREE..

VERY, VERY, VERY SEVERE

By launching, again, into print with the story of what was happening on our farm, I attracted the attention of the world's journalists who, like everyone else in the country, wanted to know what was really happening on Zimbabwe's farms. Our first visitors were three French women who happened to call when we were out. They arrived at the now permanently locked, electrified gates and interviewed Emmanuel, a loyal and trusted worker who had been with us almost a decade. It was with great importance that Emmanuel told us of the interview when we arrived home some hours later.

'Is Mrs Buckle afraid?' they had asked him.

'Oh no, we are not scared here.'

'Is she worried about her safety?'

'Oh no, we are not worried here.'

'Are the war veterans nearby?'

'Oh no, they are far away,' Emmanuel replied. A master at the art of understatement, Emmanuel dealt with the reporters, downplayed everything and they left, never to be seen or heard of again.

My letter to the paper had also attracted the attention of a CNN Television reporter who phoned and asked if he could interview us, take some film and tell our story. At first I was keen but then decided it was only fair to ask our workers what they thought. They lived on the farm too and anything I did personally would have repercussions on us all. I called them together and put the suggestion forward for discussion. By then most of us realized the power of the pen as everyone had read my last letter to the paper. My words, in print for thousands of people to read, had caused much excitement on our dusty little farm, particularly those about the children:

> *Trying to explain all this to my seven-year-old son was not easy. His friends in Grade 3 at the nearby government school are all, as he calls them, "Shonas". His best friend at the weekends is the daughter of one of my workers and the two have breakfast, lunch and supper together as if they were joined at the hip. Richard and Linnet are inseparable. Together they wander the farm and have their adventures.*

It didn't take long for a decision to be reached. As one the workers said no to the CNN Television crew. It was too dangerous; others with cameras would follow; we would draw too much attention to ourselves and the small group of men living in our field might get angry and then the situation could get totally out of control. A couple of days after I had declined an interview with the CNN reporter, I watched the television news with horror as the very same journalist covered the situation on another farm. The war veterans became angry and both the farmer and the CNN interviewer were caught in a scuffle and pushed around. In a separate incident, a South African news crew visited an invaded farm in Karoi. The resultant film footage was horrifying as scores of war veterans became incensed at one point, surrounded the vehicle, shouting and foaming at the mouth, clubs raised, a gun in view. Later, that farmer wrote of the experience and explained how two days of filming and five hours of film footage were shown out of sequence and out of context, saying the reporters had "...resorted to sensational journalism, choosing to focus on my anger and not the reasons for it..." How easily that could have been me, how quickly things could get out of control. Much as I wanted our story to be told, I decided that television was not the way and promised myself that I would not allow any cameras onto our farm. I was determined though, not to be silenced. I knew my words were already having an effect. My sister Wiz phoned and read the words of a columnist in the *Daily News*:

> *Mobs of so-called war veterans are openly breaking the law and those entrusted and paid to uphold it watch in satanic fascination as defenceless law-abiding citizens are intimidated and victimized and their*

*property vandalized and robbed. I am not ashamed to say tears welled up
in my eyes as I read of Catherine Buckle's horrifying experiences.*

While tempers were rising on farms around the country and the world's
cameras were closing in, so too was the general outrage in the cities
growing. One of the two opposition members in the 150-seat parliament
chose this point to publish a comprehensive list of all the farms bought from
white farmers by the government since 1990. The list, running to eleven
and a half typed A4 pages, showed whom the farms had been leased to, for
how long and at what price. There was an uproar of proportions seldom
seen in our previously placid country. Front page headlines in a local daily
newspaper screamed: "270 farms go to VIPs". The opening sentence of the
report read: "More than 270 state farms were allocated to government
officials…" It went on to say: "Her list shows that 272 VIPs, including a
minister and two deputy ministers, have been allocated government
farms". It was with gaping mouths that the country read the names of all
the VIPs who had been given more than 50 percent of the farms that the
government had bought from white farmers, supposedly to give to landless
peasants. There was the speaker of parliament, a handful of permanent
secretaries, governors, high court judges, members of parliament and very
high officials in the police department.

Now, more than ever before, it became clear why nothing was being
done to protect the farmers, and probably never would be. There was
too much at stake, too many high-up people had far too much to lose.
The writing was on the wall, in capital letters.

With an increasing sense of foreboding and a feeling of growing
isolation, when we thought things couldn't possibly get much worse,
when we wondered who on earth we could turn to for help, yet
another avenue of assistance was turned into a cul-de-sac. The minister
of Agriculture was picked up by the police and arrested in connection
with fraud allegations at the country's Grain Marketing Board, the sole
buyer and seller of all the country's maize and wheat. If any of us
farmers had thought of turning to our minister for assistance with the
invasion of our land, we had to think again. With every possible surface
in our farmhouse covered with newspapers, emails and reports of the
collapse of the country, I went outside to hear from our foreman
George what he had found on his morning patrol of the farm.

'It is becoming very serious,' George said, 'They are cutting trees
everywhere, many, many trees.'

I listened with increasing depression as George described how more
than 30 gum (eucalyptus) trees had been chopped down since the day

before. The invaders had started building a hut on the farm; they were moving in and building a permanent structure. These huts are made primarily from poles that are dug into the ground a few centimetres apart. When a circle of poles has been constructed, they are strapped together and the gaps filled with mud. The structure is then topped with a frame of lighter poles onto which thatching grass is tied. George, Clemence and Isaya said they had found only one half-built house and I called Ian so that we could all go down into the fields together and film what the workers had seen. With me driving so that Ian could operate the video camera, we went down the bumpy farm track. We passed three groups of people who stared at us defiantly, young men in their early thirties and I felt really afraid at their gall, and at my reaction to it. I didn't dare stop the car and ask them what they thought they were doing. I didn't dare rattle off my usual speech that I had used so many times before: "This is private property, you are trespassing, etc etc". Instead I drove on, trying not to catch their eyes, trying not to see their arrogant stares, my knuckles white around the steering wheel. I drove past them, my head filled with swear words, my mouth tightly closed.

We stopped at the gum plantation and I just stared. There weren't any words and I angrily brushed the tears away. The plantation was being raped: huge trees that I had intended to harvest this coming winter, were gone. So too were the fences that surrounded the plantation. Poles had been pulled out of the ground, droppers stripped and the few lengths of wire that hadn't been stolen lay in tangled heaps in the dust. Everywhere there were drag marks where the felled trees had been pulled out of the plantation to be used by the invaders either for firewood or for the construction of their huts. As we drove back to the homestead we went very slowly past the blue tent. A washing line of stolen fence wire had been strung between two huge wild plum trees and their clothes fluttered in the breeze. There were four men at the tent and they all came out and stood, hands on hips, daring us to stop, to challenge them. We didn't. The following morning when George returned from his patrol, the news was even more depressing. In what can only have been an act of angry defiance at our presence the day before, the war veterans had felled an enormous indigenous tree, perhaps 50 or 60 years old. The branches had been hacked off and were strewn all over the farm road so that now we could no longer go down to our own plantations and see what was happening, unless we were prepared, or brave enough, to walk there. Twice I phoned the police in Marondera; twice they promised to come but never did.

The 23rd of March 2000 was to be yet another landmark in the calendar of Zimbabwe's farm invasions. The original High Court Ruling handed down by Justice Paddington Garwe some days previously had declared the land invasions unlawful. The ruling had ordered that all squatters and invaders were to vacate the farms within 24 hours of the granting of the Order. Nothing had happened though, and then on 23rd March the police applied to be absolved from the Court Order. If it wasn't so serious it would have been funny that a country's police force were applying to the High Court to be allowed not to do their jobs—jobs that our taxes paid for. In yet another front-page headline, the *Daily News* reported that the deputy commissioner of police had applied to the High Court for a Variance on the ruling. He said:

> *The problem is both a racially and politically charged powder-keg ready to explode, if not handled with great care and political astuteness... The solution to the land issue lies in the political domain and not with the courts.*

Instead of leaving it there and going to the courts, the deputy commissioner went on to tell the country that the Zimbabwe Republic Police had no money, or food or fuel with which to mount an operation of the size necessary to remove squatters from the farms. The country then turned its attention to the minister of Home Affairs, looking to him not only for instruction and guidance but, we hoped and prayed, for sanity. Minister Dabbing, the man the police force were answerable to said, 'My hands are tied. I have absolutely nothing to do with the police following the ruling, although I am the minister responsible.' Here was another branch of the civil service, yet more people whose salaries we paid, refusing to do anything and so we turned to another day, completely helpless.

While we waited, again, with bated breath for the court hearing and the outcome of the police request for a Variance, the week was drawing to a close and we were preparing for the now familiar influx of people onto our land. It was Richard's Sports Day at school that weekend, scheduled to be an all-day affair and again we went through the agonies of what to do. Dare we go out and leave the farm untended, dare we drop Richard and collect him later—assuming of course we weren't prevented from getting in and out of our own gates. Finally I went to the school and saw the sports teachers. They immediately said that Richard was already so traumatized by what was happening at home that the best thing would be to keep him away from the Sports Day. Here again was another little hint that everything was not all right with Richie but I'm ashamed to say that my mind was so occupied with what was going to happen at the weekend on the farm, that I didn't pick up on the words of the teachers.

Steve Pratt, our Commercial Farmers' Union representative in Mariner had phoned me a couple of times in the last day to warn us of a big invasion. Steve, a farmer himself, also trying to deal with the invasion of his own land, was up to his eyes with the farm invasions and sounded permanently exhausted. Steve said that he had heard from reliable sources that our farm had been named for a big new invasion this weekend and told us to prepare for trouble. When Ox Hacking and Julian Herbert also phoned and then visited us, the hairs on the back of my neck began to prickle. All of these men were in the front line of the farm invasions, all were well-known men in our community and high up in the CFU. All three had offered enormous support when our farm had initially been invaded. By Friday three squatter houses had been built on our fields below the house. The war veterans, most of whom were in their early twenties and therefore physically incapable of having fought in a war that ended 20 years before, had started to increase in number. They had posted guards at "their liberated gate"—previously the gate we had used to cross the road to dip our cattle at a neighbouring farm. By Friday lunchtime, instead of the normal six or seven men at the tent, there were 30 of them and I was beginning to feel really frightened. Filled with panic, I started packing.

'What's wrong Mum?' Richie said to me when he arrived home from school on Friday lunchtime. 'Where are we going?'

The dining room and lounge were a mass of boxes, bubble pack and newspapers.

'We're not going anywhere poppet,' I answered. 'We just thought we'd move some of our special things to Aunty Wiz's house.'

'Oh,' he said, thought for a moment and then continued, 'Is it in case the war vets come and try and take our house?'

I didn't know what to say so I just hugged him and told him to go and play with Linnet. So wrapped up in our own panic and the collapse of law and order, the loss of our business, our livelihood and perhaps even our home, I had paid precious little attention to the fears of our son. I had no idea he knew as much as he obviously did, didn't realize that all the horrors we saw on television, of war veterans evicting people from their homes, he saw too—and understood what he was seeing. What a mess I thought. Our lives were falling apart, piece-by-piece.

Late on Friday afternoon we moved a truckload of packed cartons and our more treasured possessions to my sister's house in the town. As an afterthought we also left my truck there so that if we had to leave the farm in a hurry, at least Ian and I could be together in one vehicle. Richie waved goodbye to us gaily as he sailed around his aunt's garden on his bicycle—probably relieved to be away from all the stress on the farm.

Saturday came and Ian and I were very tense, snapping at each other and continually peering down the fields to see what was happening with the men at the tent—in the event there was nothing more than the usual Saturday gathering. Fifty or so people sat in the grass in front of the tent. A man arrived in a car, addressed the crowd and then left. In an email I sent that night to my sister in England, I wrote:

> We had been led to believe that today was going to be some sort of a showdown but it came to nothing. Rich has had a wonderful day with his Aunty Wiz and just phoned me to tell me that he's having fried eggs, spaghetti and fried mashed potato for his supper—far better than the p. butter sandwich he would have got if he was home! ... Scary news on the satellite TV this afternoon—Peter Hain said that UK had prepared to accept 20,000 white Zimbabweans—they obviously also think this is getting out of hand.

That night a neighbour phoned to tell us what he had found out. He had asked one of his workers to drift down to the meeting in our field that afternoon and try to find out what was being said. We learnt that our farm was the war veteran's headquarters and a registration centre for the area. It was our farm, because of its strategic location on the junction of three main roads, where people were told to meet every weekend. It was on our farm where people could register with the war veterans for land both on our farm and all the neighbouring farms. Saturdays were registration days when people who wanted land could come, show their identification and pay the required amount of money for a plot of land that they would be given at a later stage. These plots apparently ranged in size from two to ten hectares and people had to pay Edward anything from $20 to $200 for their future land. Things were beginning to make sense now. No one had understood why our farm had been chosen to be invaded—the soil was very poor and the infrastructure minimal; now we understood. We were a typical case of the wrong people on the wrong farm at the wrong time. Surely when all the neighbouring farms had had all their land mapped out into plots and these had been sold, our war veterans would simply collapse their tent and go? Why they were building huts though, didn't quite make sense but I was too exhausted to think much further. It was clear that my subconscious didn't agree with my musings because my journal entry that night read:

> *It hasn't gone away as everyone said it would; it hasn't got any easier to live with or understand. The mental and psychological stress is phenomenal. The anguish and anger at our increased powerlessness increase every day. I've worked so hard these last ten years and know every inch of this farm, and the pain of seeing these people destroying it is intolerable. I feel as I imagine it must feel to be raped. Always, day after day, having to see that blue tent and the flag makes me feel violated. How can this ever end amicably? How will these people ever be made to leave this land and what will stop them from coming back again? Why has it been allowed to reach such a ridiculous proportion? I have lost all faith and all trust. I can't even sleep any more. All night I hear things, wonder where the WVs are. Are they at the fence? Will they be in the house next? What to do about all the sheep and cattle? It is now an insurmountable issue.*

As March came to an end, the country was beginning to show real signs of economic distress with diesel being in very short supply, prices of basic commodities rocketing and ordinary people beginning to wonder at the future direction of Zimbabwe. At a time when the country could least afford to give anyone anything, the government announced a 21 percent increase to the pensions of war veterans and awarded village heads, previously not included, similar packages. Announcing the increments to war veterans and new packages to village heads, one of the country's provincial governors was quoted in the *Daily News* as saying:

> *We have given you the powers so that you spearhead our goals in your areas. If we fail to get the necessary support and desired results in the rural areas, we will point fingers at traditional leaders, particularly chiefs.*

If anyone had been in any doubt before, it was becoming clear that a lot of people were being used and that the invasion of farms involved many more issues than met the eye. A leading political science lecturer at the University of Zimbabwe was quoted as saying:

This is an election ploy aimed at garnering support ... and ensuring that war veterans mobilize the povo to vote for the party.

There was a public outcry as yet more taxpayers' money was given to the very people who were destabilizing the country and more doubts were raised as to who exactly the war veterans were. Were these "real" war veterans on the farms? More evidence was being made available to show that there were many who were keen to get something for nothing. One farm squatter who allowed both his name and photograph to appear on the front page of a daily newspaper was reported as saying: "So what if we are not war veterans?" A leading black lawyer was quoted in the *Daily News* as stating:

It is quite clear that the government is trying to conceal the truth. War veterans must wake up and see that their image is being tarnished. People now see them as insensitive people who cannot realize that the economy is bad and they are now being loathed by all citizens.

Meanwhile, the government was obviously waiting for farmers to lose their tempers and President Mugabe warned of "very, very, very severe" consequences against white farmers if they tried to fight back. With now no recourse to law, police refusing to act, the minister of Home Affairs saying he could do nothing and the minister of Agriculture in gaol, what were we supposed to do? The people squatting on the farms, the large majority of whom were under 40 and therefore physically incapable of being war veterans, had been indoctrinated by someone and would not be convinced otherwise. They were determined that all whites were farming on inherited property that had been stolen from their ancestors and they were not going to go away. Our resident war veteran paid a visit to one of our neighbours. In the ensuing conversation Micky Buswell said to Edward: 'But Edward, the Buckles bought and paid for the farm in 1990, ten years after Independence. They paid their rates and taxes and levies to the Zimbabwe Government. How can you say they stole the land from your ancestors?'

'Yes,' said Edward, 'but what about the people that were there before them, and before them?'

It was a pointless discussion that ended with Edward asking Micky if he could give him a loaf of bread because he was hungry. When Micky declined Edward asked for a ballpoint pen so that he could update his land registration ledger!

In another instance, a reporter for *The Farmer* magazine visited an invaded property and spoke to the squatters who showed the same mentality to the issue of land ownership. The woman interviewed explained to the reporter how whites had allocated themselves the farms they now occupied. Referring to a situation that purportedly occurred in 1890 the woman said: 'They drove in their Land Rovers with a full tank of petrol until the petrol ran out. When they ran out of petrol they put a peg in the ground.' I was certainly not around in 1890 so cannot comment on how land was originally given to white settlers, but am pretty sure that the Land Rover wasn't invented for another 40 or 50 years. There was no doubt in anyone's mind that gross injustices had occurred in the past, that some farmers did own more than one farm and that something had to be done about making more land available to peasants, but with the mindset of the people invading our farms, it was hard to see how we could ever make sense of this mess.

During the last weekend of March, I evacuated Richard to my sister's house yet again and for the first time he started crying as they drove out of the farm gate. By early Saturday morning he was on the phone to me begging to be allowed to come home. He said he didn't feel well and wanted to play with his own toys in his own bedroom. I agreed and went immediately to collect him. In a few days' time it would be the school holidays and then Richard would have to stay on the farm anyway. He would just have to learn to play only in our garden behind the locked gates; his aunt after all did have her own job to go to every day and her own life to lead. Visible signs of stress were evident on everyone affected by the farm invasions and in the leader article of *The Farmer*, the editor wrote:

> For the first time in 20 years, grown men are talking openly about the effects of post-traumatic stress, about how their children cry when they see large groups of people and, when they hear drumming on the wireless, how the same children run away and hide.

When I read those words I realized suddenly that not only were we, Cathy and Ian Buckle, not alone in this nightmare, but I began to think about how terribly hard this must be on the men too. Zimbabwean men, renowned for their toughness, their macho-ness and their ability to cope with any situation were now unable to protect their wives and children, their land or their businesses. This was a gross violation of all our human rights.

On 1st April, Zimbabwe exploded for the first time in a long while. While on our little farm we watched our usual weekend crowd of invaders swelling to over 100 people, Harare was in turmoil. In what was supposed to be a peaceful demonstration calling for a return to law and order, crowds of people estimated to be between 10,000 and 15,000 strong marched through the streets of the capital city. Carrying placards which read: "Nations are not built on hate", "Peace in our time", and "Marching for peace, justice and reconciliation", the demonstrators were attacked by war veterans. Demonstrators had permission to march and a court injunction ordering police to protect them and yet gangs of men wielding clubs, bricks and sticks lashed out at them. The demonstrators were of all colours, ages and races and they had to run for their lives as war veterans beat them from one side and police shot tear-gas at them from the other. It was with feelings of disbelief and cold fear that I sat huddled in our isolated farmhouse that evening and watched as our little country made top world headlines on BBC Television. "There were running street battles through the streets of Harare as a march by thousands of opponents of President Robert Mugabe was attacked by government supporters. Eye witnesses say the attackers specifically targeted white protestors". All of a sudden it wasn't only white farmers being targeted by the government—now it was anyone with a pale skin colour. The words of the BBC reporter remained in my head for a long time. When asked if this was a racist, black-white issue, the BBC reporter said, 'The race card is not an issue among normal Zimbabweans.' I didn't think it was either but clearly now we were moving into a new playing field as two days later the state-owned *Herald* stated: "The governor of Mashonaland, Cde Border Gezi, has charged that some whites have accumulated massive wealth over the past two decades which they are now using to fight the government through opposition parties".

Until now war veterans and squatters on farms had been relatively peaceful but perhaps the Peace March had been the starter's pistol and suddenly violence exploded onto the farms. On a farm on the other side of Marondera, a local, well-known farmer whose wife had dedicated her life to helping Aids orphans on farms, was attacked by war veterans. Iain Kay's farm of 5,000 acres, highly productive and with 130 workers was the scene of a brutal attack that sent our entire community into shock. Again making BBC World headline news, we couldn't believe what we were seeing or hearing. Iain was interviewed as he lay in our local hospital, his face covered in blood, his back zigzagged with huge welts. Interviewed by the *Daily News*, Iain told of how the resident war veterans and squatters had ambushed and then attacked him:

> *They beat me with sticks, axe handles and fan belts tied on sticks… They also burnt my Honda 125 motorbike, stole my communications radio and cell phone. Then they tied my hands with wire and demanded to be taken to my house to see how many guns I had.*

"As Kay's son, David", the report continued "drove towards the assailants, Kay unshackled himself and dived into a nearby dam. The mob encircled the dam, throwing stones and sticks each time he came up for air". When Iain's teenage son approached, the mob ran away. My God, my God, I thought as I watched the film footage of Iain Kay in Borradaile Hospital in Marondera. I know that hospital, I know those people; I've lain in that exact room. I was overtaken by a sense of real, terror. Finally when I'd watched the film footage over and over again I changed to the local television channel and listened to the words of the president of Zimbabwe addressing an election rally. 'We cannot be expected to buy back our land that was never bought from us, never bought from our ancestors,' he was saying. Clearly farmers refusing to give in, to yield to this pressure were in line for the *very, very, very severe consequences* that had been inflicted on Iain Kay.

Four ....

THE KILLING BEGINS

By 4th April 2000, the morning after the assault of Iain Kay, 922 farms around Zimbabwe had been invaded by war veterans and, according to the Commercial Farmers' Union, 504 were still occupied. While we and about 250 other farmers in the area gathered at the Ruzawi Country Club for an emergency meeting with CFU officials, the problems were mounting on Iain Kay's farm a few kilometres away. As we asked our union officials what was going to be done about this attack on a fellow farmer and pleaded for some police protection, a young black policeman was trying to do his duty and also falling prey to the *very, very, very severe consequences* that this entailed. Twenty-five-year-old Constable Chikwenya, conducting stock theft investigations, was shot and killed by war veterans on Mr Kay's farm. Worldwide, the shooting of a policeman is regarded as an abominable offence usually creating a public outcry and an immediate manhunt. But again, as was now the case with all the atrocities being committed on farms across the country, the murder of the policeman made front-page news for one day and was then buried. We were sure that this murder would be the turning point on the land invasions, that someone high up in the government would create a furore and that now a halt to these "peaceful demonstrations" would be called. But nothing happened and it was with disgust that three days later we were told that the man who had been arrested for the assault on Iain Kay had been released from the prison cells in Marondera. As for the murderer of Constable Chikwenya—nothing more was said.

Dear God, what was happening to our country?

Farm invasions, now in their sixth week, were taking their toll on the patience of farmers and violent altercations began to erupt. As the war veterans saw their colleagues getting away with assault and even murder, their arrogance reached almost intolerable levels. Mr Swanson, a farmer in Hwedza, was severely assaulted by the war veterans resident on his farm. The squatters said that Mr Swanson's cattle had eaten their mealie meal and demanded that the farmer replace it. When Mr Swanson refused, he was attacked by ten men who kicked, punched and beat him with fists, sticks and boots. From his hospital bed in Marondera, Mr Swanson was interviewed by a *The Farmer* reporter and said, 'I just sat on the ground with my head in my hands not knowing what was going to hit me next.' Another very brave policeman, on a routine patrol, happened to be passing and intervened, possibly saving Mr Swanson's life.

The front-page headline of the weekly *Zimbabwe Independent* told the world what we were witnessing on the ground. "Violence intensifies on farms", it said, and went on to detail how farmers, farm workers and supporters of the opposition Movement for Democratic Change (MDC) were being attacked on a daily basis. A war veterans' spokesman was interviewed by journalists from the *Independent* and said: 'Violence is the resort at the moment. It's a war and we've changed our strategy. They [white farmers and their managers] are being beaten, yes, but you have to know why they have been caught up in the crossfire. They are the ringleaders and they are sponsoring people to protect their interests.' The sentiments of this man were then echoed by one of the country's provincial governors who told the *Herald*: 'These whites have made money in the past 20 years because of peace and stability promoted by the government and they are now using that money to fight us.' It was with disgust that we read of this insult to the population of Zimbabwe. The governor was now accusing white people, who make up less than one percent of Zimbabwe's thirteen and a half million people, of being the only people in the country who had money. Perhaps the governor did not see or know any of the extremely rich and successful black people in Zimbabwe. Perhaps also the governor did not see or know any of the white farmers who actually struggled to make a living, had huge debts with banks and finance houses and drove around in second-hand, rusting pickup trucks. In an editorial, which brought tears to many eyes, Trevor Ncube (editor of the *Zimbabwe Independent*) related his own experiences some years before. Entitled: *The Sins of Tribe and Race*, Mr Ncube told of how he too had been victimized simply because of his tribal ancestry and political beliefs. Intimidated, followed, harassed and then physically assaulted, Mr Ncube's editorial stated:

> *I relate this to draw parallels between the current persecution of whites and the opposition and the difficulties that many of us endured in the first decade of Independence. In both instances, a whole section of the population was targeted by a desperate ruling party intent on holding on to political power.*

Mr Ncube, my hero before, now went on to a high pedestal. I had hope for Zimbabwe—there were so many like him who dared to speak, who saw the truth. The final sentences of his piece said it all in my mind:

> *One good that has come out of all this is the unity and determination across ethnic and racial lines by the majority of patriotic Zimbabweans to rid themselves of this corrupt, arrogant and murderous lot. That day is rapidly approaching.*

The journalists were not the only ones who could see the truth behind what was happening on the farms. By the end of the first week of April, condemnation, both internal and external was mounting. One of the most influential people to make his feelings known was Thomas Mapfumo, a leading, popular and veteran musician in Zimbabwe. This man's music had inspired the people of Zimbabwe for over 20 years, his lyrics renowned for being topical to the conditions and events in the country. The *Daily News* reported on Thomas Mapfumo's recent visit to England: "What kind of people are those who do not want to accept criticism?" inquired Mapfumo. "During the struggle I sang revolutionary songs. Equally I feel obliged to criticize them when they botch things up".

Next came condemnation from the Legal Resources Foundation and top academic staff at the University of Zimbabwe. Quoted in the *Daily News*, the Zimbabwe lawyers for Human Rights asserted: "When the State refuses to abide by its own laws, and refuses to obey its own courts, then there is only one appropriate word: dictatorship". Outside condemnation for the increasing lawlessness in the country then came from Nordic countries whose spokesman called for Court Orders to be adhered to. Nobel Peace Prize winner, Archbishop Desmond Tutu added his voice to the mêlée and said that Zimbabwe's president "seems to be wanting to make a cartoon of himself". (*Daily News* quoting the *Mail and Guardian*).

Then came condemnation from Zimbabwe's nearest neighbour. For weeks we had been waiting for someone in South Africa to speak out and at last this came from South Africa's defence minister. Mr Lekota, speaking at an African Renaissance Festival in South Africa, was quoted in *The Financial Gazette* as saying he was "ashamed of the behaviour he was observing across the Limpopo". The minister's words were diplomatically obscure but left us in no doubt of his underlying condemnation. Also reported in the *Financial Gazette* was the news that European Union and African, Caribbean and Pacific States had met in Nigeria and issued a joint statement in which they called on "the European Council and the European Commission to give serious consideration to suspending non-humanitarian aid to Zimbabwe until it is seen to respect democracy, the rule of law and the rights of minorities within its borders". Less diplomatic in their wording, much stronger in their condemnation, the outside world was beginning to see the light and the World Bank then froze more than $200 million worth of aid for Zimbabwe's land reform programme. Whilst it was very encouraging to know that things were going on that we didn't know about, that across the world the condemnation for what was being called Zimbabwe's Land Grab was growing, it didn't change the situation on the ground. More and more the word "anarchy" was being used. In a cutting editorial comment in the *Financial Gazette*, the writer posed the question: "Who will guard the guards?" One sentence of the comment said it all and sent a chill down our spines:

> As the deadline for the eviction of the veterans passed on Monday, both the police chief, Augustine Chihuri, and Dumiso Dabengwa, Home Affairs minister, simply folded their arms and, in one stroke, allowed the country inexorably to slip into anarchy.

The school holidays arrived and instead of the usual exodus of farmers and their families to holiday destinations, we all battened down the hatches. Too afraid to leave our farms for fear that invaders would move in, we now had the added worry of where our children were all day and if they were safe. For the past few days a drama had been unfolding on a farm on the other side of Harare, a drama that came to a head on the first day of the Easter school holidays. War veterans and their supporters, resident on John Hammond's farm in Mvurwi, had barricaded the farmer into his house. Camped outside the security fence surrounding the farmhouse, war veterans would not let the farmer out or anybody in. I had been following the story for the past three days as it was reported by an SABC news crew who were speaking to the farmer regularly on the telephone and radio.

Then on Friday, 7th April, when too many news crews arrived at the property, the war veterans lost control and detained a local news crew. A features editor, a photographer and a driver for the *Daily News* were surrounded and force-marched to the farmhouse where they were interrogated. The *Daily News* related the details: "The youths, armed with iron bars, knobkerries and golf clubs, confiscated the journalists' two cameras, national identity cards and the government-issued press cards". Some time later the three men were released and video footage was shown on SABC of a confrontation between the farmer and a leading war veteran. The war veteran, wearing a grass hat, speaking loudly but very slowly said to the farmer: 'What I am telling you is you can finish your harvesting, do everything, but you are not going to replough because we have taken this farm for resettlement. This is our farm.' The SABC crew asked the farmer what he was going to do and Mr Hammond replied, 'Anarchy is not something that anybody can live under. Now I'm getting out.' Sitting watching the video footage repeatedly with my sister, I was overcome by hysteria. Terror turned to uncontrollable laughter and I laughed till I cried. The words of that war veteran though, were to stay with me for months until I too had them shouted at me.

That same day the BBC released film footage of a similar situation on a farm in Karoi. The BBC crew, chased and threatened by rampaging youths, stopped the fleeing farmers on a dirt road and interviewed them. My laughter of earlier was replaced by sobbing as I listened to Mrs du Toit's words. Like us, they too had put their life into their land; had built it from nothing, mortgaged everything they owned to secure their land and their future. They too had bought it post Independence, they too had a Certificate of No Interest from the Zimbabwe Government and now they had been given ten minutes to get out. What sort of insanity was this? How much longer could it continue?

On Friday afternoon I happened to look over the bottom half of the kitchen door and could not believe what I was seeing.

'Richard!' I bellowed at the top of my voice. 'Get down right now.'

There was my seven-year-old son climbing up the eight-foot diamond mesh security fence.

I raced outside as he began reversing down the fence and by the time I reached him, we were both in tears.

'What are you doing Rich?' I asked. 'What do you think you are doing?'

'I just want to go to the store Mum,' he sobbed. 'I just want to go and see my friends.'

Only days before I'd been warned by one of my regular customers at the store about keeping a special eye on Richard. He wouldn't be specific but just said that if war veterans couldn't intimidate me off the farm by squatting on the land, what would stop them from resorting to taking my child? Another pep talk was in order and it was clear that I'd have to be really firm this time.

'Can you see those people at the tent Rich? Can you see them? Some of them are there and some of them are around the store. They are bad men Rich. Do you understand me?'

As his pale little face whitened and his eyes widened, I went on. 'If you stay here everything will be okay because Mum's here, and Dad's here, and Manuel and Anna are here and nothing can happen, okay? But sweetie if you go up to the store by yourself, then I can't see you, can't see what's going on. You just can't go there by yourself, okay? If you need to go to the store then you call me and I'll go with you.'

Rich nodded quietly and I hugged him as we both looked down the field at that foul blue tent. How I hated it! How I hated what these people were doing to us. Taking the huge bunch of keys out of my pocket, I unlocked the gate Richard had been trying to climb over and we went up to the store together. Richard got his drink and crisps and we gathered up his friends and brought them back to play in the safety of the farm garden. In minutes the kids were off, racing around with a football, laughing and shouting, all tension defused. That night when I tucked Richard in and we prepared for our ritual story, he had piled up all his soft toys around both sides of his pillow. His favourite, a lion that his beloved Aunty Wiz had given him, was not enough and there was little room in the bed for him.

'They're scared Mum,' he said when I asked him why all the teddies were there.

'What are they scared of Rich? There's nothing to be scared of. We're here and the dogs are all on guard outside, and Arthur [our night guard] is going round and the electric fence is on. There's nothing to be scared of.'

Rich put his thumb in his mouth, hugged his lion closer to him and nodded as I stroked his white curls and found our favourite Noddy book, the one where Mr Plod the policeman is being particularly officious about a basket of missing mushrooms. Don't I wish, I thought as I read the story and we both giggled at the policeman's antics.

That first weekend of the school holidays was a traumatic one for Ian, Richard and me, and all our workers. I related the events in a weekly email letter I had begun sending out to family and friends.

Our squatters are still down there in the field with their blue tent and the Zim flag flying. Wednesday night we had a storm with lots of thunder and lightning and strong wind, which scared them away for a few hours but they were back the next morning. During the week our campers felled another 30 or more gum trees and did some more work on their houses. There are now six huts built but none permanently occupied (aside from the lads in the tent). The nights have been very noisy this week with the squatters drunk and shouting most nights. One afternoon when the workers went to bring the cattle in for the evening, there were seven squatters down at the little stock dam, all stark naked, fishing and shouting insults to the workers.

Saturday was, as seems to be the pattern now, an outrageous day again. People started arriving in the field from about 9am until by 11am there were what looked like about 180 to 200 people. A white Land Rover, green truck and two other vehicles drove into the field and the crowd was addressed by a loud woman for almost an hour. We could hear the old familiar political chants even from the house so were left in no doubt about what was going on. It went on all day and by 5pm most had left, with about 30 or 40 remaining at the tent and we could see beers in their hands. It was clearly pay-day and it led to a noisy night with drunken voices shouting from the workers' compound and our dogs barking on and off all night.

So far all the workers are staying strong and as most have been with us for almost the whole decade we've been here, they're not giving up yet. Particularly Jane, the woman who runs our little store, deserves a medal. She has to put up with the squatters' intimidation every day. Three of the squatters have taken to standing in the store and just staring at her—sometimes for two to three hours at a time. I've offered to close the store and send Jane on leave but she wants to keep going. She's broken out in a nervous stress-related rash all over her neck and face but remains cheerful and determined.

As each day passes we can't believe that this is being allowed to continue and would happily get in the car and leave if we could. We have seven people and their families depending on us not only for their income

but also their homes and families. One hundred and two head of cattle
worth almost a million dollars that we cannot sell. We have actually
reached the point of trying to sell our cattle but there are no buyers now.
My sheep flock have started lambing so there's no way I could sell them
now even if I wanted to.

The type of intimidation of our workers was being repeated on farms
all over the country, and a regular columnist for the *Independent* wrote a
particularly moving piece about how it was far from just the white
farmers who were suffering.

Out there in the invisible countryside, thousands of men and women live
under the daily threat of bloody and mindless violence as, under
provocation of the most extreme sort, they are forced to witness the
destruction of all that they have built and sweated over for so many years.
Many more thousands of men, women and children stand to lose the little
that they have—the people who work on these farms.

With the start of the school holidays and the increasing number of
hostile confrontations between farmers and squatters, it became clear
that we really were on our own. Whilst the rest of the country and a lot
of the outside world sympathized with the plight of farmers and their
workers, no one could actually do anything to help us. Farmers
countrywide and area-by-area established a support plan. Based on
existing neighbourhood-watch guidelines, farmers were called
together and urged to form support groups within their areas. These
groups were to provide both mental and logistical support to farmers
who found themselves in difficult situations. Volunteers were found in
each area and they became either the Talk Team or the Reaction Team.
The Talk Team members were farmers who were well versed in both
the government policy of land redistribution and the CFU policy of
being a-political and non-violent. They were men who were known
and respected in the community both by fellow farmers and local
people. They were men who were slow to anger, even-tempered and
could speak the local language. The Talk Team were the men you could
call to talk to the war veterans if they were being hostile or aggressive.
The aim of this team was just as its name implied—people who could
talk to the war veterans, try to cool tempers and defuse confrontations.

Then there was the Reaction Team that involved the rest of us. It was
a very simple and non-violent plan whereby if a group of 100 invaders
came and rattled someone's gate, the Reaction Team would simply

assemble at a safe and non-confrontational distance to offer the farmer moral support and to show the invaders a presence that would hopefully cause them to give up and leave. Names and telephone numbers were printed out and a very specific set of instructions agreed upon—where to go, whom to contact, what to do and what not to do. We were all assigned dates and times when we were on call to respond to problems and just the knowledge that this system was now in place was immensely comforting. It had taken some doing in getting the Support Team programme in place because of the 4,500 commercial farms in the country, not all farmers had been directly affected and many had not yet realized the seriousness of the invasions. In an email I sent to a friend who was not a farmer, I tried to explain:

> There is a real and increasingly dangerous division in the farming community between those who are squatted and those who are not. And again between those who have been squatted and pegged and those who still have squatters living on their properties. The feeling in the former is that if you've been pegged you're sort of okay because the law will take its course. If you're still actively squatted you see them every day and know for sure that there is no law and that you are completely alone.

The response of the government to these support teams was much as we had expected. Suddenly white farmers were accused of having arms of war and forming militant rogue armies. When a CFU official went on a routine visit to a farm accompanied by his wife and three-month-old baby, he was stopped at a roadblock by war veterans. They asked to search his vehicle for weapons and because he had his family with him the official refused. The result was that his windscreen was smashed and the door of the car damaged.

The government had by now tabled a motion in parliament to amend the constitution. The Amendment Bill sought to enable the government to acquire land compulsorily for resettlement without paying any compensation to the legal owners of the land. This amendment to the constitution was one of a number of changes the government had tried to institute in a proposed new constitution in February. The new constitution, full of loopholes and giving both the government and the president sweeping powers, had been so controversial that a referendum had been held and the people of Zimbabwe voted against its implementation. The wording of the amendment was to start a war of words between Britain and Zimbabwe and cause yet more racial tension in the country. The *Daily News* stated:

The amendment says that, accordingly, "the former colonial master has an obligation to pay compensation for agricultural land compulsorily acquired for resettlement ... if the former colonial master fails to pay compensation ... the government of Zimbabwe has no obligation to pay compensation for agricultural land compulsorily acquired for resettlement".

The day arrived for the voting on the Amendment Bill and with exactly two thirds of the members of parliament in the House, the Bill was passed. Whilst the administrative processes of the Constitutional Amendment still had to be followed, it was now apparent that short of a miracle, if the government decided to take a farm, it would do so. This was not a complete surprise to us as farmers. It had been threatened before but we had hoped, assumed that sanity and legality would prevail. That was clearly not going to happen and we would be lucky if we were paid only for the improvements on the farms we had bought, assuming of course that the Zimbabwe Government had the money to pay us. The British Government reacted in the only way it could—it categorically refused to be forced to pay for Zimbabwean land unless a number of previously laid-down criteria were met. Peter Hain, Britain's Foreign Office minister was quoted in the *Daily News*:

'This is an attempt to put a pistol to Britain's head and say: "Hand over the money". We're not prepared to do that.' Hain told BBC radio: 'Half the land that has been distributed so far by the government has gone to government cronies. Most of it is not being farmed properly,' he said.

The British were as incensed as the Zimbabweans at the absurd wording of the Constitutional Amendment. How could one country use its constitution to impose conditions on another country? Yet again Zimbabwe was on the top of all the world's news reports and BBC World Television followed the passing of the Amendment Bill with video footage of President Mugabe addressing an election campaign rally the day after the Bill had been passed. The president said to his supporters that if any white farmers resisted the takeover of their land he would not back down: 'Then I will declare the fight to be on and it will be a fight to the finish I can tell you and they won't win the fight, we will win it.' (BBC World)

Leaving the politicians to it, Zimbabwe watched in horror as war veterans and supporters of the ruling party, buoyed by yet more rhetoric from their leader, ran amok. The farm invasions were rapidly deteriorating into a free-for-all. While farmers waited for the second ruling from the High Court ordering the removal of war veterans from farms, lands near to the city of Harare were suddenly swamped by squatters. Three farms near the Harare International Airport were taken over and partitioned into thousands of residential stands. The *Daily News* detailed what their reporters had witnessed on one of the farms:

> *The residents, mostly women and Zanu PF youths dressed in party regalia, converged at the farm yesterday morning and by late afternoon, the crowd had grown to more than 3,000.*

While farmers were sure that the second ruling by the High Court would be on the side of the legal landowners, we were more doubtful than ever that the police would actually obey the orders, particularly when the weekly *Financial Gazette* covered a news conference given by the leader of the War Veteran's Association, Chenjerai Hunzvi.

> *Chenjerai "Hitler" Hunzvi yesterday shrugged off an impending High Court ruling on the seizure of private farms by members of his Independence War veterans, declaring that more would be forcibly taken shortly. 'You are going to see more invasions, and I don't mince my words,' he told a news conference in Harare. 'More invasions will be taking place—and serious ones.'*

They were all there outside the High Court in Harare, the cameras, reporters, lawyers and in only six minutes a decision, again by a black judge, was made. The application by the police for a variance on the ruling was denied and the original order for the police to remove squatters and war veterans from farms was upheld. I was ecstatic. Justice was still intact in Zimbabwe. Flicking from one news channel to another though, my joy was soon quashed as I listened to what all the analysts and commentators were saying. BBC, CNN and SABC Television all thought it extremely unlikely the police would obey the ruling. Dr Gerry Grant of the CFU said outside the High Court: 'Just a return to law and order, that's all we're asking.' A commentator for Sky News made the most chilling observation about the police force of our country, 'The choice for senior officers is whether they obey the rule of law or the wishes of the government.' Asked what would happen if the police again chose to ignore the High Courts, he said, 'To do so again risks taking Zimbabwe, one of Africa's largest economies, one step closer to lawlessness.'

President Mugabe, in Cuba for a summit, was asked to comment on the latest ruling by the judiciary and said, '[We will] see how it [the ruling] can be implemented without causing a crisis.' War Veterans' leader, Hunzvi, was on CNN and said, 'The system is not good for the people. It [of the courts] must be changed; it must be changed; it must be changed.' Again Hunzvi vowed not to back down and said farm invasions would continue. One shred of hope came with the words from the vice president of Zimbabwe. Speaking to CNN, Mr Msika commented on the Court's ruling:

> *It is now no longer necessary to continue with the demonstrations. The reasons for their demonstrations are well appreciated and understood by both the party and the government. However, in light of these recent developments, it is now no longer necessary to continue with the demonstrations.*

Although not directly ordering war veterans to leave farms, the vice president's words were encouraging. It remained to be seen if they would be backed up by the president when he returned from Cuba.

We didn't have long to wait to see what we had dreaded. The president stepped off the Air Zimbabwe aircraft to a crowd of well-dressed and extremely well-organized supporters. All were holding beautiful, new placards printed in red ink and capital letters, which said it all before Mr Mugabe opened his mouth.

> *Peter Hain and Robin Cook stop lying about Zimbabwe.*
> *Down with the naked lies of the BBC SKY CNN SABC.*
> *We do not want a donor republic.*
> And, my favourite: *Zimbabwe will never be a colony again.*

Mr Mugabe stepped forward, clenched his fist and raised his arm.

> *We as members of government regard the political problems as overriding the little matter of trespass… Supposing the police were asked to go, ordered to go, isn't there the possibility of greater violence and greater conflict and greater loss of life? Must we allow that kind of outcome to ensue from our ordering the police to go?*

The newspapers carried many more extracts from the president's lengthy discourse at the airport. The *Daily News* reported: "Mugabe, on his arrival from a Third World Summit in Cuba, immediately said, 'I know there is an expectation that I will say to the war veterans, "Get off the land." I will not say or do that.'"

Another report in the same paper quoted yet more: "There is no policeman who is going there. We have said 'No.' If the British have their own police they must send them here. Ours are not going to go there".

There was no doubt, the ruling would not be upheld by the police. Yet again we were alone.

I wept when I read an article of my mother's published in the *Daily News*. At first I felt strangely detached reading of a mother's account of her daughter's anguish and had to read it repeatedly to remind myself of all the history that had gone before in our family. History that surely exonerated us from the wrath of the president and his government. Her words showed the dreadful betrayal that was taking place. The betrayal of her beliefs and principles, and those of so many others like her.

I am a white. I am not a farmer… My friends and neighbours are all black; the students I teach are all black; the colleagues I work with are all black; my boss is black. Yes my skin is white and sometimes I have wished it were otherwise but as every day passes and more racist abuse is piled upon people of my colour, I find myself getting angrier and angrier… In our own way we fought against the Smith regime with its evil policies of racial superiority and domination. As a lawyer, my first husband fought in the courts to defend men who have since risen to the very top of Zanu PF… Many of today's cabinet ministers received their prison education because of my family's commitment to the concept of a free Zimbabwe… I was myself responsible for helping write some of the books and pamphlets that were smuggled out of the country to inform the rest of the world about what was happening inside Rhodesia. In such an atmosphere of passionate belief in justice and truth, of endless interchange and discussions among the black and white visitors to the family home, my children grew up and who is to tell me that they are not Zimbabweans?… One of those children went to the School of Social Work as the only white student. She taught in the newly integrated schools as a careers and guidance counsellor to black, brown and white teenagers… and she is not a Zimbabwean? Now she owns a farm that she and her husband bought in 1990 and paid for over the next seven years of incredible hardships. It's a poor place, fit only for grazing cattle and sheep. There are no tractors nor irrigation, no heavy machines because all the spare cash went to meet the massive repayments for the farm.

The article then detailed all the abuses and violations that Ian and I and our son had endured over the past six weeks and as a mother myself, I cried too at the pain of a parent for a child.

> *I ask: Is this really a question of land ownership or is it the landowner's skin colour that so bothers the president and his cohorts? … And when our blood mingles with the soil of this beloved land, will it matter then whether we were black or white or brown or mixed race?*

Another letter published in the *Daily News*, echoed the betrayal so many people were now feeling: "…I am embarrassed to say that my family fought for the liberty of Zimbabwe, they suffered physical attack, arrest, mental anguish, exile and even imprisonment…"

But whilst people's words were comforting, they didn't stop the abuses and violations that were going on and the squatters on our farm were stepping up their activities and digging their heels in. Every morning now the squatters herded their own cattle onto our fields, sometimes upwards of 60 head, and left them to graze our fields, forcing us to move our cattle out of their way. A white pickup truck arrived with piles of timber and with disbelief we watched the newest addition being erected on our land. Strips of sawn timber were hurriedly nailed together and in less than a day a wooden house had been built, complete with door and roof. This house, we later learned, was to be the beer hall-cum-tuck shop for the squatters. A section of our boundary fence had been opened and the grass cut short with a sickle to make a safe and easy entry point for the future patrons. Ian and I were livid, as were the workers because the beer hall had been erected directly behind our borehole and within about 30 metres of Emmanuel's house. I picked up a hefty stick and called the workers together.

'Come on,' I said, 'let's go and knock that abomination down.'

'Oh no,' George replied, 'they will not allow us.'

'I don't care any more George. For God's sake the hut is right by our only supply of water. It's right by Emmanuel's house. This is insane. I've had enough. Come on.' When no one moved I felt angry, hot tears stinging my eyes and took a step towards the workers. 'Well if you won't come with me, I'll go by myself. This is enough now. Isn't it? Haven't you all had enough? Where will they put the next bloody hut, right outside your door George, or yours Isaya? Then will it be enough?' Still no one moved and I threw my stick furiously against the fence. Everyone tried to calm me down. Someone said that I should think about what had happened to Mr Kay, or Mr Hammond or Mr du Toit. I knew they were right. Finally we settled on the video camera and Ian and I drove down along our main boundary. I stopped my truck completely as we came level with the beer hall and Ian's camera whirred quietly out of the window. Two of the 20-year-old "war veterans" were putting the finishing touches to the roof and they turned and stared straight into the camera. When we arrived home I phoned the Marondera police. They said there was nothing they could do; they had received no orders. I asked for a report number and was told that "unfortunately we are failing to find the report book." I slammed the phone down, incensed and shaking. By the next day the war veterans and squatters had begun another new project on our land. They began excavating clay and moulding bricks. They were there to stay. The words of their leader and of the country's leader had ratified that. The words of the courts were useless.

Every night since the initial invasion of our farm, our long-standing friends, Bill and Ann Glover, had phoned from Harare to see if we were all right, to hear the latest news and to offer moral support. On one occasion Bill phoned in the afternoon and from my garbled end of the conversation he must have thought we were all being slaughtered. Our black labrador had cornered an Egyptian cobra in the open drain that ran along the back wall of the farmhouse. The dog's hysterical barking and the excited yapping of the other three dogs alerted me immediately and within minutes the entire workforce had gathered in an attempt to dispatch the snake. None of them liked snakes and I was terrified of the creatures, having had more than my share of very close calls with the reptiles in the past.

While everyone chose their weapons, someone said that we should try to catch the cobra and take it down to the tent but that suggestion was met with hilarity and we closed in. To our disbelief the cobra was ready for us though and it hastily turned and went head first into the open pipe that led to one of the bathrooms in the house. It completely disappeared and would not be coaxed out. I had visions of the snake mutating itself into little slithers and coming out of the plughole inside and was determined that it should be removed. Not wanting to smash the pipe out of the wall, I sent Emmanuel to get a bucket, intending to flush it out with water from the inside. George, Isaya and Clemence stood at the pipe outlet as Emmanuel and I raced into the house slopping water everywhere. Right in the middle of all this the phone rang, I snatched it up and instead of saying "Hello" shouted down the hall to Manuel.

'No, the next bathroom Manuel. Quick before someone gets hurt.'

Poor Bill on the other end of the phone had no idea what was going on.

'Hang on Bill,' I panted, 'we've got to kill this bastard now,' and ran off down the hall to join Emmanuel.

The plan worked a treat. Two buckets of water, much shouting and cheering from outside and the snake was done for. Finally I returned to the phone. Bill was beside himself.

'What the hell's going on? Are you guys all right? Have they got in the house? Have you phoned the cops? What can I do?'

Once everything had been explained and Bill was satisfied that this was not a human invader that we were trying to kill in our house, the conversation returned to normal. Funny though, I thought, how people squatting on your land, terrorizing you and your workers, erecting beer halls and moulding bricks could be classed as "normal" conversation.

The first noticeable signs that Zimbabwe's farm invasions were beginning to have an impact on the country's economy came in mid April, a fortnight before the opening of the tobacco sales floors. Tobacco, one of the biggest foreign currency earners for the country, was the one thing that everyone had been hoping would help restore the already ailing economy. Fuel queues were lengthening, electricity blackouts were increasing and we had all hoped that when the tobacco started selling, foreign currency would spill into the national coffers and make life a little easier. The managing director of the Tobacco Sales Floors reported though that only 3,500 bales had been booked for the first day of the auctions, compared to 50,000 bales on the first day of selling in 1999. The *Independent* then reported that the banks too were becoming very concerned about the impact of farm invasions on their businesses. "Bank executives whose institutions' exposure to the farming community tops six billion dollars as at December 31st, have expressed concern over the ongoing farm invasions which they fear will affect farmers' ability to service their loans". Tourism too was being seriously affected by increased lawlessness in the country and a BBC reporter paid a visit to the Victoria Falls. The Victoria Falls Hotel, listed as one of the top 30 hotels in the world said that cancellations were increasing, bookings were down by 25 percent and people's jobs were now at risk.

All the warning signs of a country in collapse though, were not heeded by Zimbabwe's leaders. The president started campaigning in earnest for an election whose date had yet to be announced and was quoted in the *Financial Gazette* as saying: "Zimbabwe is able to go it alone... If whites want to go [leave Zimbabwe], we will offer them an escort. Do you think we cannot farm tobacco, tea, sugar or oranges?" And as political campaigning continued, the violence intensified. The leader of the opposition MDC, Morgan Tsvangirai was suddenly a household name. He was interviewed on the famous Hardtalk programme on BBC. He met Robin Cook, Britain's Foreign Office leader, and he spoke to many of the world's journalists. He said repeatedly that it was the economy that needed a shake up. People wanted food on the table; they wanted money in the bank; they wanted jobs. His speeches were spontaneous and highly charged; he said what he thought and when asked about what he thought of President Mugabe's policies, Morgan Tsvangirai called him "the founding father of Zimbabwe" who "has turned from the hero to the villain". MDC t-shirts were everywhere and their slogans stated: Land to the people, not the politicians. Zanu PF t-shirts were also everywhere but they proclaimed: Land is the economy. The economy is the land. The battleground was set and days later two MDC supporters, one of whom was Tsvangirai's driver, were killed when a petrol bomb was thrown into their car. This was perhaps the first major and tragic event that showed that it wasn't only whites or white farmers who were in the government's way. More than anything else though, it showed that the land invasions were a political tool.

For hours every day I sat at my computer sending out hundreds of emails, determined that Zimbabweans and the world should hear the true story. I wrote to embassies and ambassadors, to newspapers and journalists, to human rights organizations and the churches and soon answering everyone's letters became almost a full-time job. In an email to one of the world's most famous interviewers I wrote:

My farm is on the boundary of a communal land, which has eight villages in it and a population of approximately 4,000 people. There are not 4,000 land-hungry peasants squatting on my farm; there are seven paid men.

In another to a man in Bulawayo who sent dozens of messages of support every week, I wrote: "The saying at the end of your email yesterday: 'For evil to prosper, good men must sit down and do nothing'—that is exactly what we feel we are doing, absolutely nothing". To Amnesty International I got down on my knees:

We are at the end of our tether. We have been stripped of all our rights both as human beings and as Zimbabweans just because of the colour of

our skin. We are completely alone; our government will not help us; the
police will not help us. Is there anything you can do to help us?

War veterans, clearly outraged that even with the promises and
rantings of their leaders, farmers were just not prepared to give in to
the intimidation, stepped up their campaign. Their next move was to
attempt to get farm owners to sign over their land. On a farm in
Mvurwi, the *Financial Gazette* spoke to a war veteran:

'If he refuses to sign over the farm, we are going to wage war against him.
That is that. We are not going back,' a representative of the squatters said
as his colleagues, wielding axes, danced to revolutionary songs.

On another farm, the owner was forced to sign over half of his land.
Reported in the *Zimbabwe Independent*, he said: "I had only one
option—violence or peace. I opted to bow under pressure for peace".
The report continued with a description of the activities on the farm:

[The farm] produces tobacco, sunflowers, maize and coffee as well as
cattle and sheep ... provides full time employment for 100 families. Local
leader of the war veterans ... said the plan was to carve the land up into
15-acre plots for the landless masses—although the veterans would get
more land than the others.

On Saturday, 15th April 2000, three days before Zimbabwe's 20th
anniversary of Independence, the country reeled in disbelief as a
farmer was murdered by war veterans and five others were abducted
and beaten until they were almost dead. The reports were garbled,
terrifying. Even those on the overseas television stations could not
really make sense of what had happened. The words went round in
my head: "point blank range, abducted, still missing, armed,
rampaging mobs". Finally, days later, pieces of the horror were put
together and the CFU reported the incident as it had been told to
them by deeply shocked and traumatized survivors. They published
it in *The Farmer*:

Friday 14th April, evening: *"War vets" beat up some of Mr Stevens'*
farm workers on Arizona farm, Macheke after weeks of intimidation.
Saturday morning: *The workers retaliate and chase the vets away. The*
Zimbabwe Republic Police arrive and detain some workers for assaulting
war vets after the vets lay charges.

Saturday late morning: The vets return with reinforcements from Murehwa Growth Point, with the intention of taking Mr Stevens into custody. Some are armed. Mr Stevens believes he can negotiate with them. John Osborne is on his way to help him negotiate.

[But before Mr Osborne arrives] Mr Stevens is overpowered and tied up. He is taken to Murehwa Growth Point in his own Land Rover, in a convoy with two other vehicles carrying war vets: a BMW Cheetah sedan and a minibus. Five of Mr Stevens' farming friends arrive as the war vets' convoy leaves Arizona. They follow the convoy to Murehwa Police Station. Their names are Ian Hardy, Steve Krynauw, Stuart Gemmill, Gary Luke and John Osborne. As the convoy approaches the Zanu PF headquarters in Murehwa, a war vet leans out of the window of his vehicle and fires at the convoy of farmers with a .303. The farmers seek refuge at the Murehwa Police Station.

Saturday 4.30pm: A large group of war vets walks into the police station and takes the five farmers out of police protection. They are taken to the Zanu PF headquarters in Murehwa. They are arranged into pairs: Dave Stevens and John Osborne; Steve Krynauw and Gary Luke; Stuart Gemmill and Ian Hardy. Messrs Stevens and Osborne are taken out into the bush and assaulted severely. Mr Stevens is shot in the presence of John Osborne. Mr Osborne has his life spared by a young man and a woman who persuade the mob not to kill him. Mr Osborne and the body of the deceased are taken back to Murehwa Growth Point. Osborne is allowed to leave. Meanwhile Gary Luke and Steve Krynauw are tightly bound with wire and escorted to Mr Stevens' vehicle. They are driven with the body of the deceased in that vehicle to a hill north of Murehwa where another mob awaits them. They are severely assaulted. They are then loaded into a Toyota pickup and driven further north. The pickup breaks down. They are assaulted again and left for dead. Meanwhile Ian Hardy and Stuart Gemmill are severely assaulted in the Murehwa Zanu PF headquarters and taken to an unknown location south of Murehwa. They are assaulted and detained overnight.

Saturday 10pm: John Osborne is brought into Borradaile Trust Hospital.

Early Hours of Sunday morning: Messrs Luke and Krynauw regain consciousness and walk to a distant farm. The farm has been abandoned by the owners because of the security situation in the area. Messrs Luke and Krynauw make their situation and position known and are evacuated to Borradaile Trust Hospital. Gary Luke has a fractured cranium. CFU president, Tim Henwood, and its director, David Hasluck, hire aeroplanes to help the search and rescue effort for Messrs Stevens, Hardy and Gemmill.

They fly over "at least 80 percent of the homesteads in the area at two to four hundred feet", looking for any signs of the deceased's body and his vehicle and any sign of Messrs Gemmill and Hardy. They notice that Arizona Farm workers' village and grading sheds have been burned. Vice President Colin Cloete and Deputy Director Richard Amyot speak to farmers in the area and liase with Dispol, Propol [District and Provincial Police] and other government agencies to assist in locating the missing farmers.

Sunday late afternoon: *Messrs Gemmill and Hardy are found by a ZRP Murehwa detail and delivered under police escort to Borradaile Trust Hospital for treatment. At the same time, the police general headquarters notifies the CFU Marondera that Mr Stevens' body has been found at St Paul's Musami Mission.*

Dave Stevens leaves a wife, Maria, and four children, including a pair of young twins.

There were no words, none at all. Just terror.

FIVE ....

TRAIL OF DESTRUCTION

The five farmers abducted and beaten while trying to rescue David Stevens began arriving in our little town hospital. We sat at home on the farm watching BBC Television, watching what was going on fewer than 12 kilometres away. Bloodied, bruised, barely able to walk, the men were interviewed. Deeply traumatized, they told of their ordeal and of the killing of their friend and neighbour. Hour after hour, Zimbabwe was the top television news headline all over the world as the tragic events were exposed. The country and the world waited for a reaction and response from the government of Zimbabwe. The farmers waited for guidance and reassurance but were met instead with anger from the leader of the war veterans. As if trying, almost begging white farmers to react violently to the tragedy, Chenjerai Hunzvi was filmed by the BBC's cameras. 'We don't want to be provoked and we don't care what the British are going to say. If they want to fight with us, we will fight them. And not only here but in the UK too.'

Zimbabwe's minister of Health, Doctor Timothy Stamps, happened to be in London and the BBC asked him for a response to the killing of David Stevens. It was 'unacceptable,' he said, but continued by attempting to excuse his party and government and justify the actions of the war veterans by saying, 'It's the failure of everybody involved in redistributing the land that has caused this exacerbation of feelings of resentment.' The minister's description of heightened feelings of resentment hardly explained though why mobs of war veterans and government supporters then went on the rampage and burnt Dave Stevens' farm to the ground. Not satisfied with killing David Stevens, they burnt his entire crop of tobacco drying in the barns; they ransacked and then burnt his home; they destroyed most of the village in which Mr Stevens' workers lived. Zimbabwe's *Financial Gazette* reported what they had found:

After careful and delicate negotiations [with the veterans at the farm] we were denied interviews but allowed to tour the burnt-out ruins of what had been the farm compound and buildings—under escort. From the small anthill where I was standing, I could count 20 workers' huts razed to the ground but many more lay ruined in the midst of the still-smouldering tobacco barns. Millions of dollars worth of tobacco, or in Zimbabwe terms, millions worth of desperately needed foreign currency must have gone up in flames as farm workers fled in panic after the veterans and the youths struck. We advanced a few more steps into the charred ruins and my eyes caught a half-burnt hen among the rubble... It was a panorama of destruction and desolation... For a moment I forgot where I was. Turning to the leader of the team that was escorting us, I confronted him: 'So what is all this destruction meant to achieve?' All eyes turned on me. I had made a mistake. They looked at me in silence. I got the message that my question did not need an answer.

Forty-six farmers and their families, on the advice of the CFU, evacuated their homes in the area surrounding the burning farm and headed into the relative safety of Marondera town. Those of us on the west of the town checked our windows, doors and padlocks, jumped at every sound, wondered if we would be next. The next day was the 20th anniversary of Zimbabwe's Independence and we all prayed that the president would say something, anything, to stop this. As we waited for his televised address to the nation, we flicked from one news channel to another and were horrified to hear that another tragedy was taking place on a farm outside Bulawayo in the south of the country. BBC World Television reported that a second farmer had been shot; at that time it was unknown if the farmer was alive or not.

A mob of between 100 and 120 war veterans and others had arrived at Martin Olds' farm outside Bulawayo in a convoy of 12 vehicles. In what was obviously a planned and organized manoeuvre, the invaders set up roadblocks to prevent anyone coming to the aid of the farmer. A group of war veterans then surrounded the farmhouse and opened fire on Mr Olds. The farmer, shot in both legs, called for help from the police, his workers, the neighbouring farmers, the ambulance service. None were allowed past the roadblocks manned by the war veterans. The farmhouse was set on fire and Mr Olds apparently retreated to the back bathroom of the house to get away from the smoke and wait for help. None came. He was smoked out of the house and shot in the head. Again, I sat in horror listening to all the reports that flooded the television news channel. "It was clear they didn't want to seize his land, just to kill him". "The fire brigade arrived eight hours late". "The country is teetering on the brink of anarchy". As we had done in Marondera over the past few days, farmers in Bulawayo gathered in dazed, terrified groups, looking shocked and traumatized. The BBC commentators summed up what we were all thinking: "Any farmers that do stay here [on their farms, or even in the country] must wonder if they'll be next".

Again the *Financial Gazette* filled in the details of this callous and pre-meditated murder.

> *A farm worker … says he saw the war veterans arrive at Compensation Farm in convoys of 12 vehicles shortly after 6am on Tuesday. 'They surrounded the farmhouse and the next thing I heard was the sound of gun fire.' …According to homicide officers of the Criminal Investigations Department who collected his body three hours after his death, the veterans had riddled Olds with bullets and then finished him off with iron bars and other weapons such as axes… Spent cartridges and petrol bombs from beer bottles lay strewn around the farmhouse.*

Finally, at midday on Zimbabwe's 20th Anniversary of Independence, the president of the country made an address to the nation. As the national anthem played, the visions in my mind were not of freedom, liberty, democracy or national pride, they were of blood, bullets, petrol-bombs and dead bodies. While my seven-year-old white son and Brian, his black friend, tipped Lego all over the house and giggled as they rough and tumbled, I wondered if this was the real Zimbabwe in my lounge, or if it was the 100-plus war veterans converging in the field below our house, on our land. I didn't know any more but listened to the words of my president, a president clearly clinging to the past. His speech was full of the same old rhetoric that was supposed to stir up national pride, but was now merely empty words that caused only anger. 'Oppressive settler colonial rule … years of bitter, protracted struggle ... how many had to die ... men, women and children cut down in cold blood.' ...And so it went on.

A hint of anger came into his speech when Mr Mugabe said that after extending the hand of reconciliation to white Zimbabweans, they had rejected it. 'We reject the persistence of vestigial attitudes from the Rhodesian yesteryears, attitudes of a master race, master colour, master owner and master employer.' The president went on to praise the achievements of Zimbabwe's government over the past two decades. He read out endless statistics of schools, colleges, universities, literacy levels, enrolment, academics, housing, water, roads. If everything had been so wonderful then, these past 20 years, why did Mr Mugabe suddenly admit, for the first time, that all was not roses with the country's economy. He said, 'Economic growth has been erratic ... interest rates are high, as is inflation ... export performance has been dismal.' The president offered no reasons or explanations for a country with almost no fuel at all, inflation between 60 and 70 percent, unemployment at over 50 percent and interest rates at over 60 percent. He did not mention the rampant corruption throughout every sector of the country. He did not mention the $28 billion debt owed by the National Oil Company of Zimbabwe to its suppliers. He did not mention the $28 million scandal in which his minister of Agriculture had been implicated. He did not mention the fraud investigations in the country's Grain Marketing Board, which ran into figures in excess of $320 million. He did not mention the looting of the War Veterans' Compensation Fund of over $500 million. He did not mention the raiding of a housing fund, which had been looted and abused by senior government officials. He did not mention the looting of $4 million by senior government officials of the District Development Fund. Nor did our president tell us why our local schools had so few books that groups of up to ten children had to share one book. Why those same children had to have their lessons taught under a tree because there were no classrooms. Why our local clinic had no drugs whatsoever except aspirin. Why nurses did not have gloves to wear. Why contraceptive tablets and injections were not available for local people. Why telephones remained unrepaired for up to three months at a time. Why electricity cuts ranging from four to six hours a day were now the norm. Why more than 76 percent of Zimbabwe's population lived below the poverty datum line.

There was so much that the president of Zimbabwe did not tell us in his 20th Anniversary address. Twenty-three minutes into a 26-minute speech, President Robert Mugabe spoke about land distribution in

Zimbabwe. Calling the land issue "emotive and vexed", Mr Mugabe again blamed the whites. Explaining that his government had hoped to take five million hectares of land from commercial farmers and give it to the landless he said, 'Sadly this was not to be as the commercial farmers contested the matter [of compulsory acquisition] in the courts, forcing government to abandon the acquisition process.' The president said that even the British had let him down, reneging on promises of money for land redistribution. He did not say why the British had stopped aid for land reform; he did not explain why a host of other donor countries had suspended all aid for land reform in Zimbabwe. He did not explain why he had leased or given acquired farms to senior government officials. He did not explain why the government had abandoned the "willing seller, willing buyer" programme. He did not say why the Zimbabwean government had not bought farms as they came on the property market in the past two decades. He did not say why his government continued to issue Certificates of No Interest to properties when they came up for sale. He did not say why court rulings were disobeyed, why police refused to do what our taxes paid them to do, why the minister of Home Affairs had not been allowed to do his job or why he had amended the country's constitution after the majority of the population had said no to proposed changes. Instead he said that the resistance of white Zimbabwean farmers to giving away their land, livelihoods and homes had 'led to the current spate of farm occupations by the war veterans and sporadic clashes in which two lives have regrettably been lost. Land,' he said, 'is the last colonial question … we are determined to resolve it once and for all.'

To farmers, as Zimbabweans, perhaps the most dismaying fact of the president's address was that he did not say why perpetrators of violence were not being arrested. That he did not even mention the shooting of a young black policeman by war veterans. Did not mention the assaults and beatings of black farm workers. Did not mention the killing in a petrol bomb attack of two black Zimbabweans. My president could not even find it in himself to mention the names of the people that had died, been killed in this "last colonial question". What shame I felt. What despair for the families of David Stevens, Constable Chikwenya, Tichaona Chiminya, Talent Mabika and Martin Olds.

Minutes after the conclusion of his address to the nation, President Mugabe held an impromptu news conference with Zimbabwe Television reporters. Gone now were the pages of carefully chosen words, the calm and controlled facial expressions. About white farmers he said:

Our present state of mind is that you are now our enemies because you really have behaved as enemies of Zimbabwe. We are full of anger. Our entire community is angry and that is why we now have the war veterans seizing land and this will require a real transformation on their [the whites'] part.

At first I wasn't sure what this "transformation" meant, was the president implying a racial change, an attitude towards land ownership change? As I watched the same news report later on Sky Television, they ran more of the president's interview and it became clear that it was a political transformation that was being demanded of us, enemies of Zimbabwe. Clearly referring to the government's defeat in the February referendum, Mr Mugabe said, 'Their mobilizing, actually coercing, their labour forces on the farms to support the one position opposed to government, has exposed them as not our friends, but enemies.' In other words, if we dared to believe in democracy, dared to demand our legal and constitutional rights, dared to ask for an end to corruption, dared to support anyone except the ruling political party, we would have to face the consequences.

Zimbabwe's 20th Anniversary of Independence would be one remembered for a long time. A day of grief and mourning, of pain and bloodshed, of disbelief and despair.

Independence Day was a public holiday on which I traditionally closed the farm for the day. Two workers would come in early, milk the cows, take the sheep and cattle out to graze and then they would go off for the rest of the day. We always kept our trading store closed and this year had been no exception. Our neighbour over the road who operated a butchery and general dealers' store, however, often stayed open when our store was closed to pick up the extra business. He clearly made a judgement error when he decided to open on Independence Day this year. The war veterans and their supporters had gathered at the tent in our field for their usual meeting as we had watched the president on television, telling the country that whites were enemies of the state. A few beers under their belts, the war veterans had then set out on a walk around the neighbourhood. Seeing the butchery open for business, they mustered their supporters and a gang of them stormed into the little building.

'Why are you open today?' they demanded of the owner. 'Don't you know what day it is? Close now or we will burn this butchery down.'

Within minutes the butchery was closed, the workers sent home, customers asked to leave, gates closed and locked. The war veterans had the supreme authority now and whatever they said had to be obeyed if you were going to survive. Two days later the weekly *Independent* came out and in a front-page article told Zimbabwe what we had all suspected for some time. "Government deploys army to direct invasions", the headline read.

Sources told the Independent that the military officers were responsible for coordinating logistics to ensure that there was reliable food and other essential supplies. This explained the use of AK-47 assault rifles and other automatic weapons by those invading farms and police inertia in reacting to reported instances of violence and murder on the farms. Nobody has been arrested for the murder of two farmers in Macheke and Nyamndlovu. Sources said some of the army officers were using trucks to transport food to the invading war veterans and Zanu PF supporters. 'The plain-clothed army officers stationed at the occupied farms disguise themselves as war veterans and they have played a very influential role in the upkeep of the invaders,' a source said.

There was so much going on that we didn't know about, and probably never would. It possibly explained the perpetual grin on the face of war veterans' leader, Chenjerai Hunzvi.

On Wednesday, 19th April 2000, Chenjerai Hunzvi appeared again in the High Court. In a case brought by the Commercial Farmers' Union, Hunzvi was being charged with contempt of court for inciting farm invasions after they had been declared illegal by the country's judiciary. Appearing in front of Justice David Bartlett, Chenjerai Hunzvi was found guilty and given two weeks to show proof that he had actively sought to end farm invasions. According to the *Financial Gazette*: "Hunzvi refused to take questions from journalists after yesterday's court appearance. 'I will play my game quietly,' was all he said before he was led away by one of his aides". The BBC cameras though got a closer position to the man and he grinned into their lenses. 'He was led like a sheep to the slaughter,' Hunzvi said, struggling not to laugh. What on earth that meant we didn't know; it was another one of those things we would never understand. In an editorial in the *Daily News* entitled "Victory for Law and order", the editor wrote:

Hunzvi's conviction is timely. It demonstrated to the motley band of vocal farm invaders that in the eyes of the law they are like any other citizens and should not expect to be accorded special treatment, only because they fought for the liberation of this country.

Chenjerai Hunzvi left the High Court in a black limousine and was chauffeur-driven immediately to State House for a meeting with President Mugabe and the leaders of the Commercial Farmers' Union. This was a meeting that all farmers were hoping would finally produce results. A meeting, face to face, for the first time since farm invasions began, that could see an end to the violence, the intimidation, the beatings, the killings. On television we watched the CFU leaders followed by Hunzvi drive into the grounds of the president's residence. We looked at our watches and prayed that sanity would prevail. The minutes and then the hours ticked by. Six and a half hours later a press conference was called. Surely, after that many hours, some agreement had been reached; some major breakthrough had been achieved. Again our hopes were dashed though as the BBC journalists told us what had happened.

The first five hours of the meeting had excluded the leaders of the Commercial Farmers' Union. They had been confined to talks between Mr Mugabe and Chenjerai Hunzvi. The BBC reporter said, 'After several hours of talks not much has changed. There will be no withdrawal of war veterans, no putting of police in to affected farms.' At the press conference President Mugabe looked tired and angry. He said the meetings had created an "atmosphere of understanding" and in the manner we were now so accustomed to, he continued: 'What are the farmers prepared to do? What land are they prepared to yield?' Tim Henwood, president of the CFU looked tense, bunched-up, grim-faced. Choosing his words with great care he said, 'We've had a good meeting.' Chenjerai Hunzvi, relaxed and beaming, said, 'Hostilities should cease.' The double talk, diplomatic non-statements and ambiguously worded phrases meant nothing.

With a country clearly confused about who was in charge, who was actually at the helm and making the decisions, people began to panic. Amazingly enough though, it wasn't the farmers and outspoken opposition supporters who took fright. It wasn't those of us who had our lands invaded, our livelihoods threatened, every move we made watched, our colleagues murdered and beaten—we were still resolved and strong but the people in the towns began to panic. Perhaps they knew something we didn't? In the Property Report of the *Financial Gazette*, a staff reporter wrote:

> *Real estate firms this week said the market was awash with properties because of an upsurge in the number of sellers while most buyers were taking a wait and see position. … Another property agent said: 'When police can no longer protect the country's citizens from being attacked*

and having their properties seized and the government starts creating pieces of legislation to take properties without paying anything, then investors will rush to dispose of those properties before they lose them.'

Who were all these people trying to sell their houses in the towns and cities, I wondered. Where was their patriotism? What did they know that we didn't? Did they really believe this was going to go on forever? Were they mad or was I? Perhaps it was only because Ian and I were receiving so many letters of support every day that we were still as positive as we were. Most of these letters came through on my email, some from friends but most from strangers.

A friend I hadn't seen for 25 years wrote from Belgium:

It is sad and infuriating. It is so very reminiscent for M and me of our time together in the Philippines in the year before Marcos fell. ... The exiled leader of the opposition, Ninoy Aqino, was shot dead as he descended the stairs of his aircraft. This unleashed the movement that became known as people power and had people sitting down in front of tanks and finally leading members of the military breaking away to join the opposition. It was a time of despair, courage and hope. Clearly Zimbabwe travels a similar path at present ...

From my brother in England:

Every one of my friends who have met you or Ian (plus lots who haven't) are appalled by what they have seen and read in the press and all send messages of support. As for me I'm shit scared that you are all going to be okay and I hope that none of you will be too brave.

From a stranger in Australia:

Reporters constantly remark that it is incomprehensible that Robert Mugabe continues with this course when it is clearly abhorred by the international community. Don't ever think that you are on your own. Lobbying is going on all over to the respective governments. The emails are flying everywhere. Keep your chin up and above all keep safe.

From a cousin in England I hadn't heard from for 15 years:

I cannot begin to imagine what it must be like to have gangs of drunken squatters occupying the farm. The plight of white farmers across the whole of Zim seems to be a staple of the nightly news over here right now—so at least some comfort (scant though it is) might be gleaned from the fact that there is a world out there that is aware of what Mugabe is up to.

From a stranger in Bulawayo:

Please try and hang in there, which I know is easy for me to say. Help is on its way and try to believe that the ever-growing majority of Zimbabweans are on your side, also feeling helpless enough in not being able to provide you the comfort and support that you so badly need... You are constantly in our prayers and constantly in our thoughts. We will not desert you.

There were, however, the few messages of dissent:

Don't you think it's time you guys decided to leave? I think the writing is on the wall. There really is no future in Zimbabwe.

Buoyed by the messages of support and encouragement, depressed by the messages of doom, our moods swung up and down. The continuing invasion of our land, the upset to our lives and the deaths of our colleagues were taking a heavy toll but I was as determined as ever to keep on trying to tell the world what was going on. The mailing list for my weekly email letter to family and friends was growing and just before Easter I called it "Starting to sink in", as Ian and I began seriously to doubt our future, not in Zimbabwe, but on our farm.

Dear family and friends

Every week the list of people wanting copies of my weekly dose of depression gets longer and longer. Thank you all for your support. Reading back my last circular letter dated 17th April, I can hardly believe how the situation has declined in only five days. I think for Ian and me and probably hundreds of farmers all over the country, it has finally started to sink in that this is not going to go away; it's not going to stop; no one's going to help us and it's probably going to get worse still.

Ian and I sat last night talking about how we were going to manage to start again. In our middle age we were just beginning to think that we had the formula right and were set up for the future. We have finally paid off all our debts, the property is ours and the livestock worth a million plus. Well I think now the bubble has burst. God knows where we will go and the thought of again having nothing—no home, no assets and no security—is totally depressing. Our morale, as well as that of our neighbours who haven't yet left, is at its lowest. On a national level, the violence and intimidation have been horrific in these past five days. Subsequent to the murder of Dave Stevens and torture of five of his neighbours in Macheke, our entire district went into shock and then panic. Marondera town is full to bursting with homeless, aimless people wandering around in a daze. The town is crawling with journalists and reporters. Outside our Marondera Farmers' Union office we've had BBC, CNN, Sky, SABC, ABC, Reuters, The Daily News, Paris Match and others. Everywhere you walk in town there are foreigners with large fluffy microphones desperate for someone to talk to them. None of us have anything to say any more so the cameras have resorted to taking photographs of our wrists—seeing how many of us are chain smoking in an attempt to deal with the stress!

The violence after the murder of Dave Stevens raged down from Macheke—exactly as we had feared—to almost the entire Ruzawi River area, where gangs of 200-strong armed thugs and co overran a local security company outpost, and the farmers evacuated. Then it came right to the boundaries of Marondera town as gangs rampaged along the North Road, which is fewer than two kilometres from the centre of the town. There were horrific beatings and atrocities in workers' compounds and according to eye witnesses the screams could be heard from three kilometres away. From there these gangs moved onto the Bridge Road (about ten kilometres from where we are) and again started their beatings and intimidation in compounds. At that point two of our neighbours left, which leaves now only a couple of farms between them and us and puts us in the front line. (If we aren't already in the front line with our group of squatters 300 metres from the house).

The very day after the meeting between the president, the CFU and Chenjerai Hunzvi, the security situation newspaper reported:

Commercial Farmers' Union president, Tim Henwood, yesterday ordered all commercial farmers in Matabeleland to immediately evacuate their farms and move into Bulawayo as more clashes with war veterans are anticipated over the Easter weekend. ... The CFU has received reports that about 350 war veterans are on their way from various parts of the country destined for Matabeleland North as reinforcements for those already transported there from Harare.

We too had been warned that the Easter weekend might be bloody. There was so much gossip though, so many rumours, that we did not know what or who to believe any more. Our workers had said that they had heard talk that Sunday, Easter Sunday, was the day when whites were going to be killed en masse; it was, after all, the president of Zimbabwe who had declared us to be enemies of the state. It was more than likely that this was speculation; tempers and emotions were at fever pitch. Ian and I decided to stay on the farm, keep the gates locked and see what happened. I wondered at the wisdom of our decision when I read the daily situation report from the CFU when it came in on the email two days before Easter:

> *Although the following areas have been evacuated, we believe that this is not necessary in most areas and careful consideration of the situation is necessary before a drastic decision is made: Headlands, Wedza, Virginia, Macheke, Enterprise, Matabeleland and Midlands. Please do this according to a plan.*

It went on to detail the latest evacuation nearest to us:

> *In Wedza there are reports of invaders gathering in large numbers around the area. The Igava road has been totally blocked off with trees etc. Julian Herbert has called for an evacuation of the lower Ruzawi farms and they have managed to get through the back road there.*

That night I went to bed feeling very anxious and managed to get even less sleep than normal. I had told our night guard to keep a special watch and the electric fence was of course on. I woke at 4am to hear Richie moving around and went through to his bedroom. He was soaked and his sheets and blankets were wet. My seven-year-old son had wet his bed, something that he hadn't done for about four years.

'I'm sorry Mum, I'm sorry Mum,' he repeated again and again as he stood looking down at his feet.

Taking Richie in my arms I held him tightly and stroked his curly head. 'What happened Rich?' I asked quietly.

'I was too scared to go to the bathroom Mum. I'm sorry.'

Lowering my head so that my son wouldn't see my tears, I gently stripped off Richard's wet pyjamas and got some dry ones out of the cupboard. We changed his bed together and then I climbed in next to him. As Richard lay snuggled in my arms with an entire gallery of teddies looking on, I felt so ashamed and closed my eyes so that he wouldn't see my pain. What was I thinking of, as a parent, a mother, allowing my son to keep living like this? How much longer could any of us stand this pressure? Were the "peaceful demonstrations" by the people all over our land going to leave permanent scars on Richard's mind, on mine, on Ian's? I was already badly stressed and remembered how I had panicked the afternoon before. Walking back from the store I had heard singing, loud singing from a lot of voices nearby. Immediately thinking that it was war veterans on the rampage I had panicked and started running towards the house, my hands shaking as I unlocked and re-locked gates. Anna and Emmanuel were in the garden and asked me what was wrong.

'They're coming,' I panted. 'Can't you hear them? Lots of them are coming.'

We all listened and Anna shook her head.

'It's a funeral,' she said. 'Look, just a funeral.'

I felt such a fool as the three of us stood watching the stream of cars slowly rounding the corner. Turning, I looked down the field at the blue tent and its seven men. They too were watching the cortege; it made a change that they had something to watch other than me. Is this what life in Zimbabwe had come to?

Good Friday, instead of being the normal, peaceful, family day of reflection, was another tense one for us. The men in the field started gathering early and the numbers built up rapidly. By ten in the morning there were about 150 people in the field around the squatters' tent. Someone brought along their cattle and 50 or 60 head grazed in the fields where once our cattle had grazed. Vehicles started arriving and they were the usual ones: the burnt orange Peugeot, the green station wagon, the grey pickup truck, the bright red car with the tinted windows. Ian picked up his video equipment and went off to film the gathering from what had now become his usual hiding place. When he returned, he told me of a chance meeting he had had with a young black lawyer. Perched up a tree, Ian filmed a car rounding the corner. Suddenly, seeing the crowds in our field and all the vehicles, the car braked, did a hasty U-turn and stopped where Ian was.

'What's going on?' the man asked. 'Is this a land invasion?'

'Yes, another one. They've been here for weeks now but every weekend we have these big gatherings. Some sort of political meeting or something.'

'My God,' the stranger said, 'this is unbelievable, disgraceful. What are you going to do? Have you phoned the police?'

'No, there's no point. They won't come.'

'But that's your land isn't it?' the man continued. 'This is just unbelievable.'

Ian and the stranger talked for a while longer before the young lawyer carried on, driving very fast past the gathering in our field. When Ian related the story to me I felt really encouraged. Here was a normal, ordinary Zimbabwean, appalled by what was going on; I don't know why but it gave me hope that this madness would end. A little while later a neighbour phoned to tell us that there was a large group of people down in our field and that he had phoned the police on our behalf. The member in charge of Marondera Rural had said, 'Unfortunately we are failing to find a report book, but please, wish Mr and Mrs Buckle a happy Easter.' You just had to laugh—or you'd have a mental breakdown.

There was nothing much else to do over the Easter weekend except sit tight, car keys at the ready, emergency suitcases packed, and read the mountains of emails and newspapers that had piled up in daunting amounts on every possible surface of the house. I didn't feel very encouraged by page three of the *Zimbabwe Independent*. "Msika says war veterans to move from occupied farms", the headline read. I'd heard that before but read on anyway.

Vice President Joseph Msika yesterday reaffirmed his statement that the war veterans who have invaded farms across the country would be removed... 'They will leave bit by bit,' said Msika. 'That's the strategy. We will talk to them to move out when the time comes but we will allow them to go back to the farms for campaigning...' Asked if there was any contradiction between his statement and the president's, Msika said, 'No. It's not that. I was talking to the president a little while ago. When he said that they are not withdrawing from the farms, he was telling the British that the ex-combatants would not be evicted wholesale. But we will talk to them to move out gradually,' said Msika.

More gobbledegook double talk, meaningless words to confuse us even more about who had really said what.

Then, the height of insult, I came across an article in the *Zimbabwe Independent* called "We are here to stay. Tough luck to Rhodesians—war vets". I couldn't believe what I was reading. The very war vets squatting on our farm had given an account of their actions to the newspaper when reporters had called, unbeknown to me, at our farm.

*A Zimbabwean flag was flying high at Watershed/St Michael's Farm
[other names by which our farm was known] about 67 kilometres east of
Harare in a scene reminiscent of a Viking conquest of foreign land. ...
'Consider yourself lucky that you are here, but we just want you to go
and tell the nation that we are here to stay. Tough luck to Rhodesians,'
Edward Muswaka, a war veteran said.*

*Muswaka was registering the new settlers at Watershed Farm. All
ages were congregating on the farm to get a share "of their motherland"...
'We want to live in harmony with the white farmer,' said Andrew Nyoka,
a disabled man on crutches. 'We have left the other side for him to till; it is
enough for him to make a decent living.' Nyoka was honest enough to tell
the Zimbabwe Independent that he was not a victim of the liberation war
but that he had been disabled by a road accident in the late 1980s.
Courtesy of the land invasions, Nyoka now has a small piece of land to
farm at Watershed Farm... Despite being disabled, Nyoka said he is
determined to produce potatoes that he will sell and make a decent living.
Another invader, Justin, is just 25 and determined to start farming
tobacco on the plot Muswaka demarcated for him. ... Another man in his
thirties, Moffat, has already set up a tuckshop on the same farm. The
Independent visited his plot, which is adjacent to the house of I. Buckle,
farm owner. 'It is not possible for anyone to remove me from here,' Moffat
was firm before telling the reporter to mind his own business... However,
none of the new settlers had the necessary agricultural implements to
start farming. Their argument was that the government would provide
because the state was fully behind the invasions. But can the
cash-strapped government afford that? It is a sad tale of a country that has
quickened the pace in its charge for the precipice ... the invaders, who
prefer to be called "liberators", believe they are repossessing their land
from colonizers. It hasn't dawned on them that those they are
dispossessing might be white but they are Zimbabweans nonetheless and
most of them bought the land at commercial rates.*

So now I knew the fate of our farm: potatoes, tobacco and a tuck
shop—all to be undertaken by a group of unemployed youngsters,
who were in their nappies when the War for Independence was being
fought, who between them couldn't even afford a pack of cigarettes, let
alone tools, implements, fertilizer or anything that went into running a
business. What a crying shame, I thought, that youngsters could have
been deceived like this. Where did they think the government was
going to find the money to get them started? It didn't even have money
to buy fuel to run its own vehicles.

Edward, our resident war veteran, was obviously a lot happier with the reporters and cameras than I was because a few days later I was visited by a news crew from the American Broadcasting Corporation. They wanted to interview and film us but I declined; like so many other farmers now, we were very nervous about having our names or faces on television. The publicity might have been good for exposing the land invasions for what they were, but they led to repercussions that left farms on fire, properties looted and homes evacuated. The ABC crew were determined though to hear my side of the story and told me apologetically that they had already visited and filmed Edward and his friends down at the tent. Edward had been delighted to see them—he had just received his weekly payout and took the Americans down to the local beer hall to show them off to the locals. The Americans shook their heads and laughed as they told me that Edward had proceeded to get "rat-arse pissed" and shout his mouth off about whites, Rhodesians, colonialists and land for the people. So drunk did Edward get, that he gladly allowed the ABC to film him sharing out the money he had been given by his backer to pay him and his friends for squatting on our farm for another week. The ABC cameraman offered to show me the video footage of this but I declined, knowing that I'd never be able to keep my composure. As with all the other journalists we had now spoken to, the ABC crew were sympathetic to our plight, not because we were white, but because we had been born in Zimbabwe, had bought our land and were being stripped of all our human rights. Eventually they left, filming, through the locked gates, Richard, Brian and Linnet as they played Robin Hood games on the lawn and our long-suffering dogs dodged their arrows.

Whilst we had a relatively uneventful Easter weekend, war vets went on the rampage on farms much closer to Harare and the world's cameras showed footage of farms burning, tobacco bales smouldering and terrified farm workers running away from axe-yielding mobs in all directions. As the week wore on and each day seemed like an eternity, more and more people were beginning to speak out about the repercussions on Zimbabwe's economy. A CFU official was quoted in the *Financial Gazette*:

'This is threatening investment as well as production. This has totally halted preparations to plant winter crops such as wheat and barley'… Zimbabwe's average annual wheat production of 320,000 tonnes is worth \$3 billion at the primary producer level alone, with downstream industries adding more billions.

An article in the *Daily News* made even more dire comments:

> *What is going to happen to the banking sector in the event that large sections of the farming community refuse to, or more likely, are unable to service the loans/overdrafts? ... This money belongs to the people who hold deposits with the banks. The money does not belong to the bank... I urge people hell bent on destroying crops to desist from doing so. The 110 tons of tobacco destroyed last weekend on a farm would have provided sufficient foreign currency to purchase at least 850,000 litres of petrol.*

The country's annual tobacco sales started, and hopes that we may have had for signs of economic recovery were dashed again. The *Daily News* said it all:

> *The flue-cured tobacco sales began on a very low key yesterday with disappointing prices while growers stayed away because of the current political violence, recent farm invasions and a fixed exchange rate.*

Meanwhile, professional people appeared to be looking seriously at their future in Zimbabwe, particularly those employed in the civil service. A lawyer in the Attorney-General's office resigned from his post:

> *'The Office of the Attorney-General has been rendered non-existent by the current state of lawlessness in the country. The government no longer respects advice from this office. This constitutional crisis hurts my conscience as a lawyer,' he said. (Daily News).*

For a moment our attention was drawn away from the deepening crisis on the farms and the steady collapse of the economy when the offices of the *Daily News* in the capital city were bombed. They reported their own near demise:

> *A powerful bomb exploded in an art gallery situated on the ground floor of Trustee House, next to Karigamombe Centre on Samora Machel Avenue on Saturday night... The attackers did not make their motive known, but it is widely believed the attack was launched in a bid to silence the Daily News, which is regarded as being critical of government. The Daily News has been strong in its criticism of corruption and the disorderly invasion of commercial farms by war veterans. Nyarota [the paper's editor] said yesterday that the attack had not come as a complete*

surprise to him. He said he had received a death threat on Wednesday 19th April. The letter [threatening Nyarota's life] reads: "We are tired of your daily news about the farm invasions and your lack of respect to our dear president. All your effort is to embarrass the president and make him the object useless and harmful to the nation. (sic) … If you fail to abide by our command, please prepare yourself a highway in the skies before we descend violently on you and your imperial organization". Mr Nyarota joined a growing list of people who had been receiving death threats; before it had mainly been farmers under attack, now the web was widening to include professionals and even priests, anyone who dared speak out about lawlessness.

There were many, though, who were still patriotic and courageous enough to speak out. At the memorial service for Martin Olds, the Presbyterian minister did not mince his words, as reported in the *Zimbabwe Independent*:

I believe that the government and the president are to blame… By condoning criminal action, by disregarding the courts he puts himself alongside the criminals. He indeed is a criminal; he is the enemy of the state… Do not keep quiet, speak out; the truth shall set you free.

Perhaps taking courage from the words of those that dared to speak, other voices let themselves be heard. Patrick Kombayi, a war veteran and successful businessman, bombarded all the free press publications with a series of half-page advertisements condemning land invasions, lawlessness and the highly questionable governance of the country. Fay Chung, former minister of Education in Zimbabwe and a freedom fighter from 1975 to 1980 in the Independence war, reacted angrily to the slaughtering of Martin Olds. 'It was therefore with a sense of shock that I learnt that Martin Olds has been murdered on his farm in a racist attack by purported ex-combatants…' (*Zimbabwe Independent*).

Possibly the most damning voice came from a veteran freedom fighter, nationalist and close friend of President Mugabe. In an interview with the *Daily News*, James Chikerema who had grown up with the president, gone to primary school with him and been involved in African politics since 1948 said:

It shows how desperate the president is. He has to hire Hunzvi who has to hire the war veterans, former fighters who are on the criminal fringe of that organization whose leadership has criminal court cases pending… It is not spontaneous; it is organized and orchestrated. The whole thing is an exercise in a state of anarchy. (Daily News).

Everyone now knew what was really going on. The press was full of it, day after day, and perhaps because now the war veterans didn't have to hide anything any more, they went on the rampage on the farms. On a large number of properties within 30 kilometres of Harare, great clouds of smoke could be seen. Farmers evacuated in their dozens as truckloads of war veterans and their "rent a mob" supporters went into a frenzied orgy. Workers' compounds were destroyed, doors smashed, property looted, buildings set on fire. Women were raped, men abducted and everywhere people fled from the mobs who seemed to have become frenzied with the blood on their hands. People had paraffin poured over them and were set alight; others were whipped and kicked; yet others had arms and legs broken. Two farmhouses were completely trashed, belongings strewn on the lawn, domestic dogs beaten to death as they lay in their kennels. The war veterans were clearly determined to show Zimbabweans how powerful they were.

How was this possible? How could a peaceful and prosperous country collapse like this? It was, after all, only 62 days since the farm invasions had begun. By 30th April 2000, two months and two days since the madness had begun, over 1,000 farms had been invaded. Five thousand and seventy-eight violent incidents, on and off Zimbabwe's farms, had been documented by human rights organizations. This included 1,012 people assaulted, eight women raped, 19 people murdered, 417 cases of house and property destruction. How was this possible?

RIVERS OF BLOOD AND TEARS

This is as close as it's safe to go now,' said the BBC commentator. Barely 20 kilometres from the centre of Harare city, the reporters and camera crews gathered to report on the rampage that the war veterans and their supporters had embarked upon. White-skinned journalists were now the targets of much hatred from the war veterans. Accused of misrepresenting interests and biased reporting, they had their cars stoned and were chased by stick-wielding gangs. The *Zimbabwe Independent* teamed up with foreign journalists and reported on their encounter on one of the burning farms just outside Harare:

> *Armed war veterans and youths wielding sticks, machetes, axes and knobkerries ready for a kill were visible everywhere. ...We were suddenly confronted by the armed militiamen who advanced towards the vehicle and demanded to know what we were looking for. They had no problem with this reporter because I was black but the immediate problem was, what exactly was I doing with a foreign journalist in their territory? ... One of the foreign journalists accompanying us paid for our freedom. He handed over a few US dollars, which were enough to calm down the flaring tempers. From a distance, revolutionary songs could be heard as threats were being unleashed against the farm workers.*

On another farm the situation was much the same:

> *Getting close to the scene of the incident was terrifying. Despite the repeated warnings from the surrounding commercial farmers, the Zimbabwe Independent made for the burning compound to have a glimpse of the latest form of "peaceful demonstrations" by the war veterans. Over 50 families were moving out of the compound. They said the war veterans, armed with AK rifles, were up in the mountains, hunting down the commercial farmer ... who had already fled the scene of the incident to Harare... The salvaged property of the workers was strewn around: radio sets, wooden furniture and clothing. Amidst the mayhem, rumour filtered through that the war veterans were coming to finish off what remained of the compound. As reports came out that the war veterans were advancing towards our car, we sped off at high speed heading north, passing streams of families carrying the few precious belongings they could salvage... In a convoy of five vehicles, we proceeded to town like a funeral cortege. We had nothing to bury—except the reputation of our country.*

With the situations on and around the farms deteriorating, war veterans then began to move in closer to the cities and wield their new-found power whenever it suited them. Their reign of terror, previously limited to farmers, their workers and opposition activists, now expanded to include anyone who stood in their way. The *Daily News* reported that:

> *War veterans and Zanu PF supporters, now occupying farms along the High Glen-Chitungwiza road, have banned all buses belonging to the Kukura Kurewa Bus Company from using that route. ... 'We are giving them a strong warning not to even dream of using this road, otherwise we will set the buses alight.' A bus driver said the war veterans and the residents had boarded the bus but refused to pay their fares, saying they deserved preferential treatment because they fought for the liberation of Zimbabwe. 'They refused to pay and that was when the trouble started ... passengers on the bus joined in to beat them up.'*

In another area of the country a group of 80 war veterans arrived at the Ruenya Granite Company in Mutoko in four government-owned District Development trucks. They demanded to see the mine manager and when told that he was not there, the mob went wild. The granite company, which in 1999 exported US$300,000 worth of stone, was visited by reporters from the *Financial Gazette* who interviewed the dazed and terrified workers.

> *They ransacked the place and fought over bread and tinned beef. They were really like wild dogs... The marauding gangs broke into a fowl run, grabbed four chickens, cut their throats and barbecued them as they watched the house they had set on fire burn down... When no one among the workers admitted to supporting the MDC, the attackers then went on the rampage ... they grabbed clothing, food items, money and anything valuable they laid their hands on... When the attackers were drunk from the three crates of beer and a large assortment of spirits and wines they had found ... they then set the place on fire.*

Ordinary members of the public then saw for themselves the reaction of the country's police force, a reaction farmers had been experiencing for the past two months.

> *Just about then two police trucks arrived on the scene... they did not arrest any of the attackers but instead watched them as they lifted their loot away. 'This incident has left us wondering who will protect us because the police just watched and did nothing as these people carried away stolen goods.'*

There was no doubt in anyone's mind now that Zimbabwe had descended into anarchy. All over the country people were mourning at funerals of farmers, of opposition activists, of ordinary workers caught up in the killing fields. The national ZBC Television, instead of showing us footage of burning homes, of looting mobs, of terrified people running for their lives, of a nation in tears, ran as their top news headline an incident where 12 youths stoned a house belonging to Robert Mugabe. The youths had left the funeral of an innocent victim slaughtered by war veterans and had stoned a house owned by the president. Police action was immediate: all 12 were arrested and in custody in fewer than three hours. A police spokesman said on National Television: 'We are a-political ... the police do not take sides ... this crime is very serious.' A shocked nation turned their televisions off in disgust. Breaking windows was a "serious crime"—what about rape, murder, beating, torture, looting, arson, abduction?

The outside world was as shocked as Zimbabwe at this sudden and catastrophic deterioration of the situation. There were widespread calls for the war veterans to be reigned in, for a return to law and order and for the police to do their jobs. Leaders of the Commercial Farmers' Union again met with Chenjerai Hunzvi. Barely a week before, Hunzvi had said that "hostilities should cease". Now he was more specific. BBC's television cameras filmed him saying to a crowd of his supporters on an invaded farm, 'What I would want to say to everyone, be it a war veteran or a farmer, is that violence is not needed. The violence should stop forthwith. The criminal element that has been taking place of late will be dealt with severely.' To the cameras of the SABC, however, Hunzvi said, 'If MDC comes to provoke us, we can work together to discipline them. The war veterans know the best methods of disciplining someone and it will be discipline forever.'

Chenjerai Hunzvi had again shown his true colours as he contradicted himself by calling for peace on the one hand and insinuating "permanent discipline" on the other. Hunzvi and the leaders of the CFU had apparently brokered a deal in their latest talks. A strange and very one-sided deal where again the war veterans were in a win-win situation. The deal was simple: squatters would stay on the farms, the violence would stop and farmers would no longer be allowed to support opposition parties. Many other farmers and I were furious when we heard of this "deal". Surely a deal comprises both sides yielding something? I was very suspicious of this deal in view of the fact that a number of other issues were involved. One of these was that Hunzvi had been found guilty of contempt of court and was about to be charged for his crime—unless the CFU withdrew their charges. Hunzvi was angling for exactly that as was reported in the *Daily News*:

> Hunzvi said, 'As the leader of the war veterans I have already been convicted of contempt of court charges over farm invasions. How do commercial farmers expect me to engage in serious dialogue with them if these charges remain? They must drop the charges immediately.' Apart from his contempt of court charges, Hunzvi is on remand on allegations of defrauding the War Victims' Compensation Fund of $467,660. Police are investigating him in connection with fraud amounting to $2.7 million at Zexcom, the investment arm of the war veterans' association.

Even though the deal was in place and Hunzvi had said that "hostilities should cease", no one drew much comfort from his words, suspecting that they were just meaningless platitudes. We all began to wonder if in fact Chenjerai Hunzvi was still in control of his members and their supporters. *The Farmer* told us of yet another indiscretion in one of Hunzvi's encounters with the cameras.

And while Hunzvi called for peace on the farms, he said that the invasions had taken place for two reasons: 'One is to get the land back,' he said. 'The other is to keep Zanu PF in power and if those things do not happen there will be no peace.'

Hunzvi's deal with farmers did not apparently extend to anyone else though, as the *Daily News* reported:

War veterans abducted eight MDC supporters from Nyamhunga Township in Kariba and assaulted them. A Zesa security guard, Luckson Kanyurira, died as a result of injuries sustained in the assault. His corpse was displayed [by the war veterans] on the veranda of a shop.

The screen of my computer was overflowing with messages from people all over the world. What's going on? they asked. Have you made plans to evacuate? Like us, they too thought the country was about to erupt into a civil war. In my weekly letter, which I called "The gods must be angry", I updated our own situation.

Watching the country we've lived in for 40 years disintegrate before our eyes is just too horrific. We don't know whom to trust any more. I never talk to my customers in the store now because the squatters from our tent have taken to wearing MDC t-shirts and hanging around in the store to see whom they can trip up.

...Many farmers are outraged at the recent deal brokered between the CFU and the leader of the war vets. The deal is that the squatters are allowed to stay but they won't commit any more acts of violence. In return for this we—as farmers and employers—have been told that we are no longer to support the opposition political party... We are required to attend—and take our workers—to Zanu PF rallies, raise our fists and "pamberi" and be berated for being "bad Zimbabweans" for daring to differ. There have been three of these rallies in our neighbourhood in the past three days—none of which I have attended. Our neighbour attended one, terrified of repercussions if he didn't go, and came back with all the stories. That meeting was chaired by three local war vets who introduced themselves as Prince, Satan and Stalin. I'd rather let them liberate my house before I attend.

...About a month ago—in a moment of hysteria (of which I seem to have a worrying increase lately)—about a week after the first High Court Order had been won, we had a terrific storm here with huge winds and a lot of rain. The squatters in our field had their tent flattened and they

evacuated during the night. We all laughed and I told our workers that the gods were angry. Then, after the second High Court ruling was made ordering them off, and still they didn't go, we had another storm. No electricity for 23 hours, thunder, lightning, heavy rain and hail. The next morning the squatters were still there but only just and this time the workers told me that the gods were angry and again we all laughed. This week winter suddenly arrived on our farm and the night temperatures have plummeted. We've had days of mist, typical drizzle and guti and strong cold winds. Now, you've guessed it, the gods are really angry!

This next stage of the war veterans' reign of terror was soon to be known as "re-education" and it extended across the country. The farms were the obvious place for the veterans to operate from—they were isolated, out of public view and contained large numbers of already terrified people who had little access to national or international media. Also, in some farming areas the war veterans had completely taken over. Farmers had fled and the war veterans operated over three or four properties in blocks, declared them "no-go" areas and were virtually untouchable. Every now and again a journalist or camera crew managed to get in and report what was going on. There was little film footage but what we did see was spine chilling. War veterans, wielding sticks and axes forced people into lines and made them march and chant for hours on end. The people, looking mesmerized, defeated, exhausted did what they were told. Young and old, men and women, sick and healthy, teenagers and children—marched and chanted "Zanu, Zanu, Zanu, Zanu" until virtually hypnotized. With terror, cold terror, we read the reports of re-education camps in the *Financial Gazette*. Reporters spoke to two farm workers near the newly liberated Gem Farm.

They confirm that there are at least 500 men, women and children at Gem. And more are arriving all the time. Lorries laden with people can be seen turning off the main road led by young men clenching their fists in the Zanu PF salute. Hundreds of Zanu PF supporters are patrolling the camp armed with sticks and knives. 'We were ordered to sing yesterday from 2pm until deep into the night,' says Samuel. 'Then we started again and sang until 6am this morning.' He describes the sleep and rest deprivation and the boot camp routine. Everyone was kept awake overnight. 'We must jog for hours, then we eat the food stolen from farms just to get the energy to jog again.' Joseph says that no one spoke to them of land. They were simply ordered not to vote MDC. In rural villages all

*over the country Zanu PF is warning people that it will know from
numbers printed on ballot papers who voted MDC and that these people
will be punished later... Forty minutes drive north at Mvurwi, labourers
were re-educated two days before the Concession camps were opened.
Here more than 1,000 workers were trucked into the huge Forrester
tobacco estate in vehicles commandeered from surrounding farms... At
the camp workers were encouraged to turn on one another. 'We were told
we must beat anyone wearing an MDC t-shirt' ... Twenty people were
beaten with electric cables and rubber truncheons.*

On our farm in Marondera we had nothing like as organized an affair
as the re-education camps in other areas of the country. The
knowledge that it was going on, however, was frightening enough.
The war veteran and his supporters on our farm were not as well
organized and perhaps not as politically indoctrinated. As the cold
winds blew up our fields and battered their tent, they became more
and more uncomfortable. Edward took to spending hours at a time in
our little trading store where it was warm and dry and he could listen
to the radio. He told Jane that he'd had enough of living in the tent and
camping out. It was cold, he said, there were too many mosquitoes and
it was smelly. Jane and I laughed till we cried at Edward's statement
that it was smelly in the field where they had made their headquarters.
For two months, crowds of up to 200 people met in the field, defecated
wherever they felt the need and dropped their litter everywhere. Of
course it was smelly. One morning George called me to come and see
what was going on.

'They're leaving,' he said with a grin on his face. 'See, they are taking
their blankets.'

'I don't believe it George. Why would they leave now? There isn't
even an election date yet.'

'But look, they are carrying their things, blankets, pots and pans, big
water containers, duffel bags.'

'I'll believe it when the tent goes George!'

For the rest of the day the squatters traipsed backwards and
forwards across the field carrying their belongings. It certainly did look
promising. When I went up to the store at 3.30 that afternoon to help
Jane close up for the day, I stood out on the veranda and looked across
the road at the butchery. I could clearly see Edward leaning against the
wall of the butchery. And the other man who always wore the heavy
black jersey with the eagle on the back; the old man with the navy blue
overalls and red leather cap; the two youngsters with their faded blue

jeans—they were all there and they watched me as avidly as I watched them. Through the window of the store Jane called me to come inside.

'What's going on Jane? Have you heard anything? How come they're all over at the butchery?'

'They are moving in to the butchery now.' Seeing the disbelief on my face, Jane went on. 'It's true. All day they have been bringing their things there, plenty of things and they have told the owner of the butchery that he must give them room.'

'You're joking!'

'No, it's true. They want to live inside now.'

Every couple of minutes I looked out the window but they weren't moving. It seemed that our war veterans really had moved in over the road. Walking back from the store, for the first time in two months, I had a spring in my step. I had always loved the five-minute walk back from the store to the house through the forest of gum trees. Trees I had planted with my own hands, pruned and nurtured, now stood high above my head and their leaves quietly rustled and whispered overhead. If I was really lucky I sometimes saw the barn owls flying low through the trees as they prepared for their nightly patrols. Often there were Kurrichane Thrushes and Arrow Marked Babblers hunting through the leaf litter on the ground and it was always cool and quiet. I stopped when I reached Richard's tree. As the trees had grown up, Richard had carved his name into the bark of one of the gums. I ran my fingers over his name, the bark smooth and cool under my fingers and for a moment lost myself in the memories of a decade.

Richard had been born on this farm and although, as Zimbabwean farms go it wasn't much to write home about, I loved every inch of it. I could remember pushing Richard in his pushchair up to the store between these same trees, remember watching as a jackal had trotted through here every evening for weeks through the dreadful drought. Could remember my adored little wild cat, whom I had called Crazy Cat, getting stuck up one of the trees and we had had to rescue him with a ladder. Could clearly remember Richard's experiment with matches here a year ago. More than anything he loved going with me when I burnt the fire-breaks around the farm, loved being allowed to squirt at the flames with the nozzle of the knapsack sprayer, loved being given a branch and swatting at the flames with it. The previous year, on a Sunday morning, Richard had taken a box of matches, broken off a branch to use as a fire beater and started his own little fire, sure he would be able to put it out by himself. The first I knew about it was when he appeared at my side in the kitchen.

'Mum, come,' he'd said, his face flushed crimson but deathly white around the edges.

'I'm busy Rich. What is it?'

'Come Mum, please. There's a fire.'

Fire! The words always made me run and when I saw the smoke twisting and swirling out through the top of the gum trees, I ran. Before I'd even reached the forest, the smoke had turned a thick choking yellow and the leaves popped and hissed as they spat out their eucalyptus oil. Yelling at the top of my voice I called for help. Isaya and Clemence were soon with me and it took us an hour to extinguish the flames and clear the leaves away from the smouldering ashes.

So many memories. If the men from the tent really were leaving, perhaps there would be more. Perhaps, after all, there could be a future for us on our farm.

When I got up the following morning and went out to see the night guard just after dawn I couldn't believe what I saw—nothing! The tent had gone, and the flag and all sign of the squatters. It was over! Throughout the day I kept going back to look down the field, to see if they had returned, but they stayed away. I went to the store and tears of laughter poured down my face as I saw what they had done. The blue tent had been erected in the yard of the butchery and, right next to it but at a very precarious angle, the Zimbabwean flag. It was Saturday, the day when normally 100 or more people gathered in the field for their weekly meeting. By 9am there were about 15 people in our field, sitting where the tent had been, just sitting, waiting, confused. Others drifted in and out. Three vehicles arrived, drove across the field and then left. At midday the familiar grey truck drove across our field and down to the grove of Msasa trees. Three men got out and started chopping branches off the trees and loading them into the back of the vehicle. Then they pulled out some fence poles and tipped those in the back of their truck too. Through binoculars I watched this and my hands shook with anger at this open and blatant theft. There was nothing I could do.

Later in the afternoon I received a phone call from a neighbour who had a message for me from our local CFU; "Cathy and Ian must go, and take their workers, to a re-education meeting at a nearby farm". NEVER, I wrote in bold capitals across the page of my ledger. They can "liberate" my farm, my house even, but never my mind.

On Sunday morning a truck drove across our field loaded with asbestos roof sheets. Edward's superiors were very angry with him, we heard through the grapevine. They had bought some roofing so that he could put it over a derelict house further down our farm. Edward had been instructed to move back onto our farm. This wasn't over—not by a long way. The flag came back, the people came back, the fences began falling down as more and more poles were pulled out for their campfires. Silly though, it was even worse now that I couldn't actually see them. At least when they'd been at the tent I knew where they were and what they were doing. Now that they were out of sight it was more frightening. I felt even less in control.

While Edward and his merry men settled in, the country held its breath as regional heads of state converged on Victoria Falls for a mini summit. According to the local press, this meeting was only to discuss the war in the Congo. According to all the political analysts, four regional leaders were meeting to discuss the rapidly deteriorating situation in Zimbabwe. All agreed that it was highly unlikely that the leaders of South Africa, Mozambique and Namibia would openly or publicly castigate Mugabe. As the BBC reporters observed: 'They are unlikely to publicly break ranks with President Robert Mugabe. They have a long history together of fighting for freedom and against white minority rule.' When the four leaders emerged from the closed-door meeting, President Mugabe looked tense, tenser than we'd seen him for a long time. Nothing was said though. They had, however, unanimously agreed that Britain was liable for any money that was to be paid to any farmer whose land the government acquired. Junior foreign minister in Britain, Peter Hain, responded immediately on BBC Television. He said that Britain would help

'if we see a serious programme of land reform that is within the rule of law and addresses the problem of the rural poor ... we will not help, however, if violence and defiance of the law continually put an ultimatum up in front of us and just tell us to hand over the money.'

Britain's foreign minister, Robin Cook, spoke on Sky Television.

'The choice is the government of Zimbabwe's. This week they can decide whether to return to the rule of law and to establish a fair programme of land reform that will help the rural poor, or not.'

Both men were responding to the pronouncements of Africa's leaders that Britain should hand over money—unconditionally and regardless of circumstances. They were also talking about a meeting scheduled to be held in London between Britain and Zimbabwe to discuss Zimbabwe's land crisis.

Zimbabwe had not found any relief from its turmoil at the Victoria Falls Summit and we carefully watched the deliberations in London. Zimbabwe demanded that Britain hand over the money. They refused. Britain demanded an end to the violence; an end to intimidation and killing; the transfer of land at free and fair prices; the removal of illegal squatters from farms. Zimbabwe refused. Three top Zimbabwean ministers and their aides, three nights in five star hotels, numerous first class air fares, numerous chauffeur-driven limousines, eight hours of talks—all for nothing. The only thing that both sides had agreed to was that there would be more talks once the violence in Zimbabwe had ended. Home Affairs minister, John Nkomo, summed it up succinctly to the television cameras: 'We do not accept that there are any conditions.'

Farmers and Zimbabweans alike were back to square one. Nothing was going to change. The state-run *Herald* had obviously followed another set of talks though because their headline was: "Ice broken at Zim land talks". Whilst these talks were going on, Zimbabweans watched in undisguised delight as the leader of the MDC returned from a trip abroad. How refreshing to see a man of his importance carrying his own red duffle bag, walking alone across the tarmac to his vehicle. We were so used to masses of people, convoys of shining limousines, armed soldiers and red carpets. How humbling to see this man being just an ordinary man. This man whose influence and effect on ordinary people had struck terror into Zanu PF was like you and me—just an ordinary man, tired and crumpled after a long overseas flight. He met the journalists and spoke, as always, off the cuff with no pomp and ceremony:

> 'Zimbabweans of all races must feel that this is their home and that they have a future in this country—black, white, yellow. Confidence must be given to the citizens of Zimbabwe, no matter what their race is.' (Sky Television).

The MDC leader, Morgan Tsvangirai, left the airport and attended the funeral of one of his supporters. A few hours later, full of grief, briefed on the reign of terror that had gripped the country, he called a press conference. He too had had enough of the violence and the killings. Five MDC supporters had been murdered in five days and Mr Tsvangirai said:

> 'We know who is involved. Now we are taking this violence to their doorsteps. All those MPs who are sponsoring violence, we know where

they are; we know what they are involved in; we know they have protection from the police.'

Fewer than 24 hours later Zimbabwe's police commissioner, Augustine Chihuri, also called a press conference. He announced that he was invoking the Law and Order Maintenance Act. This Act, dating back to the 1960s, had been commissioned to repress black nationalists by Ian Smith's government. Now it was being resurrected to repress anyone who dared oppose those same black nationalists. The Act gave extra powers to the Zimbabwe Republic Police, it restricted movement to and from political meetings, and barred all political meetings unless the head of that party was personally present.

The following morning President Mugabe launched the official Zanu PF election manifesto. This was the same man who had sent his three top ministers to London to demand that Britain hand over £36 million for land reform and yet the pivotal point in his two-and-a-half-hour speech was that Zimbabwe wanted nothing to do with Britain.

We will determine it [our destiny] ourselves, the people of Zimbabwe, not from Downing Street, not from the British parliament. And let those who are pretending that they can determine our future, realize that we have fought for it; we can still fight for it.

His closing words: 'Down with British imperialism and neo-colonialism.' (ZBC Television).

Later that same day the South African Rand fell by three percent and Britain revoked all arms export licences to Zimbabwe.

The campaigning was about to begin in earnest and the editor of the *Zimbabwe Independent* gave us some chilling words. Referring to the president's attacks against whites, farm workers and opposition supporters, Trevor Ncube wrote: "It must be remembered that it is this sort of bigotry and racial prejudice that drove Hitler to exterminate millions of Jews and saw the deaths of nearly a million Tutsis in Rwanda in 1984". The war veterans, in charge of running the election campaign in the rural areas of Zimbabwe, turned their attention now to the second biggest foreign currency earner in the country—tourism. If any tourists had still been brave enough to travel to Zimbabwe, perhaps the attack on the Makuti Hotel would make them change their minds. According to the *Zimbabwe Independent*, a group of 60 war veterans and their supporters descended on the Makuti Hotel, angry that the owner had attended the funeral of farmer Martin Olds. The guests and tourists at the Makuti Hotel checked out immediately. Another group of war veterans attacked tourists at two backpackers' lodges near the Harare International Airport, effectively closing Zimbabwe down as a desirable destination.

It was now the end of the first week of May 2000. Parliament was closed; the president was ruling by decree and no date for elections had yet been set. Could it really get any worse? Hadn't this nightmare gone on for long enough? Wasn't it time to wake up? It could worsen though and did very rapidly, as the war veterans ran out of money. Chenjerai Hunzvi, the rural campaign manager for the government, had been given a budget of $20 million at the end of February. By May the money was exhausted and there was only one way to replenish the coffers. War veterans and their supporters embarked upon their next strategy which was simply to demand that farmers give them what they needed—or face the consequences. The *Independent* reported that war veterans "have run out of resources and are now forcing farmers to provide them with basic supplies to enable them to remain in farms".

Over the past two months demands had been made for water and firewood; now they were extended to include food, mealie meal, fuel and even transport. The daily situation report from the Commercial Farmers' Union concurred with this newest development:

> *War vets/Zanu PF have demanded that farmers provide food and transport for the numerous rallies that are taking place. The demands are accompanied by threats that non-compliance could lead to an escalation in "problems". In the case of vehicles required for transporting people to rallies, several farmers have been warned that if they did not comply, the vehicle would be destroyed.*

Then, as Edward had done at our local butchery, they began demanding that farmers supply accommodation. Winter had arrived and it was cold in makeshift shelters on open land. Every day there were new reports: a cottage should be emptied, a guesthouse vacated, a manager's house be given over to the war veterans.

People that were not farmers could not understand why we were putting up with this. First our land was taken over; then we were intimidated, beaten and killed; our workers forced to sing songs and march all night. Then we were forced to go to re-education rallies and shake the hands of the people who had committed all these offences. Or "ordered to come forward and look into the eyes of the men who have invaded their land". (BBC TV). But still that's not enough. Then we have to give food, vehicles and accommodation to these same people. Everyone we met, wrote to or spoke to, said to us: 'Why on earth don't you refuse, phone the police, get them evicted, imprisoned?' It just didn't work like that though. The police almost never attended the scene when we made a report, told us there was nothing they could do as "this is political". They refused to take official complaints, refused to give police report numbers. If we told a mob of war veterans, or whoever they really were, 'No, I'm not giving you any food, any fuel, my car etc,' what would they come and do to us that night? Would they burn our houses down? Abduct our children? Kill us?

The war veterans had the farmers exactly where they wanted them. We were non-citizens, had no legal rights, no recourse to the law. All of us had to decide to play along in this evil political game, to stand up for ourselves and face the consequences, or, to leave. None of the choices were very attractive and it was more and more becoming a case of every farmer for himself. From area to area the situations were completely different. On Stow Farm we had to contend with Edward whose main preoccupations seemed to be psychological intimidation and beer drinking. In other areas the war veterans were seemingly intent on taking as much as they could; on yet others it was a determination to obtain a particular piece of land. Sometimes it was political mania. There were no rules or footnotes. It was an ongoing game of Russian Roulette.

Whilst the war veterans continued to make demands on farmers, their counterparts on the outskirts of Harare engaged in some aggressive fund-raising. They began allocating and selling stands on peri-urban farms that they had invaded and liberated. The *Daily News* reported:

> *Between Harare and Chitungwiza an estimated 50,000 people have paid amounts ranging from $50 to $350 for plots of land. Urban police clearly had the same orders as their rural counterparts: Police remain helpless spectators at invaded peri-urban farms around Harare ... film [of cameramen] was confiscated in the presence of senior police officers, who just looked on as the scuffle ensued.*

No one knew if all these people buying plots and stands were doing so voluntarily, or if they were also playing the same game of Russian Roulette as the farmers. When the veterans made speeches threatening war, the voluntary aspect became very doubtful.

'If Zanu PF loses this election, you will not say that I did not warn you. If we lose, we will get out our guns. We cannot allow the MDC to sell our country,' said a leader of the veterans occupying the farm, who identified himself only as Comrade Zimbabwe. 'We will be at the polling stations,' he said. 'If Zanu PF loses, there will be war. You will witness our strength in the coming weeks.' (Daily News).

Asked for comment about war veterans selling plots and stands, Chenjerai Hunzvi said he knew nothing about it, he was not responsible. His men on the ground insisted, however, that the money raised from the selling of plots was going into the Zanu PF coffers. On Stow Farm, Edward had been selling plots for over two months and it appeared that most of the revenue went directly to the beer hall—perhaps it was an official, government-owned collecting centre!

On our farm the situation suddenly became very frightening when Edward emerged from a taxi outside our store with his head swathed in bandages. The rumours and gossip about what had actually happened were confusing. Some people said that because Edward had taken the tent away and moved into the butchery, the local villagers were angry with him. They said that they had paid him money for plots of land on our farm and he was no longer guarding their investment. Most people seemed to think that even though the derelict house on our farm had been roofed, Edward was not living there—he was sleeping in comfort over at the butchery. Others thought that he'd been attacked by war veterans who were angry that Edward hadn't done sufficient fund-raising for Zanu PF. We will never know what really happened. In my weekly letter to family and friends I related what little I knew:

There was a very worrying development yesterday afternoon. Our local war vet emerged from an ET [local taxi] with his head swathed in bandages, limping and clearly with something wrong with his back. It turns out that he's spent the last two nights in Marondera Hospital. Local villagers got very annoyed that he wasn't guarding their plots and demanded their money back. When he told them he didn't have their money, they lured him down to the nearby beer hall where he was set upon and beaten badly. So Edward came back yesterday with reinforcements. A white Peugeot arrived outside our store and four big men got out, one armed with, as my storekeeper described it, a very long gun. They set off into the nearby village to find the people that had assaulted Edward. We haven't heard any more yet but word travels very fast so we can only hope

that everyone keeps their doors locked and mouths shut. It is becoming
really scary though and I imagine there are more stories than will ever be
told when and if this thing ever comes to an end.

A combination of factors then forced Ian and me to make one of the
hardest decisions since the farm invasions had begun. Edward had
liberated our grazing, left us with two small fields in which to graze
over 200 cattle and sheep. He had liberated our three small dams
forcing us to water all our livestock in troughs to which we had to
pump water at vast cost from our only borehole. He had claimed all our
timber plantations, depriving us of the income we had budgeted on
from the sale of poles. He and his followers had stolen thousands of
dollars worth of firewood and encouraged nearby villagers to do the
same, depriving us of our regular winter income from the sale of
firewood. He had forced our neighbour to remove his cattle from the
bottom third of our farm and deprived us of the grazing per head
income. The grazing we had left was stale and fetid, smothered in urine
and faeces, the sheep and cattle were losing condition and we were
forced to make a decision.

The bank balance sank lower and lower and there was no money
coming in at all any more. We had to make a decision and our choices
were very limited. We could borrow money from the bank (at 60
percent interest) to buy stock feed. We could lay off some of our
workers. We could sell off some of our cattle and use the money to buy
feed and hope for an improvement in the situation. Borrowing money
wasn't an option. Which bank manager would lend us money using
title deeds as collateral when it was no longer clear how long the title
deeds would be ours? Laying off workers who had nowhere to go, no
chance of finding other jobs and who had been loyal and dedicated
team players with us for so long was also not an option. With very
heavy hearts we contacted an auctioneer. Some of our cattle would
have to go and sadly the only people now buying cattle were the
butchers. No one was buying breeding stock; no one had the
confidence to go into long term cattle-breeding projects.

I was so sad, but also very angry and wrote in my ledger:

So this is it. This is what we've come to after ten years of heartache and
backbreaking work to get this farm going. We had lunch with Micky and
Myrtle today and all agreed that now it's enough. We should sell off all
the cattle before it's too late. Even if this is ever resolved and we are
allowed to stay on this farm, it will never be the same again. I don't think

I'll ever be able to trust our communal neighbours again. My blood boils when I see people sitting in our field, people that I recognize, people I've chatted to in our store, whose children I've given sweets to. I know I'll never be able to trust them again. How could they have done this to me? The cripple and his bloody beer hall—how many times have I spoken to him all these years and now he just walks in and takes what he says belongs to his ancestors. And Edward himself—for ten years I've been a friend to his family. Giving money for their Independence celebrations. Going to that big party at his father's house the year they had the bumper harvest. All the firewood I've given to them when they've had a funeral and all the buckets of milk to make tea for the mourners. All the poles I've given them to repair the fences around their maize crop. And just this last season—three times I went with all the workers and the knapsack sprayers and helped put out the fires raging through their communal grazing lands and villages. I feel betrayed. How could my neighbours do this to me?

A deal was made and I sat in the lounge staring out at nothing as Ian loaded the lifeblood of our farm onto two cattle trucks. First to go were our 12 magnificent Charolais heifers. Born and raised on our farm, we had carefully selected them to keep for breeding, fed and nurtured them for 18 months. Next our two massive pedigree Brahman Bulls. When Richard had been a bit younger he'd helped me choose names for them. One was Barry and the other Huffy—because he always huffs at us Mum. Then 23 Charolais and Hereford cows. When Ian had finished he came in the lounge and sat next to me holding my hand. We had nothing to say to each other; there were just no words.

Ten years we had struggled to build up our breeding herd of cattle. Every winter we had scrimped and saved and gone without to buy feed for the cattle. Each one had a story to tell—the ones that always thought the grass was greener on the other side and permanently broke fences; the ones whose teats were so big that we had to hold the calves onto them; the ones that had three red stars in my files, that got really cheeky when their calves were born and charged everyone; the ones whose calves we had to bottle feed; some that always needed help delivering their calves and we'd go out with ropes and buckets of hot water. Oh God, so many memories, so much hard work. The income from the sale of these 37 cattle would buy enough feed for the remainder of the herd, for all the sheep and their lambs, for the wages and other expenses for another four months. Perhaps by the end of September the madness would be over and we could start again.

Ian and I were not alone in our decision, far from the only ones financially and emotionally affected. Hotels in Harare reported occupancy of less than 40 percent. One of the largest car dealers in Harare said they were being forced to downsize, lay off workers and try to ride the storm. Other companies had to start putting their employees on three- or four-day working weeks. An agricultural equipment distribution company in Marondera reported an 80 percent drop in sales. A major stockfeed company cautioned shareholders as it reported a 60 percent downturn. A polythene manufacturing company in Marondera closed its doors and laid off all its workers. Political instability, almost no petrol or diesel and no foreign currency were forcing companies into liquidation. SABC reported that over 2,000 people had emigrated to Botswana in the past two months and the Australian and New Zealand Embassies said that immigration enquiries had increased dramatically.

On Monday, 8th May 2000, another farmer was attacked. Allan Dunn was beaten outside the back door of his own house. His wife and three children heard his shouts, his moans as, unarmed, he tried to shield himself from the blows of a gang of war veterans wielding chains and bricks. In minutes it was over and the assailants fled. When help arrived, Mr Dunn was unconscious and rushed to hospital but it was too late. Again the community was shocked. Mr Dunn was called "a man of the people". He was a good man, helped everyone in his community, treated his workers well, looked after their welfare, served on the Beatrice Rural Council. Chenjerai Hunzvi was asked to comment on the murder of Mr Dunn. He was the man leading these murderers; they were answerable to him. Hunzvi said, 'There is nothing to say; he's dead.' (*Daily News*). Hunzvi didn't say he was sorry, didn't say he regretted it; didn't say it was a tragedy; didn't offer any solace to Mrs Dunn and her three children; didn't offer jobs to Mr Dunn's workers and their families; couldn't even find it in himself to say anything diplomatic to show remorse for yet more blood on the ground.

As people gathered to mourn for Allan Dunn, others grieved at home for opposition activist Peter Kariza; only his widow, eight children and a handful of family were allowed to attend his funeral. The *Financial Gazette* revealed the tragic story:

There were no friends, not even a priest at the burial of opposition activist Peter Kariza... 'People have been told by Zanu PF allies and war veterans that no one must mourn a member of the MDC. If they do they'll be killed' … Kariza's 25-year-old daughter said at what used to be their home… 'Kariza's widow Vena must now look after her eight children alone.' Rivers of tears slid quietly down her cheeks as she sat on a blanket. That and an old metal frame bed that did not burn when her home was set ablaze, were all that was salvaged from the invasion. Her cows and goats were taken by the killers. 'The men said we are looking for Tsvangirai's people. Your husband was one of them. They hit him on the head. Pulped him with big sticks, beating and beating like people thrashing millet [grain], until he was dead,' said Kariza's widow.

The school holidays came to an end and rather than signalling a return to some sort of normality, war veterans and their supporters turned their attentions to teachers. They were stoned, beaten, had their homes burnt down, and were chased out of classrooms. Teachers fled and sought refuge in towns and the schools that opened operated under very tense conditions. I wrote to family and friends describing Richard's first few days back at school:

It has been a very traumatic week for us here on the farm as the school holidays came to an end and we had to ease Richard back into the routine of going to school every day. On the first day he threw a tantrum of the sort I hadn't seen since his nursery school days: crying, kicking and then sobbing, begging me not to take him to school. He cried all the way in the car and when we arrived there, he wouldn't get out of the car, pleading with me not to leave him. I tried all the usual "mother tactics", but he was really inconsolable, finally spluttering out his fear: 'What if something happens to you and Dad while I'm at school?' … On the second morning he quizzed me very seriously about what would happen if he became sick at school. Would I come and fetch him if the school phoned me? I reassured him, promised that I would come the moment the school contacted me and off he went again, albeit reluctantly. Mid morning the school did phone to ask me to come and get Rich—he was sick. This had never happened before and I guess I broke the land speed record in driving rain on the 16 kilometres to school. I found him in the school clinic sitting wrapped in a blanket sucking his thumb.

There was nothing wrong with Rich but I took him home anyway. Perhaps he'd been testing me, seeing if I really would come immediately; perhaps he was just reassuring himself that I was all right.

The opposition MDC called another press conference. This couldn't go on, they said, they would have to consider all the options to stop this killing. Perhaps a boycott of the elections was the answer. There was an uproar from everyone who longed for freedom and democracy. Had all these people died in vain? I sent an email to one of their activists:

We are devastated to hear that the MDC are considering a boycott of the elections. For ten weeks we've tolerated every one of our human rights being stripped. Has our patience and dignity been for nothing?

Two rural schools on the other side of Marondera were closed today after teachers were stoned and intimidated... We've had Hunzvi in Marondera yesterday, still not giving an inch, grinning and saying he's going to take more properties. Our beautiful little town is crawling with foul people in the so familiar leather, big bush hats and trench coats. Surely a boycott isn't the way?

Mine was one of thousands of letters and proved without a doubt that there was massive popular support for a change in government. The MDC said they wouldn't boycott but would send all their activists underground until the last minute. Anything rather than the wholesale slaughter of their supporters and activists.

In mid May 67 Marondera farmers were called to an emergency meeting. Another farmer had been shot; we knew none of the details. Travelling one behind the other we made our way to the Ruzawi Club. I had never seen such low morale, such depression and resigned despair. Everyone was in a state of shocked paralysis. The fighting spirit had gone. I related the events of the meeting in an email to friends.

A lot of winter crops are not being planted, tobacco seedbeds are not being established, vegetable seedlings are not being started. There is a huge destocking of beef and dairy cattle and there is a major fear of a country on the brink of starvation. We were told at this meeting that the president of Zimbabwe is very concerned about hunger and that it's now up to the farmers to decide which farms the government can have... It was all about who has had enough, who wants to sell and who's prepared to be a sacrificial lamb. It's all a farce really because although 35 percent of farmers in one small area of Marondera are happy now to give up their farms; it's got to be done with compensation. Compensation, we were told, is not an issue that's been discussed yet because there isn't any money. What the government have suggested is that farmers would be given an IOU and then, funds permitting, they would pay us out over a five or ten year period. These comments were met with the scorn and disgust that they deserve. What hope would any of us have of ever being paid out, and how would we survive in the interim?

Each one of us had to decide if we were ready to give in and throw our livelihood away or take the chance of being the next victim, the next corpse in the river of blood that was in full flow across the country.

SINS OF THE FATHERS

John Weeks was shot in the abdomen during an armed robbery at his farm in Beatrice. He shot back and one of the perpetrators was injured but escaped in a vehicle with the four other criminals. No one knew if this was "just" an armed robbery, if it was conducted by war veterans or common criminals—or what the difference between the two was any more. Mr Weeks was rushed to hospital but died later. His attackers were not found or arrested, even though one of them must have gone somewhere to be treated for bullet wounds. There was almost no media coverage on the death of Mr Weeks, no gory film footage, no eyewitness reports. This was the first sign that international attention was waning, or perhaps the foreign journalists had had enough of being threatened and abused. Possibly the friends and family of Mr Weeks were wary of journalists and their cameras. Their presence on the farms certainly seemed to infuriate the war veterans and exacerbate an already explosive situation.

The people squatting on our farm, now that their tent had gone, moved their attention at this time to intimidating me in my store. Jane was used to their stares and snide comments by now but I found it a very nerve-racking experience. Every afternoon when I went up to the store, there would be three or four of them waiting for me. Sometimes they would be on the veranda and just stared at me; mostly though they would be standing inside, leaning up against the counters. They were youngsters, possibly in their mid to late twenties and the Shona custom of respecting your elders was certainly something their mothers had never taught them. They were always in groups of three or four, egging one another on and every day their tactics were different. Some days they were dead quiet, just staring and sneering. Other days one or two would stand right at the hinge door that led to the counter. They knew that I had to keep going in out of the door to replenish stock, take away empty bottles, carry in crates of drinks to fill the fridge. They wouldn't get out of the way and every time I had to ask them please to move so that I could pass. This amused them enormously. They often pretended they couldn't hear me and I would have to ask them two or even three times to move. My blood boiled but perhaps it was my fear that made me hold my tongue. Jane would keep glancing across at me to see if I was on the point of exploding, which we both knew was exactly what they wanted, and we learnt to communicate with eyes and eyebrows. I know mine were spitting out volumes of swear words and I'm sure hers were saying: calm down, just ignore them. Another tactic was for one man to buy one cigarette and then lean up against Jane's spotless counter, blow smoke in her face or mine and then flick ash on the yellow Formica. On one occasion when he stubbed the cigarette out on the counter top I really lost control and ordered him to get out of the store. That caused an explosion of hilarity from his friends and they all went out clutching one another and roaring with laughter. I shut up shop immediately and leant against the doors with my hands over my face.

'Don't you worry,' Jane said with her hand on my shoulder. It's just electioneering. Don't you worry about them—they are just rubbish.' I knew she was right but it didn't make it any easier. On another occasion one of the watchers had plucked up his courage to talk to me.

'I need milk,' he said. 'I am hungry.'

'Seven dollars a cup,' I replied coldly. Whilst I often gave people things, this man was not on my list of charitable causes.

'You give it to me.'

I don't know what came over me but I was tired of them, day after day after day.

'You help me by getting off my farm and then maybe I'll help you,' I said quietly, looking right into his eyes. He looked away, obviously embarrassed, turned and left the store, closely followed by his friends.

The next day he was back.

'I need this store,' he said.

His needs had increased dramatically from a cup of milk to a store!
'It's not for sale.'

'But I need it,' he repeated.

I ignored him and went into the little storeroom and he followed me
in with his friend.

My sweat turned cold as the two of them stood blocking the only
door of my storeroom.

'You give us this store; we want it.'

'This store is not for sale, or for rent. Sorry.' I turned my back on them so
they wouldn't see the panic in my eyes and thanked God for Jane who
managed to hustle them out on the pretext of coming to get something.

A couple of days later they were back again. I had been having a sort
out in the house and had great boxes of bits and pieces: old books and
magazines, Richard's unwanted toys, some of his old baby clothes,
excess china from the kitchen. As I pushed the boxes of second-hand
things across the counter for Jane to unload, the watchers started
rummaging through them. I asked them politely to wait until we had
unloaded the things onto the shelves.

'We can't wait; we need these things now,' one said. 'You think we
haven't got money; look we've got money.' He pulled out a couple of
filthy notes and shoved them at me. 'We need these things now. We are
very happy,' he said, pausing to blow smoke in my face. 'We can see we
have won. You are going. You are selling all your things. We are very
happy now that you are running away.'

I was shaking with anger and only managed two words: 'Get Out.'

That night I wrote about the encounter in my ledger but cannot
reproduce it here. Every third word, or was it every second, was a
swear word. There is only one section that I dare repeat: "Seeing these
... drunks for what they really are—unemployed and probably
unemployable, layabouts totally intoxicated with eight weeks of
anarchy. Never have I hated people as much as I hate these maggots".
It was so painful to be feeling this hatred. It wormed its way into my
system and I couldn't understand why anyone would degrade
themselves to such a point where they would intimidate someone else
for money. How humiliating it must be for these youngsters. Do they
really sleep at night? I wondered. This wasn't a racial hatred—it was a
people hatred. No matter what their skin colour, I would have felt the
same and if I was their mother I knew exactly how I'd discipline them.

Whilst I was dealing with these comparatively minor irritations in
my store, the leaders of the farmers' union were again meeting with the
war veterans and the president. The CFU were still desperately trying

to negotiate an end to the violence and President Mugabe announced the formation of a Land Commission. This was apparently to work hand in hand with the Land Acquisition Committee and was an attempt to reach agreement on which farms would be taken by government. Then, supposedly, war veterans would be moved onto those properties only. The president again called for violence to cease and said that farming operations should not be interfered with by war veterans. Within 24 hours of this Commission having been agreed upon though, war veterans invaded yet more farms and everyone now wondered who, if anyone, was in control. Asked to comment on the continuing violence, the leader of the opposition, Morgan Tsvangirai commented, 'It is a demonstration of the lack of control by Mugabe and his government over the war veterans. The police are helpless because he compromised the role of the police in the whole exercise. Now the chickens are coming home to roost.' (BBC TV).

More proof of lack of control from above came when war veterans raided customs offices in Harare. According to the *Financial Gazette*: "A mob of war veterans last week forced the Department of Customs and Excise to release two vehicles belonging to ex-combatants which had been impounded for non-payment of duty". Ironically, the customs offices are situated approximately ten metres from Harare Central Police Station. The acting director of the customs offices wrote an official letter to the police requesting protection and told them what had taken place: "A group of more than 30 war veterans stormed my office and used all sorts of threats to gain the release of a commercial truck ..." (*Financial Gazette*). The officer commanding crime in Harare Central, responded to the request:

> *We indicated to him that it was not possible to give such kind of security to his department. But, however, in the event that the war vets return to make further demands, we can swiftly move in to make arrests if we are called in time.*

'The country's in meltdown,' everyone was saying. 'The economy's on the verge of collapse.' But amazingly Zimbabwe managed to stagger on from day to day. The tobacco sales were well underway now but the volumes of produce being sold were low, almost as low as the prices being offered. Farmers were accused of deliberately holding back their crop to sabotage the economy. Minister Joyce Mujuru took the accusation a step further when she said that farmers were setting light to their own tobacco barns and then blaming the war veterans. Asked by an interviewer on SABC how farmers were supposed to conduct normal business with war veterans running wild everywhere, and a US dollar rate that had been pegged for 18 months, Minister Mujuru said:

> *There is no invasion; I can't call it off because I didn't create it… Once the dollar is devalued between now and the elections everyone will revolt against the ruling government… Our commercial farmers just want government to pray to them, to beg them, which we are not going to do.* (SABC Africa TV).

It then seemed too much of a coincidence when war veterans started forcing tobacco farmers to take their crop to the auction floors.

> *Zimbabwe's Independence war veterans, backed by state security agents, have swooped on the country's tobacco-growing regions in the past two weeks to force farmers to sell their crop despite sharply depressed selling prices… The strategy is aimed at ensuring that there are unbroken inflows of foreign currency into Zimbabwe so the government can continue to pay its fuel bills as well as service some of its external debts.* (Financial Gazette).

Another arm of the foreign currency-earning sector was then also eroded by the marauding war veterans. "Border Timbers closes as war vets run amok" was the headline of an article in the *Financial Gazette*.

> *In a tersely worded statement, the timber giant employing 3,500 workers, mostly in the Eastern Border Districts bordering Mozambique, said all its plants had discontinued operations "other than where a critical export order is being processed". The managing director of the company told the newspaper that Zimbabwe stood to lose millions of dollars but explained the sequence of events that had forced him to take such drastic measures. He said a mob of about 40 Zanu PF supporters entered the Charter sawmills early on Tuesday and forced workers to drop everything and attend a rally for more than five hours at the premises. During the rally many were beaten and one worker was severely injured. The police officer in charge of Chimanimani … said no arrests had been made. He said his officers managed to quell the violence and took the injured workers to hospital.*

Amidst all this violence, the security head of the Commonwealth arrived in Harare. New Zealander, Don Mckinnon, had earlier in the month been interviewed on BBC World's Hardtalk programme by Tim Sebastian. I had been so angry after watching the programme and hearing McKinnon's evasive answers that I immediately sent an email to Mr Sebastian.

> *Right-minded Zimbabweans—and not just whites—are disgusted at the continuing reaction of both the Commonwealth and the EU. If they honestly believe that we can have free and fair elections after what we are being subjected to, they don't deserve to hold positions of world leadership. We need overseas observers here now. There has not been a de-escalation of violence at all; if anything it has increased. These thugs are now openly getting away with rape (eye witness account from a policeman who has since resigned), burglary, public beatings with rubber hoses and murder. I am appalled. What on earth can the threshold be? It is simply not good enough for someone in the position of McKinnon to say that he will send a "recce team" soon. Will that be a "recce team" in a 5 star hotel in Harare or will they come out on to the farms and talk to our terrified workers, go to the areas where ordinary people are being forced to goose step to the tune of war veterans whose names are "Prince", "Satan", "Stalin"?*

McKinnon arrived and got a taste of our frustration when he was made to wait 24 hours before President Mugabe would see him. After a 45-minute meeting with the president and the minister of Foreign Affairs, Mckinnon said: 'He [President Mugabe] genuinely wants to see a lessening of the violence. He genuinely wants the international community to see a free and fair election.' (SABC Africa TV) No one will ever know what was discussed in that short 40-minute meeting and no one was fooled. McKinnon had done exactly as we feared—spent his entire visit in his hotel and at State House. I wasn't the only one angry. In the leader article of *The Farmer*, the editor wrote:

> *He then indicated that he was happy that Zimbabwe's septuagenarian president, Robert Mugabe, was doing what he could to restore the rule of law and, defying everyone else, he claimed free and fair elections were a possibility. Oh sure. If Mr McKinnon had taken the time to travel a few kilometres out of the capital, say to Arcturus, he'd have seen for himself just how free and fair these elections are going to be. So Mr McKinnon is either a fool or playing a game so subtle that none of us can see it. ... The Commonwealth will send 40 observers to check on some 4,000 polling stations. Perhaps Mr McKinnon believes that Zimbabwe's blind faith in*

Top left: The author, with fellow graduates from the School of Social Work, Zimbabwe 1979.

Top right: President Robert Mugabe reacts to a question from a reporter at a press conference. *Per-Anders Pettersson/iAfrica Photos*

Bottom: National fuel shortages started in early 2000. Here, hundreds of people queue for paraffin for cooking in central Harare. *Per-Anders Pettersson/iAfrica Photos*

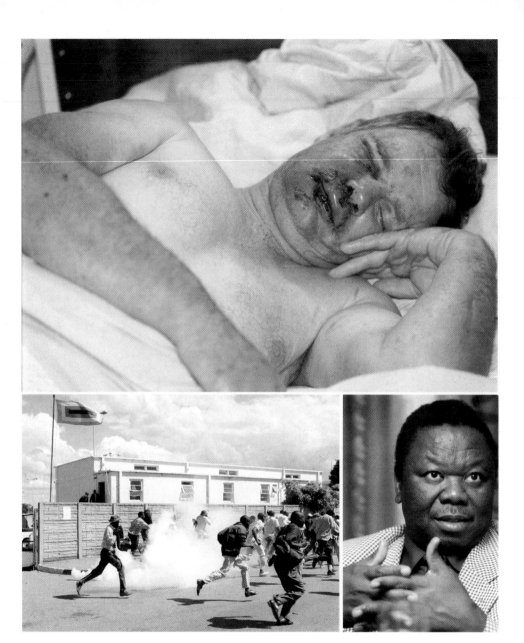

Top: Steve Krynauw, a farmer from the Macheke area who was abducted and assaulted by war veterans. Krynauw had gone to the aid of David Stevens, the first white farmer to be killed by land invaders, April 2000. *Eric Miller/iAfrica Photos*

Bottom left: Zimbabwe ruling party ZANU PF's flag flies high as war veterans flee from ZANU PF offices (background) as teargas is fired at them by Zimbabwe Riot Police. *Howard Burditt/iAfrica Photos*

Bottom right: Morgan Tsvangirai, leader of the main Zimbabwean opposition party, the Movement for Democratic Change (MDC). *Adam Welz/iAfrica Photos*

Top left: May 2000. Hundreds of Zimbabweans, mainly students, demonstrate in Cape Town against the degenerating situation in their home country. *Eric Miller/iAfrica Photos*

Top right: Zimbabwean liberation war veterans on their pegged-out land claims on Unadale Farm, south of Harare. *Eric Miller/iAfrica Photos*

Bottom left: Zimbabwe police clear barricades from the streets during food riots in the capital. *Howard Burditt/iAfrica Photos*

Bottom right: Behind sandbags and under siege. Zimbabwean farmer Paul Retzlaff describes how hundreds of war veterans attacked his Arcturus farm and homestead. *Eric Miller/iAfrica Photos*

Above: The road to nowhere? (Kezi district, southwestern Zimbabwe). The future for the country appears bleak. *Richard Jansen van Vuuren*

Top left: Storm clouds gather over the commercial maize farms.

Centre: Harare's unemployed. Job seekers peep vainly through the closed gates of a Harare factory.

Bottom: Farm homestead in the Kezi district. This commercial farm, now decaying and unproductive, was designated for resettlement and is now owned by a member of the ruling political elite. *Richard Jansen van Vuuren*

an institution as venerable as the Commonwealth is so great that the nation will sleep peacefully knowing that each observer will cover 100 stations.

McKinnon's visit to Zimbabwe did, however, produce one positive thing—an election date was finally announced and set at the 24th and 25th of June 2000. With little over a month to go, everyone wondered how free or fair these elections could be after the intense intimidation of the past two months. Although the dates had been set, voters' rolls were not available for inspection, nor were the constituency boundaries defined. These were still being worked on by a special Delimitation Committee, which had been appointed by the president. The whole thing was shrouded in suspicion but we could only hope that as international observers arrived, the violence would decrease. BBC World Television interviewed Jonathon Moyo, the Zanu PF campaign manager, and asked if he thought the elections could be free and fair. 'We've had regrettable incidents of violence … exaggeration and misrepresentation by the international media … there is peace here…' I found myself listening to Moyo's increasingly frequent and lengthy monologues in snatches but he said what we all knew he'd say. Of course they'll be free and fair. For his party anyway!

At this time the religious leaders in Zimbabwe at last decided to come out in the open and admit that everything was not rose-coloured. The Catholic Church's Archbishop, Pius Ncube, took out a half page advertisement in the *Daily News*.

We strongly deplore the lawless invasion of the farms, sometimes by villagers who are being forced against their will to settle on the farms; we see anarchy growing in the country. The economy is deteriorating with shortages of fuel and rising prices. People lack food and are unable to afford transport or procure accommodation. Young people are unemployed. Hospital fees are expensive. People lose their houses to auctioneers. The Congo war continues. Destitution grows and misery increases. The decline of the economy is largely owing to corruption and nepotism in the government. People in the rural areas are being forced to buy party cards and being threatened with return of the 5th Brigade.

These were indeed very strong words, although it had taken two months of hell before the churches had come forward. The Evangelical Fellowship followed suit:

Our people and our institutions are being harassed, threatened and intimidated left, right and centre. There is chaos reigning at Mnene mission in Mberengwa, which is our biggest mission. Members of staff were yesterday abducted from the hospital and beaten up. Groups of youths have come threatening people. We are concerned about the situation in the country and particularly in our institutions. (Daily News).

Regardless of whatever Jonathon Moyo said, there were clear indications of coming disaster. Everyone knew what was happening and we could only hope that international observers would be able to see it too.

President Mugabe justified the violence by comparing it to what Zanu PF had had to endure in the elections of 1980. At his weekly Cabinet meeting, the president announced that he had used the Presidential Powers Act to sign into law the compulsory acquisition of farms in Zimbabwe without payment of compensation. All legal obstacles had now been removed. Farms could now be acquired without government having to pay compensation for the land. He spoke to the gathered reporters after the announcement and took great pains to explain what he and his members had endured in the 1980 elections. I watched with shock as the leader of our country, the man whom my parents had risked their lives for, justified the violence sweeping through the country.

I listened carefully to the president's words and could remember so well when, as a first-year student at the University of Zimbabwe, Ian Smith's government had had me, an 18-year-old, followed because of the ongoing work my parents were undertaking to bring freedom to Zimbabwe. I remembered so well the fear I had felt as I rode home from lectures on my bicycle and always they were there, following me to see where I went, whom I spoke to. I also remembered the terror of being caught in a "cordon and search". Just before the 1980 elections the police conducted regular and unannounced cordon and search sweeps of the city. They would block off all exits to a street and whoever happened to be there was then made to stand still while they were searched by Smith's police and their dogs. Bags had to be emptied and arms raised as a police detail physically frisked you for weapons or explosives. I remembered too the terror of driving out of the cities in convoys. Great snaking lines of vehicles would drive in convoy for safety in case of ambushes by freedom fighters. I also remembered the one occasion Ian and I had stayed for just one more drink at the Marondera Hotel and missed the convoy. At that time Ian drove a

Suzuki 500 motorbike, which had a genie in its engine and went like the wind. We still laugh today as we proudly boast that we made the 67-kilometre trip from Marondera to Harare in 23 minutes. My maths isn't good but we were travelling very fast, so fast that I could hardly breathe as I hung on for dear life and the visor of the helmet pressed into my face. We had decided to risk the journey without the convoy, Ian's thinking being that if we drove fast enough, even a sharpshooter wouldn't be able to hit us!

With these memories I listened to President Mugabe:

> They should look at other environments elsewhere. We had bombs being thrust, thrown at us in 1980 across the nation and some of my own members were hit by bazookas. And in the course of campaigning I was missed by several bombs it will be known. I had hand grenades thrown at my house in Mount Pleasant but elections were still declared free and fair. Now, we haven't started real campaigning. We are only now going to start… We are all appealing for non-violence, for peace and stability in the country, not only because of the elections but because violence mars the harmony in society…' (SABC Africa Television).

So now we knew exactly where President Mugabe was coming from. This was pay-back time. He had not been able to forgive or forget what Ian Smith's white government had done to him and now it was apparently all right for him to get his revenge. The worst thing was though, that the president of our country was not only hurting people with white skin—he was unleashing his reign of terror on his own people, his brothers, the very people who had suffered so much to bring him to power. This, to my mind, was unforgivable. In a letter I wrote to family and friends in mid May, I said:

> It's an awful thought, but when this began three months ago and they were bashing whites, it was almost understandable—perhaps, I thought, we are paying for the sins of our fathers and grandfathers. … Now though, when the rent a mob are bashing everyone, it's an unforgivable crime for which they will be made to pay the price when this is over.'

This was certainly not a case of white people paying for the wrongs of their ancestors. It was a leader and his government desperate to hold on to power, whatever the cost. If they lost, heads would roll, corruption would be exposed and many of our leaders would not be able to retire gracefully to the countryside. They would have to answer for the collapsed economy, the fraud, the theft, the murders; they would perhaps retire to gaol cells.

For Ian and me, our financial future as farmers was almost finished. We were both middle-aged and had sunk everything we had, and didn't have, into Stow Farm. We thought we were set for the future. We had obeyed the three Ls my sister said were the prerequisites to life: to live, to love and to leave a legacy. Lived—we had; loved—we had, but the legacy was sitting on the edge of a precipice. Neither Ian nor I came from wealthy families. We hadn't inherited anything and life had been a happy but continual uphill struggle to get to where we were now. We both had a deep love for wild life and Zimbabwe's beautiful countryside and with our farm we had managed to capture a tiny part of it. This little farm was going to be the legacy we would leave to our son. Ian had planted hundreds of indigenous trees. We had had reedbuck, duiker, steenbok and even kudu on the farm. The birds were exquisite, attracted by Ian's wild fruit trees, and in a three-month period I had recorded over 100 species of birds in our garden. This little piece of our heaven was to be for Richard and it broke our hearts to think that we might lose it all for someone's political survival.

I lobbied even harder, sending out dozens of emails every day to people all over the world, determined to expose this "land grab" for what it was—a dirty political ploy to get votes. How confusing it was though. There was a burning need for land to be given to peasants, but why had it taken two decades for the government to do something? And why had they done it like this? My emails attracted a lot of attention and before I knew what was happening, this book was born. This, perhaps, would be the legacy I could leave to Richard, and to the people of Zimbabwe. Someone once told me that I wrote from the heart and it was this that people obviously wanted. A New Zealand newspaper, the *Waikato Times*, published one of my letters, then *Fair Lady* Magazine in South Africa and then in the weeks ahead, the *Daily Telegraph* in England, the *Washington Times* in America, the *Standard*, *The Farmer* and *Tobacco News* in Zimbabwe. There were requests for interviews from *The Times*, *Channel 4*, *News Night* and the *BBC*. By coincidence I discovered that my words had found their way onto the Internet and were on the web sites of *Sky News Online*, *Zimbabwe News*, *The Zimbabwe Situation* and *The Zimbabwe Democratic Trust*. The emails came in thick and fast and I felt so encouraged that complete strangers took the time to write to me. I was more than a little overwhelmed when I read these letters and spent hours trying to reply to them all.

Some that gave both Ian and me the strength to go on, came from strangers:

> We keep you in our prayers and the international support is growing every day. I mail your letters to over 1,500 people worldwide including human rights groups, the full House of Commons, all the Australian MPs and even Hilary Clinton ... (Zimbabwe).

> Thank you for your wonderful courage and the human insights provided by your inspirational emails on the tragic situation that besets our nation ... I unashamedly wept when I read one of them at 2.20 am ... (Zimbabwe).

> We find we are waking up every Sunday and checking our email to see if you have made it through another week of what seems unimaginable to us in our safe little world, but at the same time appreciating that your reality could easily become any one of our realities in an instant. ... Zim is no longer in the news here and you are the only source of information we receive ... (Canada).

> I really cannot imagine how you manage to keep your chins up. I can only thank God that G and I are not in the same boat as you ... (South Africa).

> ...your weekly updates are riveting... I cannot fathom how you all must feel in the midst of such uncertainty and being forced to give up your lives like that ... (America).

> I cannot begin to imagine the reality of what you and your loved ones are living, it sounds like some hideous dream from which you must surely wake soon ... (England).

There were hundreds of letters every week and they came from Africa and America, Europe and Australia. My words were touching people and their responses gave courage and inspiration, particularly this one from a friend, a black professional living in Harare:

> I do not understand what's going on in this country. Is it the end of the world? I read your letters and every time I feel so guilty as if I'm a part of it all. My colour would not allow me to pop in and say hello and maybe have a cup of tea while the farm is under siege like this. I'm sure you do understand...

Here was the reality of what the "peaceful demonstrations" were doing to race relations in Zimbabwe. When two women of the same age but with different skin colours dared not meet for tea and a chat as friends, what hope was there? There was so much support, so much encouragement but through it all there was nothing anyone could do except sit it out.

On Sunday, 21st May, we were forced to close our store and give all our workers a day off—on full pay. The minister of State Security, Sydney Sekeramayi, was the candidate for the coming elections in Marondera East Constituency and was holding a campaign rally in the town's football stadium. Aside from the fact that we were not in Minister Sekeramayi's constituency, we had been told by our resident war veterans and Zanu PF activists that no business was to be conducted at all on Sunday. All stores were to be closed, no companies were to operate, no employees were to go to work. Everyone was told to go to Marondera to the minister's rally. If we didn't go, they said, they would know, and would return and deal with us later.

All week the youngsters had been threatening and intimidating the entire farming neighbourhood and surrounding villages so that by Sunday everyone was too afraid not to go to the rally. Buses started arriving outside our store early on Sunday morning and we could hear the whistles and calls from the touts. 'Come and get in for the rally. Everyone must come now for the rally. Come for free food and drink at the rally.' People lined up and filed quietly into the buses. Cowed into submission, told that the consequences would be severe if they didn't attend the rally, almost everyone did what they were told. The farming communities were not the only ones being forced to attend the rally. Three times in the preceding week, gangs of youngsters had marauded around the residential areas of Marondera town. Shouting, whistling, throwing stones on roofs, they had issued the same threats—come to the rally, or else. My sister Wiz had phoned a number of times, frightened, asking me what she should do, telling me they were throwing stones on her roof again. The *Daily News* covered the story:

Marondera was at a standstill yesterday after Zanu PF youths forced businesses to shut and residents to attend a Zanu PF rally by the ruling party's parliamentary candidate for Marondera East constituency, Sydney Sekeramayi. Shops, fuel stations, market stalls and even tuck shops in the town's high-density suburbs were closed. People were not allowed to leave the town as buses were barred from ferrying them... Zanu PF youths, in trucks, went from door to door yesterday morning ordering residents to attend the rally. Teachers at Watershed College and Grasslands Primary School, who had not complied with the order to attend the meeting, were assaulted... Sekeramayi, the minister of State Security, said that Rudhaka had never been that full since Independence. About 10,000 people attended the rally... Mashonaland East province, the province most affected by political violence, had the largest number of "No" votes in the referendum for the draft constituency in February... Yesterday people were not allowed to leave once they gained entrance into the stadium... 'After the votes we will see who has been cheating us and we will deal with each other,' he [Sekeramayi] said. He warned teachers against teaching politics saying they should stick to the syllabus.

As dusk fell on Sunday afternoon we saw our workers straggling back to their houses. I went out to hear their stories. They were hot, thirsty, hungry and exhausted. The buses had taken them to the stadium and there they had sat the whole day. There was nothing to eat or drink (not for the ordinary people like them, they said); they were not allowed to leave and when at last the rally had come to an end, there were no buses to bring them home. The 16-kilometre journey back to the farm was a long walk for them but at least they'd been seen attending the rally they said; at least now they could sleep easy that night. In the tired faces of my workers I saw the reflection of a nation broken, cowed into submission, a people who would do anything to avoid another war. Fear was their ruler. Again I cried for Zimbabwe.

Similar tactics were being used around the country to force people to go to rallies hosted by Zanu PF candidates. The threats were continuous and the Kariba Zanu PF candidate was not diplomatic in his choice of words. Addressing a crowd of 1,000, which included five whites, he said:

'Let me assure you whites here, that once you support MDC, Zanu PF is not going to treat you as business people, but as politicians. Then if you are treated as politicians, it is like signing your own death warrant. The political storm will not spare you. Let you be informed (sic) that our reserve force, the war veterans will be set on you.' ...

Hotels and holiday outlets have begun retrenching hundreds of workers while others have been put on forced leave. A premier tourism resort in the town particularly felt the impact last month when it was rocked by scenes of unprecedented violence, which saw a sharp decline in the number of visitors to Kariba. 'Tourism is the lifeline of this town,' said one hotel manager at the rally. 'We are having a more than 80

*percent downturn in business forcing us to lay off workers. We are
surprised the people who instil tourist confidence are fuelling violence
making the political temperatures rise again.'* (Daily News Online).

One by one Zimbabwe's top leaders stood at the podium and spat
words of hate and anger at the people as the election campaigning
continued. In other countries, candidates would promise the moon to
attract votes; in Zimbabwe they promised death. It was a campaign of
hate and anyone who dared speak out became a target. It became more
difficult to find out what was really going on as foreign journalists got
thinner on the ground and the war veterans intensified their campaign
against the free press. Just finding the local *Daily News* became difficult
and we spent hours every night reading the *Online* edition. War
veterans banned sales of the newspaper in Murehwa and Shurugwi,
threatened vendors and truck drivers who delivered the papers and
even confiscated it from people who were seen reading it. It was no
longer wise to be seen with the newspaper and civil servants were
banned from taking the publication into their government offices.
Freedom of thought was alive in Zimbabwe though as daily circulation
figures of the one-year-old *Daily News* rocketed to over 100,000 by late
May, overtaking the 100-year-old state-run *Herald*.

Farmers watched anxiously as Chenjerai Hunzvi appeared in court
again to face contempt of court charges. He was supposed to show
proof that he had told his followers to vacate farms. Hunzvi had no
proof to give and had somehow persuaded the Commercial Farmers'
Union to call for a minimum sentence. He was found guilty of
contempt of court, fined a paltry $10,000 and given a three-month jail
sentence—suspended for twelve months. This was indeed a ludicrous
sentence for the man who had encouraged his supporters to bring the
country to its knees and effectively destroyed commercial agriculture,
not to mention the beatings, tortures, rapes and murders. The
Commercial Farmers' Union justified itself:

*'We opposed a custodial sentence for the simple reason that we feared
increased violence on farms if that sentence was effected,'* CFU director
David Hasluck told the Financial Gazette. *'We had to take into
consideration the safety of our members.'*

I was incensed, speechless. Of course farmers' safety was the first
consideration but we had not even been consulted. Here had been a
chance to rein in the leader of the war veterans. Perhaps his

incarceration would have led to more violence; perhaps though it would have sent a signal to squatters that no one is above the law.

The lawlessness was again allowed to continue and in the last week of May 2000, the *Financial Gazette* ran a front-page story entitled: "Six thousand villagers flee rural terror".

> *More than 6,000 villagers had by mid yesterday fled Zimbabwe's countryside into Harare and other cities as armed bands of former independence war guerrillas and Zanu PF youths stepped up a terror campaign against the opposition in rural areas... The Zimbabwe Human Rights Organization ... said, 'Some of them claim that their relatives have been tortured and murdered' ... ZimRights Offices in Harare, Mutare, Kwekwe and Bulawayo had been inundated by villagers seeking shelter and help.*

Others though could not escape in time and they too told their story in the *Financial Gazette*:

> *'You can imagine our shock when at midnight on Tuesday a group of people came bashing our doors and demanding that we come out. My husband was trying to dress up when they broke into our bedroom and dragged him out. They immediately started beating him,' she recalled. 'One of them made sure that he was no longer breathing and ordered me to carry his body into the house. They then said they were going to deal with my eldest son. I could hear Onias' cry for help as I stood helplessly in my own yard,' said the old woman, tears streaming down her wrinkled cheeks.*

Onias Mushaya died at midday. Onias' son picked up the story:

> *Pointing at the mountains that separate Zimbabwe and Mozambique, he said his family and others here had provided nourishment to Zimbabwe's Independence war fighters as they criss-crossed the border on missions during the 1970's campaign. 'Even then several people died at the hands of the guerrillas, most accused of being sellouts. We now have a black government—a government that is staffed with selfish men and women who think nothing of shedding blood, all because they want to remain in power,' he said.*

Teachers, nurses and civil servants were next in the systematic exorcism of political opponents to Zanu PF. A nurse and a teacher were abducted from a mission in Mberengwa. The *Zimbabwe Independent* told the story.

> *'They were picked up and frog marched to Texas [farm],' the hospital official said. 'They were stripped naked. We are told they were forced to climb up trees from where they would force them to jump down from about three metres. They were beaten up with electrical cords, sticks, and they used guns to threaten them with death,' he said. 'When they came back they had swollen faces. One of them, the nurse, could hardly talk.'*

And at another school: "They descended on the female head and threatened two male teachers before setting the library on fire". Teachers and nurses, like all other civil servants had just been awarded a 65 percent pay increment, possibly to buy their silence.

> *'We have been suppressed and have suffered for too long,' a secondary school teacher said. 'The increments cannot make up for the desperation and troubles we went through over the years. How can we be remembered now before the crucial parliamentary election?' he asked.* (Zimbabwe Independent).

Nearer to Harare, the problems were intensifying on the peri-urban farms occupied by war veterans. The Harare City Council's Department of Works issued an internal report to the town clerk, concerned about the implications of the haphazard subdivision being undertaken by war veterans.

> *The nature of the allocation has been clandestine in most cases. Along Airport Road on the farm that Council has approved a casino complex, 900-square-metre stands were being pegged and allocated. Consideration is not being made to provide for infrastructure such as roads, water and sewers... Most of the farms [occupied] are ecologically fragile. About half of them are vlei and would require efficient drainage systems and a waterborne sewerage system... The problem requires urgent attention before settlers commence construction at which stage it becomes more difficult to address. The occupations being part of a national phenomenon require a high-level solution.* (Zimbabwe Independent).

Chenjerai Hunzvi, the conductor of this "national phenomenon", was on television the next day. He arrived at the squatted farms, camera crews in tow, looking castigated. Perhaps for once he'd had his wrist slapped? Wearing a bright red jacket and looking very serious (were those beads of sweat on his forehead?) he told the leader of the squatters:

As you know there are so many accidents at airports throughout the world. We would like people to be a little further back [waving vaguely to the horizon behind him] and this area will be designated for aviation training courses. (SABC Africa Television).

For well over a month Hunzvi's men had been on these farms, which had to be passed by every tourist and visitor arriving in the country as they made their way towards the capital city. Perhaps now with international election observers arriving, Hunzvi was wise in asking the people to move back a bit. The squatters refused though and began building more permanent structures both on the farms along the main Harare Airport Road and the Harare Chitungwiza highway.

Desperate for something to smile about exactly 30 days before the elections, The *Daily News* found just the right story: "Lions attack war vets".

A group of war veterans who invaded Malilangwe Conservancy in the Gonarezhou National Park escaped death by a whisker when a pride of lions attacked them. Police in Chiredzi confirmed that about 100 war veterans who invaded the conservancy had to run for dear life when a pride of angry lions attacked them.

It wasn't funny though. No one seemed to have any sort of control any more and the banks were repeating their warnings of economic collapse and food shortages. Farmers apparently owed the country's banks an estimated $25 billion and Standard Chartered Bank published its latest report.

As agriculture is the mainstay of the economy, the rate of economic decline would accelerate after the elections ... winter wheat plantings were down by about a third from last year. Vegetable prices have gone up by 200 percent because of the shortages arising from the current turmoil... Food imports will increase in the final months of the year and food prices will increase sharply over the next few months, pushing inflation higher than previously forecast. (Daily News).

Chenjerai Hunzvi responded immediately, not by telling us what we were going to eat, even if we could afford it, but by saying, 'We will not inherit the farm debt.' (*Daily News*). When asked how the war veterans would finance their new farming ventures, Hunzvi said that he would approach the minister of Finance for assistance.

In the final days of May, horrific reports emerged of the torturing of opposition supporters in the centre of Harare. Chenjerai Hunzvi, a Polish-trained medical doctor, operated a surgery in the suburb of Budiriro and the *Daily News* told the story.

> *Hunzvi's surgery in the Budiriro neighbourhood of the capital looks innocent enough at first glance... This former place of healing has become a torture centre. A week and a half ago, about 50 men calling themselves war veterans moved into Hunzvi's surgery compound and began sending out gangs to kidnap local residents they suspected of supporting the opposition.*

The *Daily News* interviewed a man who had been one of the victims.

> *His captors had tied a rubber strip tightly around the tip of his penis and kept it bound for the 13 hours that they held him in the surgery preventing him from urinating... 'About 12 of them picked me up near my friend's shop at about noon,' Emmanuel, 28, said. 'I had no chance. They said you are MDC and drove me to Hunzvi's surgery.' Two other men were already on the floor naked and bruised. His ordeal began at once. 'They beat me with electric cables and wooden poles like table legs,' he said.*

While Zimbabwe seemed to be collapsing around us and our minds were filled to overflowing with the horrific details of beating and burning and torture, life did actually go on. We tried as best we could to carry on with day-to-day activities but it was becoming more and more of a problem. On our land, farming had virtually come to a standstill. Our grazing and timber plantations liberated, a third of the cattle sold, we had no plans to make for the months ahead. We tried to work on repairing some of the fences closer to home but the war veterans made this an impossible task, shouting insults, threatening and intimidating our workers. The fences that we did manage to repair lasted only a day or two; as fast as we erected them, they took them down, pulled out poles and stole the wire. It became increasingly difficult to find enough work for our three men to do, so we resorted to cutting and stacking firewood close to the house in the hope of finding a buyer in June when winter would be at its coldest.

This was a task Richard loved to help with at the weekends, picking up sticks and logs and piling them into cords, chatting incessantly to the workers. He was a lot happier now that the school had put an evacuation plan in place. Earlier in the week he'd come home with a letter from the school and told me happily that it was "about what we're going to do if the war vets come to the school". The seven-year-old that I thought could just manage Janet and John, told me that he'd read it and that if anything happened at school the children would be taken to a big shopping complex in town where they could be collected by their parents. Richard knew what was going on now; that was all he'd wanted—to know where he stood in the event of an emergency. Very carefully, and of his own volition, he wrote his full name, address and telephone number on a piece of paper which he stuck to the inside of his suitcase—just in case he said. This complemented the capital letters I'd already written on the top, bottom and inside of his suitcase declaring his name and telephone number!

Another thing Richard loved to do at the weekends was to come up to the store with me at closing time. While I took stock and cashed up, he enjoyed sitting out on the veranda with Brian where they'd have a drink and a cream doughnut each. Towards the end of May he stopped coming with me. He said there were "scary men" there that kept looking at him. I was glad he didn't want to come any more, particularly as I had a surprise meeting with Edward that left me very flustered. I described the encounter in one of my weekly letters:

I had a chance meeting with "Commandant Edward" in my little store this week. I was taken completely by surprise and am still laughing at the encounter. Unbelievably I didn't recognize him—he was wearing a suit and reading glasses, held out his hand and greeted me like a long lost mate.

'You don't remember me, do you?' he asked. When I said I was sorry but I didn't, he smiled and said: 'I'm Edward!'

'Oh Edward Trouble,' I said laughing, flustered. (The only times I've ever seen him he's been rolling drunk, wearing filthy blue overalls, a big bush hat and long trench coat).

'I'm not Edward Trouble,' he said, 'I'm Edward that has shown the world that blacks and whites can live together in peace and share their land.'

Shortly after my brief encounter with Edward, he disappeared. Little did I realize how I would miss having "Edward Trouble" in charge of the invasion of our farm. Those that were to follow him were less partial to the bottle and far more organized when it came to intimidation, demands and violence.

Eight...

BURNING FLESH

The invasion of farms around Zimbabwe had been going on for 13 weeks and we all expected the situation to worsen as the elections drew nearer. In just over three weeks' time the nation would go to the polls and decide if they wanted a change in government or were happy to continue with things the way they were. For a few precious days, Ian and I thought that our problems were over. Edward had disappeared and the tent had gone. The squatters' houses were still standing scattered in our fields but aside from one or two, most looked deserted. It didn't seem possible that this close to the elections we were going to be left alone and when I heard the whistling and shouting from the gate, I returned to reality sharply. They came at lunchtime. Ian had gone to Harare for the day, Richard was at school and all the workers were at their houses for lunch. Completely alone, I looked carefully out of the kitchen door and then quietly swung it closed. I could see three people at the gate and they were whistling and shouting. One was a very large woman who was banging on the gate with a hefty stick. I walked into the pantry and flicked the switch to arm the electric fence. Holding my breath I waited for the green light to come on to show me that I had a complete circuit but it didn't. It was being shorted and within seconds the alarm started blaring. I left it for a few more seconds and then switched the alarm off, leaving the power on. At least my unwanted visitors would now know that if they touched the fence again they'd receive a nasty shock. The dogs were going crazy. When the whistling and shouting continued, it became obvious that they weren't going to go away so I took a deep breath and went outside.

'Good afternoon. May I help you?' This was my standard greeting to anyone that came to the gate but it didn't elicit the usual response and returned greetings.

'You give us money for our rally,' the fat woman said.

I wanted to say: I'm fine thanks and how are you?—but thought that possibly the sarcasm would be lost on this woman who looked angry and aggressive and clearly in no mood for jokes.

'I beg your pardon?'

'Give us money for our rally,' she repeated, speaking slowly and loudly.

'And meat,' the other woman said. 'We need meat and maize also.'

Now the third one chipped in. The only man in the trio said: 'And wood, give us firewood.'

So far they'd done all the talking and frankly I didn't know what to say. They were doing pretty well without me, obviously had this whole shopping list all worked out well in advance.

'Sorry, I don't give things to everyone who walks up to my gate.'

'You don't know who we are?' The fat woman was getting really cross with me now. 'We are war veterans.' She stepped a little closer to the fence and put her hand up, possibly to rattle the gate but then must have remembered the electricity coursing through the wire. She settled with shaking her fist at me and shouting, 'We are the really war veterans. You give us these things now! Give us money now for government.'

By this time the four dogs were barking hysterically and it was hard to hear myself think let alone make myself heard.

'Have you got ID?' I asked. 'I'm not giving money to anyone through the gate. May I see your ID please? And some proof that you are collecting officially for the government.'

'We are the government,' the fat woman spat at me, hands on her hips. 'Why do you want proof? Don't you know we are the government?'

'I give money regularly to Chief Mswaka for government functions and he always gives me a letter from government and a receipt.'

This shut her up for a minute and the three went into a whispering huddle giving me a chance to look at them properly. The fat woman, in a bright, flowing floral dress and wearing a red beret, looked to be about my age and was obviously the spokesperson. The second woman was tall and thin, wearing a sleek olive green dress and probably in her mid-forties. The man, wearing well-cut trousers and a black leather jacket, had a hint of grey in his hair but also did not look to be much more than 45. None of them looked as if they were landless peasants and certainly looked nothing like the "usual" war veterans I had encountered, who seemed always to wear dark blue overalls and trench coats. I almost smiled as I looked down at my own apparel— tatty grey shorts, a stretched t-shirt and barefoot. They were certainly far better dressed than I. Perhaps they should be the ones giving out money and food.

'When did you give money to Mswaka?' she demanded. 'You tell me when you gave money, and how much. Yes, how much did you give? You show me the receipt.'

'Why don't you go and ask Chief Mswaka?' I answered crossly, getting really fed up with these ridiculous demands, which she seemed to be making up as she went along. 'You go and ask him if he knows Mrs Buckle and when I last gave him money. He'll show you the receipt.'

Fat woman was becoming agitated and began shouting again. We had a stalemate but I was determined at least to try to make a stand. I stood at the gate feeling the sweat trickling down my arms and waited until she had finished, spittle beading at the corners of her mouth.

'You come back with your ID,' I said quietly, 'and an official letter from the government and a receipt book.'

'Then will you give us money?'

'I'll see,' I answered and turned away, effectively ending the conversation.

When I returned to the house I was shaking—delayed shock at the unexpected confrontation. There were so many questions I should have asked them. Like: So what if you're a war veteran? Do I owe you a debt of gratitude, a living? Haven't I paid you enough already? Wasn't it my taxes that gave you the $50,000 pay-out in 1997? Wasn't it my taxes that paid you your pension every month? I should have asked her what she meant when she said she was a "really war veteran". What was "a really war veteran"? If she meant she was a real war veteran, then what was Edward? In fact, where was Edward? This was his patch. He'd been giving the orders round here for 13 weeks. Who were these impostors? I calmed down and then, knowing that I was wasting my time, phoned the police in Marondera. It took an age for them to answer the phone and when they did, even longer for them to find someone who would speak to me. I said that I wanted to report that three people had been making demands at my gate. The officer I spoke to, who said his name wasn't important, was not impressed with my complaint. He said this was nothing, other farmers were being forced to hand over thousands of dollars and their trucks; my complaint was not important enough and no, he was sorry, but he didn't have a report number at the moment. He did say that he might be able to find the official report later on and might phone me with a complaint number later on. He never did.

After I had put Richard to bed that night I joined Ian in my study and we peered at the blue screen of my computer reading the *Online* edition of the *Daily News*.

> *A British diplomat on holiday on a farm in Mvurwi was attacked by war veterans and briefly held hostage with his wife and two children... A 38-year-old year old diplomat based in London, was confronted on Monday night by a group of war veterans occupying the farm in the Mvurwi district, about 90 kilometres north of Harare. They called him out saying they wanted to talk to the owner of the farm. He said the owner was away. When he came out he was knocked unconscious for about ten seconds ... he managed to get back into the house where his family and a visiting couple were trapped for three hours. The siege ended when a local war veterans' leader intervened and convinced the farm invaders to leave.*

The prickly heat that had suddenly come over me increased as we printed the daily situation report from the CFU as it came in on the email screen.

> *Trelawney ... two intruders had entered the farmhouse at Skelton/ Uitzight Farm belonging to Mr Tony Oates. The intruders cut through the security fence with wire cutters, which were left at the fence. They scouted around the house and gained access by cutting burglar bars at an open window of the bedroom of the son who was not on the farm at the time. The bolt cutters used in this operation were also left at the scene. The intruders proceeded down the passage towards Mr Oates' bedroom. Mr Oates caught sight of them as they entered the room and was shot in his right arm as he reached for his revolver. He called out and his wife, who was watching television in the lounge and heard the shot, ran down the passage towards the bedroom. She was hit on the head by the assailants with a sharp object but managed to free herself. At this time Mr*

Oates rose from the bed with his revolver and let off two rounds, one of which killed the assailant yielding the gun. Mrs Oates raised the community through her radio network. At approximately 9.00pm the first farmers arrived at the scene, including a trained nurse who applied CPR to Mr Oates who was having difficulty breathing. She was unable to revive Mr Oates who had been shot through the lung and he died at approximately 9.30pm.

Leaving Ian sitting at the computer I went first to the pantry and checked that the power was activated and then moved systematically from room to room checking every window and door. Ours was a typical old farmhouse, built of farm-fired bricks. It had started out as a one-roomed house and over the years more and more bits had been added to it. As a result, there were numerous doors that led to the outside. None of the windows really closed well and I just thanked God that less than a year ago we'd found the money to put burglar bars on every window. It would be a nightmare for us to get out of the house in a hurry as all the outside doors had been fitted with heavy, barred gates, but at least it would be equally hard for anyone to get in. When I'd finished going round the house I sat with Ian in the lounge. He always watched television long after I'd gone to bed, but tonight I was too afraid to go to bed before him so I sat staring at the television. For about the millionth time I wondered how much longer we could go on like this, living in perpetual fear. My worries had increased significantly after my three visitors at the gate earlier in the day and when Ian and I finally went to bed I didn't fall asleep for hours. I was too frightened to get up and watch television by myself so I lay listening to every creak of the tin roof as it absorbed the cold night air and contracted. I must have got up at least half a dozen times to check on Richard and as the hours crawled by I knew I'd be in no state to bargain with the "really war veterans" if they returned the next day.

At lunchtime the following day, the three "really" war veterans arrived at the gate. This time they didn't shout and whistle, merely waited until the dogs announced their presence. They were not as aggressive as they had been the day before and I even received a mumbled response to my usual greeting. Today the man was doing all the talking and said he had come with the "official government" letter. I had to bite my lip to prevent the smile when I saw the letter being carefully torn out of a small school exercise book. It was an exercise book they had bought from my store. I could see my own pencilled price, $5.50, in the top corner. The letter was handwritten and had no trace of a government stamp on it. He handed it to me through the gate.

From: The War Veterans, St Michael's Farm, Watershed Headquarters.
To: All Commercial Farmers.
We require donations for a min star rally to be held at Charakupa on Friday 2nd June at 2.00pm. We require meat, mealie meal, fuel, vehicles, transport and money for this rally. All commercial farmers and their workers are required to attend.
Signed …

Undated, unstamped and unsigned. I'd asked for a letter and now I had one! I asked to see their identity documents then and the two women immediately produced their war veteran cards. The man handed me his metal national identity card.

'May I see your war veterans' card?'

'They didn't give me one,' the man muttered. 'I didn't get the money.'

The three then went immediately into a discussion among themselves about the reasons why the man did not have a war veterans' card, why he hadn't been given the $50,000 government gratuity in 1997. It was obviously a very sore point and I left them talking and took the letter and their documents into the house. Carefully I copied down all their names, identity numbers and "heroes" details and reread the official letter. The slim woman was Caroline, the large woman, Netty and the unpaid man was Isaac. I knew that I'd boxed myself into a corner by now and would have to produce something for their "min star rally". I hadn't made sense of what a "min star rally" was at that point but eventually decided on giving them $300. I returned to the gate, handing their documents, letter and the money to Isaac.

'May I have a receipt please Isaac?'

He looked at me with what seemed like surprise that I knew his name. He said something to Netty who dug around in an enormous handbag while he counted the money.

'Aah, it is only $300. It is not enough.'

I'd been waiting for this and had a little speech already prepared. I cleared my throat to get rid of the quaver I knew would be there.

'No, it's not much Isaac, but it's all I can afford.' I saw his eyebrows go up but didn't give him a chance to say a word. 'You know for over three months your comrades have been on my farm. They have taken all the grazing for the cattle and I have to buy all the food now from National Foods. They have taken my dams so I have to use electricity to pump all the water for the cattle. And the trees, look!' I pointed to the plantations within view—all showed clear signs of having recently been raped, dry brown branches lying on the ground where their poles had been stripped. 'Look at all the trees that have been stolen. I should be selling these trees for poles and firewood Isaac. But for three months now I haven't sold even one stick of firewood. We cannot even find the money to pay wages now Isaac so I'm afraid even $300 is more than I can afford.'

'Sure!' he exclaimed.

'Sure,' I repeated.

By this time Netty had finished writing my receipt and I watched as she tore the first counterfoil out of the brand new receipt book.

Also undated and unstamped the receipt said: Received from Miss Buckle 300 dollars for min star rally.

Now that the official business was over I asked them what had happened to Edward.

'Edward?' Isaac said, his brow furrowed.

'Yes, Edward. He's been the war vet in charge of this farm since February. What's happened to Edward?'

'Oh, we're in charge now. We've thrown him away!'

'Oh,' I murmured, not daring to ask more, not daring to find out what "thrown away" meant. 'Okay,' I said and turned away.

'What about your small truck?' Isaac called after me. 'We need it for the rally at the weekend.'

I stopped and my heart thumped.

'My car?' I repeated stupidly. 'No, sorry you can't have my car, I need it for farm business.'

'It's only for taking people to the rally. We can even bring a driver.'

'Sorry, no.' I walked away quickly, my hands shaking.

'We'll come back tomorrow to see if you've changed your decision,' Isaac shouted.

I didn't turn round again or say anything, just quickened my pace.

Oh God, this was getting out of hand, I thought as I fumbled with the catch on the back door. I thought I'd got away lightly. For weeks I'd been reading the daily CFU reports on how farmers had been forced to give money, fuel, vehicles to war veterans. I'd vowed I'd never give in, never do it and now I'd already made the first big mistake. By giving the $300, I'd played their game and now didn't know how I could stop it. What were the options though? Refuse to give anything and find the house burning down? Find the sheep and cattle slaughtered, the store looted, or, God forbid, the workers assaulted or Ian, or Richard. This was insanity. I decided that I'd now given more than enough and that under no circumstances would I give them my small pickup truck. I was ashamed of myself, disgusted that I'd given them anything—but it was done. Perhaps tonight I wouldn't have the nightmares again; perhaps now that I'd given in I'd be able to sleep.

For the past three weeks my nights had been plagued by two recurring nightmares. The first was one that was very familiar to me, although I hadn't had it for over 20 years. There was fire everywhere outside. The house was completely surrounded by flames. I was alone in the house with a toddler and raced with the baby to the bathroom to fill the tub with water so that we could protect ourselves. I bent down to put the plug in and the flames shot up through the plughole and then they came in through the ventilation bricks and the overflow pipes. Flames roared in to the house above the pelmets and between the windowpanes. Then I would wake up, not knowing whether I'd managed to save the baby or escape from the house.

The second nightmare was a more recent occurrence and had begun after the war veterans had held one of their weekly meetings down on the field. In the dream I was lying on a hammock in the garden with Ian. Richard and Linnet were in the kitchen playing with their Lego on the floor and it was almost dusk. Suddenly coming towards us were eight white men. They all wore blue boxer shorts and carried rifles and said they were soldiers and that we should get inside quickly. We tumbled off the hammock and ran inside, followed by the eight men. Everyone was slipping and tripping over Richard's Lego as we hurried to close windows and doors and switch off the lights. Richard and Linnet hid under the kitchen table and were both screaming, and screaming and screaming when the shooting started. A bright red car with black-tinted windows drove round and round on the front lawn. The car's windows were open and out of each one was a rifle that spat bullets at us, at the house, and the windows were exploding and shattering all around us. Then I woke up, again not knowing what had happened, if anyone had been killed, if Richard and Linnet were all right. Paying the $300 to Isaac and Netty and Caroline did not stop the dreams. Clearly my nightmares were not for sale.

The following day I sat at my desk writing more letters and trying not to think about the impending return of the three new war veterans. I had begun to make sense of what was going on and had pieced all sorts of things together. The "min star rally" was easy. It was a mini rally. Whether it was called a "min star" because it was going to be a small rally or was going to have a not-so-famous speaker, I wasn't sure. I knew that a "star rally" was one where the speaker was someone of great importance—a top minister, the vice president, even the president. I didn't know who might be called a "mini star" at the political rally scheduled to take place a few kilometres from our farm that weekend. Everyone now knew about the coming rally and I had already told George that they should finish work at lunchtime so that they could attend the rally if they wanted to. As for Isaac telling me that Edward had been "thrown away", that was a bit more of a puzzle. There were so many different stories that it was hard to know which one to believe. Some said that Edward hadn't been giving the money he raised from plot sales to the government; others said he was really sick; yet others said the war veterans in Marondera had replaced him because he wasn't powerful enough. I really had no idea which of the stories was true, or why he was suddenly being thought of as not a "real" war veteran.

When I went to the store at 3.30 that afternoon, I thought I'd got away with it, thought that my three new keepers had forgotten about me. They hadn't. All three were waiting for me at the store. Netty stood outside on the veranda and was knitting. Nothing was funny any more, but I did smile inwardly as I knew the bright blue wool she was using had been bought from my store. Part of my $300 had reverted to me! Caroline was inside the store and was in the process of paying Jane for three house plants that she'd just selected from my display—more of my money coming back! Isaac was leaning up against the counter, a drink in one hand and a pack of cigarettes in the other. I nodded to him and he immediately ushered me out onto the veranda.

'We came to check if you have made your decision.'

'Decision?' I echoed stupidly, knowing exactly what he was referring to, trying to play dumb.

'Of your car. We really need your car for the weekend.'

'I'm sorry Isaac. I already told you my car is needed at the weekend.' I really didn't want to go any further with this conversation that was already attracting attention from people waiting at the bus stop right outside the door, so I turned and went into the store. Jane, dear, clever Jane, immediately began a lengthy story to me about some problem with a bread invoice. She knew exactly what was going on with Isaac, Netty and Caroline and was yet again bailing me out. She babbled on about figures and tapped things into the little calculator until she saw the three leave and then suddenly stopped in mid flow.

'They've gone!' she grinned as she pressed the "cancel" key on the calculator and we both began laughing as we slapped hands in the African way. I hadn't told her anything about these three but she knew everything already. A farm is a small place, gossip travels very fast and everyone knew I was in trouble.

On Thursday afternoon Isaac was waiting for me at the store again. Now he'd worked things out in his mind. He'd obviously been watching us and knew that Ian too had a vehicle. It was also a one-ton pickup truck, much newer than the one I used on the farm and much faster.

'What about your husband's truck? I have got a driver if you are both busy.' Isaac announced the moment I arrived at the store.

Again I managed to fob him off; again Jane came to my rescue but with the rally now only two days away I was becoming really nervous that we were going to be forced to surrender one of our vehicles. The moment I'd closed the store, I ran home and Ian hid my truck. With some very impressive reversing, Ian managed to squeeze the truck between a very overgrown flowerbed and the back of his workshop. It was invisible from the driveway and the gate. We tipped the wing mirrors down so that they wouldn't glint, took out the battery and locked it up. I was distraught by the end of the week, crying a lot, short-tempered with everyone and we decided, for the first time in three months, that we should get off the farm. We agreed it would be better to be away so that we wouldn't be forced into a situation over which we had no control. After Richard had gone to bed on Thursday night we packed our bags and I phoned friends in Harare to beg three beds for the weekend. Bill and Ann were only too pleased to have us and I slept a little better that night.

First thing on Friday morning we bundled all our things behind the seat in Ian's truck and I gave my cat and the dogs an extra long cuddle, really not knowing if we'd still find them there when we returned. I ran through everything one last time with George and Emmanuel who were going to stay in the house in our absence and we drove out. For once I was really glad of the tinted windows in Ian's truck because on the corner outside our gate was a group of war veterans. They would hopefully think that Ian was just taking Richard to school, would not know that the whole family was in the vehicle. We dropped Richard at school, promising great adventures of a weekend in Harare, and went into Marondera town to waste the morning. We found a diesel queue outside one of the service stations and joined it to while away the time. Then we went to the only restaurant in the centre of Marondera town and spent the rest of the morning with our neighbours, Micky and Myrtle. They too were leaving their farm for the weekend. As we always did, we talked about the farms, the war veterans, politics, the daily CFU report. There was nothing else to talk about. These things consumed our lives—every waking thought was about farms and war veterans; anything other than this was trivial, inconsequential. When we'd finally wasted the hours to lunchtime, we said a tearful goodbye to Micky and Myrtle, collected Richard from school and headed for the capital city.

This was my first time off the farm in over three months and it felt strange. As the miles sped by it seemed almost as if I was in another country, everything looked so normal. Children waved to us, other drivers smiled, businesses were open, and there wasn't a war veteran anywhere in sight. None of the people we passed wore blue overalls, big hats and trench coats. When we approached the outskirts of the city of Harare, everything looked completely as it should. There were no plastic shacks in sight, no half-built huts. It was as if nothing was wrong with the country. On Saturday morning Ann and I went to a very popular and up-market fresh produce complex so that Richard could play on the swings and eat the biggest slice of chocolate cake he'd had in his life. After we'd negotiated our way through the luxury 4x4 and Mercedes vehicles in the car park, we sat in the open-air coffee shop. If I'd been in shock before, it intensified a hundred-fold now as we sat drinking our coffee and I eavesdropped on the conversations going on all around me.

These were the elite of Harare: diplomats, former patriots and people from the middle and upper classes of our society. They were black and white people but to me it was if they were from another planet. They didn't look worried or stressed; they weren't talking about farms or war veterans or the breakdown of the rule of law and order. They weren't discussing the horrific abuses of teachers and nurses, the beatings and rapes of people that weren't as fortunate as they were. They weren't talking about the murder of Mr Oates or the assault on the British tourists. They weren't even talking about the elections, which were only three weeks away. I became angrier and angrier and was at the point of standing up on the table and screaming at them: 'My God, are you Zimbabweans? Do you live in the same country as me?' My fists were clenched and my eyes full of tears as I watched Richard working his way through his monstrous piece of cake. For him, because of him, I could do nothing, say nothing and I felt a really deep sense of both shame and despair. If the farmers, teachers, nurses and opposition activists had to depend on the likes of these people to save Zimbabwe, then there really was no hope. I turned away so that my son wouldn't see my tears. As we left with the remnants of the chocolate cake in a doggy bag, Richard whispered to me: 'Mum, I'm as happy as a butterfly.' Then I couldn't hold back the tears any more.

At the end of the weekend, for the first time ever, I didn't want to go home. We left it to the last minute and reached the farm just before dark. Emmanuel was waiting for us. Everything was all right, he told us. Jane wasn't feeling too well, but she'd be fine by the morning. When I said I'd go up to her house to see if there was anything she needed, Emmanuel told me Jane wasn't at home. She'd gone to the clinic. Jane had ongoing problems with an ulcer and I assumed that this must be the problem.

On Monday morning as soon as I went outside just after dawn, I knew that something was seriously wrong, something had happened during the weekend. First I asked Arthur, the night guard. Oh no, he said, everything is all right. I asked him how Jane was feeling and he wouldn't look me in the eyes as he said that she was much better. Thirty minutes later George, Isaya and Clemence reported for work. Isaya and Clemence mumbled their good mornings, eyes to the ground, and went past me into the dairy.

'George, what's happened? Is everything okay?'

George too wouldn't look me in the face; he just shook his head.

'Come on, George, tell me what's happened. Is there something wrong on the farm? The sheep, the cattle?'

'All the animals are okay.' George paused. He knew me so well, knew that I wouldn't let this go until he'd told me.

'It's only the storekeeper,' he said at last.

I frowned, wondering why George wasn't referring to Jane by name. I waited for him to go on.

'She has hurt herself,' George said at last.

'Hurt herself! What do you mean George? How has she hurt herself?'

Now suddenly George looked me in the face and his voice changed slightly. It was more assertive.

'We don't know what happened. She just hurt herself.'

By now Emmanuel had arrived and was standing listening to this non-conversation.

'Maybe she fell down,' Emmanuel announced. 'Yes, maybe she fell down.'

'Okay, you two go and get on with your jobs. I'll see Jane in a minute.' It was obvious that they knew something but either didn't want to tell me or were too afraid to. I stood at the gate waiting for Jane to come down and collect the basket with the books and money for the store. I found it impossible to believe that no one knew anything. Usually when something happened there would be a great to-do with everyone speaking at once, all eager to make their contribution. Now though it was if they all had a secret and were frightened. Their houses in the workers' compound were all close together; there was a communal tap; their children played together and often they ate their meals together. It was impossible that no one knew anything.

At seven o'clock I saw Jane coming towards the house. She was bent over and limping, walking very slowly, clearly in a lot of pain. As she came nearer to me, Jane lifted her hand and tried to cover her face. I put my hand up and gently lowered her arm.

'Jane, my God, what's happened to you?'

Jane turned her face away and again tried to cover her mouth from my stare. She didn't answer me, just slowly shook her head.

'Jane, please tell me, what's happened.'

'I can work,' she whispered, barely able to speak as her face and mouth were so enormously swollen.

'Come Jane, come inside with me,' I begged. 'Come and tell me what's happened.'

Still she shook her head. 'I will be all right. Maybe I'll go to the clinic later.'

'Jane no, come on, come and tell me what happened. You can't possibly work like this. At least let me drive you up to the clinic.'

Jane's eyes widened and filled with tears. She looked nervously over her shoulder.

'Please, I can work, please.'

I just stared at her. Something really bad had happened and Jane was terrified, of what or whom I didn't know. On her cheek was a large, dark bruise and running through it were two jagged cuts. One of her eyes was swollen and bruised. Her mouth though, was enormous, her lips almost completely enclosed in a massive swelling. Between the base of her nose and her upper lip was an open wound, which she had packed with cotton wool and which oozed blood and plasma. Jane's eyes were red, her hands were shaking badly and she kept rubbing her lower back. As I stood helplessly looking at this broken woman, Jane looked at her watch and then again over her shoulder. There was some reason she wanted to get to her job in the store and she clearly didn't want to be seen to be late. For now there was nothing I could do. Jane didn't want to talk to me, didn't want to tell me anything and I couldn't force her. I called to Emmanuel and asked him to carry the basket to the store for Jane. She tried half-heartedly to protest but I insisted.

'You stay with her Emmanuel please. Make sure she is okay and help her to open up the store.'

Emmanuel nodded, took the basket and the two went off, not talking, one behind the other. What could I do? I couldn't force Jane to go to a doctor. I couldn't force her to tell me anything. She must have a very good reason for what she was doing.

Before long Micky and Myrtle were sitting in our lounge drinking coffee with us. They too had been away all weekend and knew nothing about what might have happened to Jane. They did, however, tell us about the events of the weekend. The Zanu PF youngsters had been around, door-to-door, farm-to-farm, village-to-village telling everyone to attend a big meeting on the Buckle's field on Saturday morning. There had been over 300 people in our field apparently and they had been told that everyone must attend the rally that afternoon at Charakupa. If they didn't go, they would have to pay the consequences. Everyone had to have a Zanu PF data card and would have to show it at the rally. For hours the people had filed to the front to buy this data card. None of us had ever heard of a data card before and from what we could understand, it was an updating of all Zanu PF members. It recorded name, age, marital status, dependants. That afternoon there had been 300 to 400 people at the rally. A farm register had been called. 'Stow Farm,' the leader had called out and all those from our farm had to stand up. There were only two from our farm and they were interrogated about where the other workers were. They had to show their newly purchased data cards, swear allegiance to Zanu PF and denounce the opposition. Then they could sit down as the spotlight moved to another farm or village or household. If an opposition supporter was suspected, he was called to the front, told to take off his shoes, shirt and trousers and was publicly berated. One man had been forced to lie in the dust while others poked him with sticks and threw stones at him.

In the middle of the morning I walked up to the store. Jane had closed for lunch so I went straight to her house to see how she was. I found the place locked and Jane not there. I asked the women in the neighbouring houses where Jane was. They all said they didn't know, hadn't seen her. They too were paralysed, struck dumb with fear. After lunch I went back to the store and found Jane. She looked shocking. The wound on her mouth had been covered with plaster, her forehead was beaded with sweat. There were a couple of customers in the store and I waited for them to leave.

'Let's close up Jane,' I said, hoping she'd be too tired to resist. It was a little after two o'clock and we always closed at 4.30.

Jane looked at her watch but didn't say anything so I took the keys and locked the outside gates and we cashed up in silence. When we had finished Jane collected her jersey and house keys from under the counter and a clear plastic bag. In the bag was a box of plaster, a small bag of cotton wool and a tube of antiseptic cream. I knew then that the swathe of plaster on Jane's face had not been put on by a doctor or a nurse but by Jane herself.

'Jane,' I said quietly with my hand on her arm, 'I want you to let me take you to a doctor tomorrow.' She started to shake her head but I continued. 'Please Jane, you don't have to tell the doctor what happened, or me—you don't have to tell me. But Jane we must get some proper treatment for your wound. It could go septic Jane. It really is serious. You haven't been to the clinic have you?'

'I was there,' she whispered. 'They said they couldn't treat me.'

'Okay, we'll go early in the morning to my doctor Jane.' I had begun to put things together in my mind. Jane was terrified. She had obviously been threatened, told not to tell anyone what had happened. Told not to let whites help her. It was going on all round the country. 'No one will know Jane. We'll go early in the morning, straight from school. No one will see us. I won't pick you up here. You come down to the house so that no one will see us—but Jane, we must get proper treatment for your mouth, okay?' Jane nodded, her eyes brimming with tears and I said no more. We locked up in silence and Jane went home.

The youngsters who spent their days intimidating us in the store were standing under a tree across the road watching us. I wanted to turn and shout at them; tell them exactly what I thought of them; make them strip off and lie in the dust; throw sticks and stones at them. I said nothing though and turned down the path for home. As I always did, I stopped outside Isaya's house and solemnly shook hands with two-year-old Cecilia and gave her the sweet in my pocket. Her sweet, high, innocent little voice called out goodbye to me as I trudged home but today I couldn't answer and just waved.

At seven the next morning Jane was waiting at the house for me. Richard moved to the middle of the bench seat in my truck but Jane would not get in. She said she was feeling much better. I laughed and patted the seat and we argued for a couple of minutes until she relented. Jane would not get in the front of the truck with me so I grabbed a blanket and she climbed in the back, wriggling down until she was out of sight completely. Sitting outside the doctors' rooms,

Jane was very nervous and I kept reassuring her, telling her everything would be all right, that she wouldn't have to say what had happened.

'I fell off my bicycle,' she said, not looking at me. 'It was nearly dark and I just hit a rock and fell off my bicycle.'

I nodded but said nothing. I knew Jane didn't have a bicycle. She knew that I knew. I was sure that if I had been Jane I would have wanted to stand on the tallest building and scream it to the world with a megaphone. I had no conception of the fear though. It wasn't me. I did not know what they had threatened her with.

My family doctor was wonderful. I knew she would be. She gently prised off the sticking plaster. With a pair of tweezers she painstakingly picked out the cotton wool that had stuck to the wound and as every piece came free, it bought with it a piece of flesh and the blood dripped down onto Jane's lip. I held Jane's hand and the tears ran down my cheeks as this woman beside me kept completely still. She didn't even wince and my admiration for her knew no bounds. When the whole thing was exposed I gasped. Never before had I seen anything so horrific. From the base of her nostrils to the top of her lip, and running right across the full width of her mouth there was a mush of flesh. It looked like the inside of a rotten peach.

'What did they use, Jane?' my doctor asked.

Jane didn't answer. She shook her head and turned away slightly. For the first time her eyes brimmed with tears, which she hastily wiped away with the back of her hand.

'Can you stitch it?' I asked but my doctor said she couldn't. The wound was so long and wide there was nothing for the stitches to hold on to. Gently the doctor cleaned the wound, dabbing it with neat antiseptic that must have stung dreadfully. Jane didn't move. This was the only treatment possible for a wound like this—leave it open and exposed, douse it with antiseptic and a drying agent and let nature do the rest.

When we left the doctors' rooms, Jane would not let me take her home. Still she didn't dare be seen with me so I gave her the money for a taxi and she went home alone. Perhaps that hurt me more than anything—the fact that I couldn't be seen with Jane, couldn't be seen to be helping her, couldn't show my love and concern. In the days that followed, Jane came down to the house every morning, very early, and I treated the wound for her. I never again asked her what had happened, who had done this to her and she never volunteered anything. Jane would be scarred for life and carry that and her secret with her forever.

Over the following weeks I did discover what had happened to Jane, not from her, but from the one man who was not too afraid to speak out. By chance the man, whom I cannot name, called to me one evening as I left the store and we talked quietly behind the back wall of the building where no one could see or hear us. The youths had come just before dark, he said, throwing stones on the roofs, banging on doors and windows, calling everyone out, demanding to see Zanu PF data cards. When Jane could not find her card, they entered her home and ransacked the place, turning it upside down looking for evidence of opposition literature. Still the data card had not been found and they had picked up a steel rod and shoved it into the hot coals of the cooking fire. When it glowed red with heat, they lifted it to Jane's face, holding it against her mouth. After they had gone, the man had helped Jane. He rushed her to the nearby clinic but the nurses would not come out to help her. He had taken Jane home and helped her to bed, stayed with her until she fell asleep. When the story was told, we shook hands and the man left. Never again did we speak of it. We too were party to this horror.

NINE

THIS IS MY FARM

On Friday, 2nd June 2000, our attention was temporarily drawn away from the atrocity that had taken place on our doorstep as the country woke up to a very thick *Herald* edition. On page eleven of the state-run newspaper, headed by a thick black border, began a seven-page list of farms the government intended to acquire compulsorily. In the preamble, signed by J.T. Mujuru, Acting Minister of Lands and Agriculture, it said:

> NOTICE is hereby given, in terms of subsection (1) of section 5 of the Land Acquisition Act [Chapter 20:10] that the President intends to acquire compulsorily the land described in the Schedule for resettlement purposes… Any owner or occupier or any other person who has an interest and right in the said land, and who wishes to object to the proposed compulsory acquisition, may lodge the same, in writing, with the Minister of Lands and Agriculture … on or before the 2nd of July 2000.

In the following seven pages were listed 804 properties, 41 of which were situated in Marondera. My hands shook as I looked at this obituary to commercial agriculture in Zimbabwe. The list was arranged numerically, area by area but still used the names of pre-Independence, Marondera was Marandellas. This must be because of

the wording on the Title Deeds I thought. But then I looked more
closely at the title deed numbers that showed which year the
documents had been issued. Properties purchased even in 1994
(fourteen years after Independence) were still listed under the old area
names. It was very confusing. Twenty years was a long time ago and
people born after 1980 would surely find it a mystery. Some farms had
their size quoted in hectares, others in acres and others still in morgen. I
had no idea what a morgen was and neither did my dictionary or
thesaurus. I looked first for our farm, but it was not on the list. Then I
looked for those of friends, neighbours, acquaintances, and was deeply
shocked at some of the properties that the government of Zimbabwe
intended to acquire. There seemed to be no reason, no pattern. Huge
cattle ranches were there, properties of over 33,000 hectares in extent.
But so too were smallholdings of fewer than 50 hectares. The more I
pored over the pages, the less sense it made. There were safari
companies and game ranches, abattoirs and flower farms; there were
the best dairy estates and huge tobacco properties. One of the biggest
potato-growing farms in the country was there as was a mission farm
and a mine. Even listed were farms owned by black Zimbabweans:
Madondo, Sithole, Mpofu. It almost seemed as if the list of properties
had been compiled by a blindfolded person who had stuck pins into a
map at random. Surely this couldn't be a serious list? If it was, the
consequences were dire for Zimbabwe—our economy would surely
collapse, tourism would be finished.

A couple of days later we were given a 14-page handout by the CFU.
"Notes for farmers whose properties have been listed for acquisition in
the extraordinary government gazette of 2nd June 2000". It instructed
listed farmers about what to do, what paperwork to complete and by
what date. Two small sections in the booklet were chilling, making this
all too real:

> Work out who wants to stop farming, who wants to carry on, who wants
> to move out of your area, who wants to stay, what will be left of your
> community, which community you will fit into best.
>   It is nevertheless essential that farmers endeavour to be constructive.
> Objections for objection sake will not hold and could cause you more grief
> and problems than they are worth. (Commercial Farmers' Union).

This surely was Zimbabwe's worst nightmare. To wake up one
crystal-clear, cold winter morning and see your name in a newspaper,
read that your life's work was to be compulsorily acquired, confiscated.

Although enormously relieved that our farm was not on the list, I knew this was just the first of many lists—that we could be next. My heart went out to every one of those 804 farmers. Again, as I had been so many times in the past three months, I was ashamed to be Zimbabwean.

The night the list was published, the first page of the daily situation report from the CFU contained a statement by Dr Jerry Grant, deputy director of regions. What an impossible job this man had, to try to keep the situation cool, try to encourage farmers to remain calm. Dr Grant warned though of ...

> *the likelihood of a rush of farm invasions, by war veterans and their followers, of these properties so identified today. These invasions should be treated in the normal way ... it is imperative to avoid opportunities for violent reaction from invaders. (CFU).*

The CFU leaders were as worried as we were of yet more problems. The government gazette had virtually given licence to anyone who wanted a piece of land to take it.

On the day after the list was published, there were over 100 people in the field below our house and we could only hope that they were being told to leave. I was still treating Jane's wound every morning and those few minutes were a special time between us as we could talk freely without worrying about who was watching or listening. I showed her a newspaper cutting and watched to see how she would react as she read it.

> *Hospital personnel were warned that the war veterans and Zanu PF supporters would come to the hospital and beat them up if they continued to give treatment to victims of commercial farm invasions... Staff members at a certain private hospital had to undergo special drilling, including evacuation exercises in preparation for the invasions by war vets ... (Standard).*

Jane didn't say a word as she handed the paper back to me. This was another secret she was keeping to herself. I had still been unable to find anything that would make Jane smile but finally managed when I showed her the story in the *Daily News* of the latest charges being levelled against the British by Zimbabwe.

> *The president accused the British of resorting to following ships laden with fuel destined for Zimbabwe on the high seas and offering them*

double the amount paid by Zimbabwe for the fuel in a bid to deprive
Zimbabwe of normal petrol, diesel and paraffin supplies.

The president had made the accusations whilst addressing a campaign
rally in Mbare. Jane smiled so much that her eyes watered with pain as
the skin on her newly healing mouth was stretched and pulled to its
old and much missed shape. These most outrageous and unfounded
statements made at political rallies were now a daily occurrence and
one wondered who believed them. The continuing crisis with fuel
shortages was, as the *Daily News* pointed out, probably completely
unrelated to any devious plot by Britain.

Top managers at the heavily indebted parastatal [NOCZIM—the
National Oil Company of Zimbabwe, in charge of procuring and
supplying fuel to the country] were arrested and are on remand under
charges of corruption. (Daily News).

The chronic shortage of both fuel and foreign currency in the country
was affecting everyone, companies and individuals alike—and
hundreds of productive man-hours were being lost as the country sat
in queues. The Zimbabwe Electricity Supply Authority (ZESA) now
announced that "it had resorted to emergency power rationing
countrywide because of a critical foreign currency shortage and an
increase in demand caused by the cold weather". (*Daily News*). On the
farm we were without power every day for six or more hours at a time
and I was deeply touched when the Marondera Regional ZESA
manager phoned me one morning. In the Shona way, he asked me
how I was, my husband, my family and then spoke about the subject of
the farm invasions. He said how very sorry he was to have heard that
our farm had been invaded and wanted to know everything. Were we
all right? Had we been harmed? Were our workers being harassed? He
asked, as did so many, if there was anything he could do. I asked him
what the situation with the electricity was and if it would be possible to
switch our power off in the day only. I explained that with squatters on
the land, the nights were the worst times. It was during the darkness
that we most needed power to run security lights and the electric fence.
He agreed immediately and promised he would do his best to limit our
cuts to daylight hours. There was a human being I thought, as I set my
alarm clock for 4am when I knew the power would be on and could
keep up with the mammoth task of replying to the emails that
continued to pour in.

As the elections drew closer, all sorts of people and organizations began to speak out and this was certainly not before time. Long gone were the days when this was a simple case of white farmers trying to stop "landless peasants" from regaining land "stolen from their ancestors". Every sector of the country was being affected and the International Rehabilitation Council for Torture Victims published a report of its findings. In a one-week visit to Zimbabwe, the Danish-based organization had seen what was really going on: "There is evidence that mass psychological torture is occurring... There is evidence of community disruption through intimidation and violence against health workers and teachers". *(Daily News)*.

Perhaps drawing courage from this report, others added their voices:

About 9,000 teachers particularly in Mashonaland Central and East provinces became victims of the widespread lawlessness affecting much of rural Zimbabwe. A report compiled by one of the organizations representing teachers, the Progressive Teachers' Union of Zimbabwe, and covering the past three months says that 551 schools were affected by violence and 2,096 teachers were assaulted by war veterans and suspected Zanu PF supporters. The organization documented 12 cases of rape, mainly affecting spouses of teachers and 25 abductions or rape cases of school pupils. (Daily News).

Contagious panic was beginning to spread throughout the country as not only farmers, teachers and nurses were targets any more. What had started as an election gimmick to win votes was now out of control and everyone who wasn't a "war veteran" knew they were at risk, particularly minority communities. In a letter to the *Daily News* signed by the Indian Communities of Harare, Bulawayo, Gweru, Kwekwe and Kadoma, the fears of the country were expressed. The letter writer spoke of a document in circulation, apparently from someone in high authority, stating that the farms were only the beginning of this revolutionary indigenization of Zimbabwe.

It is believed that businesses will, in fact, be confiscated and homes taken over and apparently the only compensation we will receive will be the value of the property paid at the time the land was purchased. It states that indeed all the land belongs to those who fought for the country, that the fine homes are in the wrong hands and that will change. Yes, we are afraid. Yes, we are being threatened ... black, white, brown, we are all targets and we are in fact all feeling the brunt of the violence. We are human beings and we all have rights, regardless of colour. We love this country, but how can we live in fear? (Daily News).

Zimbabwe's war veterans were creating havoc wherever they went and at last, the "real" war veterans spoke out. This had gone too far and the Zimbabwe War Veterans' Association split. A group calling themselves the Liberators' Platform dissociated themselves from their comrades and condemned the spreading lawlessness. They went public with their stance and it was reported in the *Daily News*:

Happyson Nenji, the chairman of the movement, said his group deplored the decision by the Zanu PF leadership to allow the invaders to remain on the farms during the election. 'This not only perpetuates the disregard for the rule of law,' he said, 'but also undermines the credibility of the elections... Besides being unlawful and undermining the credibility of the elections, the farm occupations have far-reaching economic consequences, which the people of this country will live to regret... It is as incomprehensible as it is irresponsible for any patriotic Zimbabwean or even the neighbouring countries to assume a posture of indifference to this unfolding catastrophe.'

The political campaigning continued though and rather than toning it down as the world's cameras again approached our borders, the two people apparently running the country, (Hunzvi and Mugabe) made even more inflammatory statements. Chenjerai Hunzvi was first and he spoke against the international election observers who were supposedly all over the country, even though we hadn't had a glimpse of even one:

War veteran leader, Chenjerai Hunzvi, yesterday said international election observers were welcome to visit commercial farms occupied by his men but must do so without speaking to farm workers. 'If you want to visit, you are welcome, but just don't speak to the workers, because you will speak about land and that is a separate issue. It has nothing to do with this election... If you speak to the workers, that is politics. That is interfering and we cannot accept that.' (Daily News).

He went on to say that the findings of election observers would not be accepted anyway:

We do not need your recognition of our election… We will fight to make sure that Mugabe remains in power by any means necessary, and it would be very unfortunate to have your findings to be negative.

The vice president of Zimbabwe, Simon Muzenda, joined the farce and told voters at a rally that even if Zanu PF put forward a baboon as a candidate, they should vote for that baboon. The press had a field day. It wasn't only ludicrously funny though—it was also highly insulting to the intelligence of all Zimbabweans. The statements made by the president of the country were far more worrying though and his words were reported in the *Financial Gazette*:

'It is not just the 805 farms [only 804 were listed] that we are looking at. We are looking at the totality of our land,' Mugabe said in a pep talk to the party's 120 candidates… 'If we allow others to own portions of it, it must be out of our own will, our own desire, our own charity. Not on the back of colonial history. So let us be clear on that,' he said. 'The nation must thank the war veterans for standing up where others would not stand up to acquire their vital resources. This is the path now and there shall be no return,' Mugabe said. 'Those of you who are going to parliament must carry the message that the revolution is yet to be concluded.'

Clearly there was no turning back now. More and more farms were being invaded, the president of the country had given his blessing to a virtual take-over of the entire country, not by Zimbabweans, but by those who had fought over two decades ago for his freedom. By mid June more than 1,500 farms had been invaded by Mugabe's brave warriors. My crazed thoughts that perhaps they would move off our farm as we were not on The List, were just that—crazed thoughts. Now it was my turn to get a taste of the terror that Jane had so recently experienced.

For some days there had been a worrying change to the situation on our farm. Instead of the usual weekend build-up of people on our farm, now it was happening every day. At about 9am in the morning people would start wandering across the field to wait under the big old Muhacha tree where the tent had been. It was a mixture of men and women of all ages and often there would be groups of farm workers there too, clearly identifiable in their blue or green overalls and gum boots. A political poster had been tied onto the tree just inside our boundary fence. It was a large black and white photograph of Sydney

Sekeramayi who was a Zanu PF candidate, but not for our constituency. Day after day the people came and usually there were 100 or more gathered, trespassing, on our land. They would sit from 10am until about 3.30, in the mist and the cold and the wind with no food or drink, made to listen to the political re-education of the leaders, not allowed to leave until the speaker had finished. On Thursday morning shortly after 10 o'clock I could hear what was now the chillingly familiar shouting and whistling at our gate. I had not seen or heard at all from any of our war veterans for almost a week, not Edward or Netty, Caroline or Isaac. Ian and the workers were all at the dairy unloading stockfeed from a National Foods Truck so I groaned and went out. This time my visitors had not come to our main, electrified gate, but instead stood at a very rusty, rickety gate, which led from the water pump down onto the farm. The gate was, thank God, chained and padlocked but from the way the seven men were rattling it, I didn't think it would hold out for much longer. Because the gate was so bent and twisted, I didn't dare take any of the dogs with me as I knew they would be under it in a second, so I was completely alone as I approached them.

'Good morning. How may I help you?' This was clearly not the time or place for my usual greeting. Just the sound of my tired and tense voice made the ringleader angry. The six others stepped back a pace or two and staggered as they did so. They were drunk, very drunk. I knew it immediately.

'This is my farm,' the ringleader said, speaking very slowly and loudly. 'This is my farm and this is my fields.'

Oh God, I thought immediately, he's been watching that CNN clip of the war veteran with the grass hat. I shoved my hands in my pockets so that he wouldn't see them shaking and just said quietly: 'Oh.' Not in an angry or defiant or even sarcastic tone, just quietly surprised. He glanced over his shoulder at the six behind him as if drawing courage, inspiration perhaps, and went on.

'This is my farm.'

'Oh.'

'This is my fields.'

'Oh.'

'This is my cows.'

'Oh.' He was running out of ideas now and turning, saw our two ostriches.

'And this is my ostrich,' he said with a grin, clearly delighted with this last acquisition.

I had no idea what to say to all his claims so I waited for him to carry on, for him to tell me exactly what it was that he wanted. He was a youngster, perhaps 25 years old, as were his followers, and I had never seen him before. He was wearing grey trousers and a black jacket, his eyes bloodshot from a night in the pub, his hair mussed, his breath stinking of beer. He stared at me and I at him. Clearly he'd done his bit, had run out of steam.

'So what is it that you want?' I asked quietly, coldly. 'What can I do for you?'

That did it. He went beserk and started all over again with the ownership claims.

'This is my farm, this is my fields, this is my grass, this is my cows.' He was getting into his stride now and rattled them all off one after the other, his voice becoming louder and louder, his speech faster and faster, spittle bubbling and gathering at the corners of his mouth.

'Yes, I understand,' I said, my voice choked, quavering. 'But what is it that you want?'

'Give me your workers, NOW!' he screamed at me through the oh so fragile gate. 'NOW, give them now.' He wanted our workers to attend the meeting that was getting underway down in the field.

'The workers are unloading a National Foods Truck.'

'National Foods! National Foods is for Africans. We are Africans. You are British. You fuck off to Britain.'

Now I was feeling really afraid. My mouth went dry and I couldn't speak.

'You know this farm? This is MY FARM! Give me the workers NOW!' he screamed, seemingly on the point of hysteria, his hands gripping the gate, shaking it ferociously. His eyes had widened and the spit was dribbling down his chin. My heart was beating so fast I thought I'd have a heart attack and I felt an urgent need to go to the toilet.

'That store there,' he bellowed, pointing vaguely in the right direction, 'that store it is for Africans. We are Africans, you whites, all you whites you fuck off to Britain.'

I stared at him through the gate. I couldn't take my eyes off the great gobs of saliva hanging in heavy distended beads on his chin. There was really only one word to describe his behaviour: rabid. He went on, unstoppable now.

'Bring workers now. This is my farm.'

I interrupted him. I'd had enough. 'The workers will come as soon as they have finished unloading the truck.'

'Now!' he screamed. 'They come now. This is my farm. Even that there, it is my house. You get out of my house now.'

This was a new one and I felt my eyebrows rising. His colleagues started giggling and I looked directly at them for the first time. They were embarrassed by my gaze and looked down at the ground, scuffing the dirt with their shoes.

'Four o'clock, hear me. Four o'clock you get out my house.'

'The workers will be at your meeting soon,' I said, wanting to end this insanity now. I don't know what got into me then but I stupidly asked: 'What is your name?'

The man on the other side of the gate became even more enraged.

'My name? My name? You want my name? You fuck off! Look,' he opened his jacket. 'You see this? This it is my gun. I can drop you right now.'

Oh God, he had a gun. This rabid, drunk, spittle-laden little shit had a gun. I could see it in his inside pocket. I could see the scratched, cold, black butt of it. Scream! I could feel it in the back of my throat, could feel it coming. I bit my lip until it hurt to stop the scream from getting out and tensed my thighs to stop any more urine from dripping out. My legs had gone wobbly and I almost put my hand out to steady myself on the gate but clenched my fists in my pocket even tighter. I could feel my short fingernails biting into my palms.

'Yes, I can take you right now. Even ten metres, or 20, or even 40 metres. I can drop you.'

I'm going to call my workers,' I whispered and turned away from the gate. They all burst out laughing as I staggered away, my legs refusing to do what I desperately needed them to do. I walked back towards my inner security fence and with every step I waited for the click and the bang—I waited to be shot in the back. I tried not to run, just walked and the 30 or so metres to the inner security fence seemed hundreds of kilometres away. As soon as I thought I was out of sight I ran. I ran and stumbled, fumbled with the gate and ran again. I was crying and babbling long before I reached the dairy, Ian, and the workers. It took a while before I could make any of them understand what I was trying to say. I was hysterical but at last they understood. The seven men had gone from the gate and we could see them walking up alongside the outer fence towards the store and the workers' houses.

'Run, George run now. Quickly, go and help Jane,' I begged.

I tipped two, or perhaps even three tots of brandy into a glass and filled it with water and drained almost half of it before I lifted the receiver of the telephone. Perhaps it was the tone of my voice, perhaps it was because I said the word "gun". Whatever the reason, the policeman on the other end of the line promised me that they were on their way to our farm. Ian came back into the house. He had been up to the store and had walked around the workers' houses. The place was deserted—everyone had disappeared. The store was locked and there was not a soul in sight. While we waited for the police I phoned the CFU in Marondera and told them what had happened. They too promised to send someone out to our farm. In fewer than 20 minutes a police Land Rover was at our gate and Ian and I went out together. Numbed, tranquillized by the brandy, I told them what had happened. There were five of them and they listened carefully, took notes as I described the appearance and clothing of the gunman. They promised to return and tell us what they had found and set off in their vehicle to the field where more than 200 people were gathered.

Nearly an hour later the police returned to the house and Ian and I invited them in for tea. They had not found the gun, they said. They had told the infant war veterans that none of them were to come anywhere near the house or me, or Ian again. They had informed them that they were not to call workers away from their jobs to attend meetings. I sat, foetus-like, hugging my knees as I listened. They knew the man who had threatened to kill me, they said, knew where he lived but I wasn't to worry, they said, he wouldn't trouble me again. He was just a youngster. He was drunk. He wouldn't do it again. They told me his name and I wrote it down. As they all sat sipping tea from my best china tea service I felt as if I were floating. They talked to Ian and laughed and I rose higher. I was on another planet. This was not Zimbabwe. I had reported a gunman to the police, a man threatening to kill me. I had described him. They knew him but didn't arrest him, told me not to worry—he was just a drunken kid. How would we ever get past this madness? I asked the most senior of the policemen who he was. He gave me his name and rank and I studiously wrote down that he was the member in charge of Rural Affairs for Marondera. He gave me all his phone numbers, at work and at home, said I should call any time, day or night, if it happened again. Great comfort, I thought, should I call before or after I've been shot in the back? When the time came for them to leave, I asked them when they were going to start doing their jobs and move these war veterans and squatters off our farm. The member in charge shook my hand and said that whoever won, all squatters would be moved off all farms four days after the elections. He was so sure, so categorically sure, that I believed him.

When the police had gone, Ian spent an hour with a man from the CFU who arrived at our farm shortly after three. I'd done enough talking for the day. Shock had set in and I couldn't stop shivering. The meeting in the field had broken up and I went and saw all my workers who had come down to the gate. For five hours they had been sitting in the freezing wind in the field. I asked them to tell me everything, to start at the beginning. Shortly after I'd met them outside the dairy gate and gibbered out my tale, they had all run to their houses. The seven men were already there, ordering the wives and children out of the houses. Everyone was told to go to the meeting in the field, immediately. No time to grab a jersey, a chunk of bread, run to the toilet. None were excused. Jane was ordered out of the store, the women dragged out of their houses, my sweet little two-year-old Cecilia had to go, as did her seven-month pregnant mother who had twice been hospitalized recently for high blood pressure. All the children too young to be at school were marched behind their parents to be re-educated. For five hours they had been lectured. Vote for Zanu PF and you will all be given land, farms, houses. Vote for Zanu PF and there will be peace, jobs, prosperity. Vote for MDC and there will be war. We will get our guns. And later the slogans, accompanied by raised fists:

Down with the whites   Down with Britain
Down with colonialism   Down with Tsvangirai
Down with the MDC.

The workers smiled though when they related what had happened when the police Land Rover had arrived. The police had shouted a lot, they said, demanded to know who had been up at the house threatening Mrs Buckle. No one would own up and the police had told all the men to stand up so that they could do a search for the weapon. This had caused a furore and the leading war veterans and police had gone into a private but heated discussion. Eventually the police apparently agreed that the war veteran in charge of the meeting should conduct the search for the weapon, which he did while the police watched and nothing was found. The story was told, everyone was exhausted, hungry, intimidated and I sent them all home. It was time to fetch Richard from school, a job that Ian usually did but today I went with him. I was too afraid to stay at home in my own house.

Jane was waiting at the gate to see me when we returned from school.

'I'm so sorry, so very sorry about what's happened,' she said, sounding close to tears. We were in this together now. Perhaps it had been the same man who had terrorized us both.

'Jane, tomorrow I'm going to check my name on the voters' roll. Would you like to come with me?'

Jane beamed. She could see I was down but not yet out.

'We will go together!' she announced and we slapped hands.

I didn't sleep very well that night, or many of the following nights. Another nightmare had been added to the repertoire and all any of us could do was to count the days, just count the days.

"Its time to stand up and be counted" was the first email message on my computer screen the next morning. "Have You Registered to Vote Yet? Only 12 days to go". Jane and I went together to the nearest polling station. We drove right past the 100-odd people gathered on our farm and felt proud of ourselves. We stood in line together, checked our names one after the other and both went home smiling. Our names were there; we would have a say. I couldn't wait. There was no doubt in my mind where I would mark my X. Twelve more days and this would be over. Or would it? The president was still at it, the rhetoric continued, intensified. He was holding a rally in Marondera that weekend. We'd all been ordered to attend but everyone was tired of it now. On the morning of the presidential rally, three empty buses arrived outside our store. The store was locked. The usually bustling corner was deserted. There were no children selling bananas; no women hawking boiled eggs; no taxis waiting for passengers.

As before, the touts got out and shouted for people to come for the rally. The drivers hooted, and hooted. Forty minutes later not one person had come out and the buses left, empty, and headed down the road towards Wedza. Perhaps there they'd find support. A little later we heard the rumbling of approaching helicopters. There were three of them, one behind the other, blue and white—the presidential aerial motorcade. I was with one of the workers when the helicopters clattered overhead. Instinctively we both took cover behind a big tree.

'There goes the president,' I said and the man laughed. He told me that apparently the president hardly ever actually goes in the helicopter himself. He uses it as a decoy and travels in an ambulance instead. The president's rally was well covered by the press:

'We would like the war veterans on the farms to remain there peacefully with no violence. This is not for the purposes of the election. In fact, soon after the election, the farm occupations will be carried out more vigorously.'

"Down with Tsvangirai, down with his wife, down with his children, down with his totem, down with his dogs, down with even the cup that he drinks his tea from" were the slogans the crowds were asked to repeat at the rallies at Chikomba and Marondera.

On Saturday from Bromley to Marondera, 30 kilometres away, all the shops, butcheries and bottle stores on farming properties along the Harare to Mutare highway were closed for business until after the Zanu PF rally at Rudhaka Stadium in Marondera. (Daily News).

Ten days to go and the president took the rhetoric a stage further. It made front-page headlines in the *Zimbabwe Independent.* "Mugabe threatens to seize mines".

'After land, now we must look at the mining sector,' Mugabe told South Africa's Independent Newspapers group at his state residence. 'This is the phase that we're going through. After the coming election that area will be addressed fully,' Mugabe said. 'It requires the political struggle once again to be kindled and the people are better united.'

Again there was an outcry from business leaders across the country but still the people at the top were not listening. Zanu PF had a great deal to answer for now: the collapse of a quarter of the agricultural sector and its downstream industries; a civil service manned by battered, bruised and raped professionals; an extremely tense mining sector; a property market in serious trouble; an increasing exodus of private businessmen and a tourist industry that had virtually collapsed.

With only a handful of days left before the elections, journalists went to see how many tourists were still brave enough to be visiting Zimbabwe, previously called the jewel of Southern Africa. Nyanga, the cool, wooded, mountainous paradise where icy streams dropped majestically down narrow gorges, was struggling to survive. A National Parks official told the *Daily News,* 'Right now business has gone down by about 70 percent. Most lodges around here are empty.' In Victoria Falls, the situation was even worse: 'In the past, our traditional dancers [in the world-famous craft village] would attract about 250 tourists, but the number is now down to four, or none, on some days.' (Daily News). In Kariba, journalists didn't have to wait long for interviews with tour operators. One said,

'We have invented a game. It is called spot the tourist... This is about survival, pure and simple...' Another said, 'I have had to retrench several

staff, put the rest on short time and we have all—starting with me—taken a 20 percent pay cut...' The manager of one nearby hotel said he would be lucky to hit an occupancy rate of ten percent in June, while in town one large hotel opened just eleven months ago had an occupancy rate of four percent. (Zimbabwe Independent).

The worlds' cameras were back in Zimbabwe as were hundreds of election observers but still it didn't stop. War veterans countrywide, clearly worried that their 15 weeks of intimidation might not work, began confiscating people's identity documents. Without proof of identity people would not be allowed to vote and again the *Daily News* broke the story. "Hundreds of war veterans and Zanu PF supporters have launched a massive door-to-door campaign in Mwenezi in which they are confiscating national identity cards and passports from villagers". The campaign moved onto the farms and the CFU advised us not to hold our workers' documents for safekeeping as this might put us at risk. It had become a case of every man for himself. It was a survival game and many people, especially whites, decided the time had come to leave the country. A lot were emigrating but many more were just going away for a fortnight, terrified that we were on the verge of a civil war. I got up on my soapbox again and told everyone we met, in shops, garages, banks and supermarkets that they must vote. I didn't say for whom they should vote, just that they should vote. I plastered the walls of my store, inside and out, with voting posters, not political posters, just voting posters. In my weekly letter, which I now knew reached over 2,000 people, I begged everyone I knew, and everyone I didn't, to vote. Again my hero was back in print, echoing my sentiments:

It has been a long and taxing wait... We have been assaulted mentally and physically. Our mothers, wives and sisters have been raped. Many dear to us have been maimed for life while some have lost their lives for their political beliefs. We might be exhausted and battered but our spirits are far from broken... While some of us have been doing everything to ensure that we are around to vote this weekend, some cowards within the white community have been making it for the borders... They are quitters and hoppers pure and simple. And I hope they never come back to Zimbabwe again... But one thing is clear: they are running away from their responsibility as citizens. They are abdicating their moral duty to a country that has given them so much. If all goes well they will be back to enjoy the fruits of our sacrifices.

Trevor Ncube, editor of the *Zimbabwe Independent* said it all, and so much more, words that I was too ashamed to say.

Time had run out. D-Day had arrived and on the eve of the elections, one day before my son's eighth birthday, I read again the one email that had moved me more than any other during this fortnight from hell. At his final campaign rally at Rufaro Stadium in Mbare, Harare, Morgan Tsvangirai had stood in front of 25 people.

I stand before you as a messenger of the people. I stand as a humble conveyor of your dreams, your hopes, your aspirations... I stand before you as a messenger of peace. I have heard your anger, your pain. I have heard what old men in dark huts say—how sad they are that the greatness of Zimbabwe is no more... The red sand of Africa is the colour of the blood in our veins. This is our home—we have no other. There is a new wind whispering through the people of Africa.

FAST TRACK
TO WHERE?

After lunch on Friday, 23rd June 2000, a great swelling of noise could be heard on the afternoon breeze. I stood outside the gate at the bottom of our driveway with the workers and we moved out of sight of the road to watch a river of singing men jog past. It was the Zanu PF youths going on their last raid and we estimated there were between 70 and 100 of them. Both the sound and sight of them was frightening, not only to me but also to the men standing next to me. We all knew what they were capable of. I was unable to warn my neighbours because the previous day our telephone had stopped functioning. I had been in touch with the technical engineer heading the telephone company in Marondera, pleading with him to repair it before the weekend's elections. He said it was out of his hands, told me that my line had been taken for a nearby polling station. This was yet another violation of my rights but what could I do? Not only was I a farmer, but also a white—I didn't have any rights any more.

The reason we were all standing at the gate was that we were trying to make a plan for getting to the polling stations the next morning. We agreed that it should be done very early in the morning, when hopefully all our local activists would still be asleep or nursing hangovers. The only problem we had was that the constituency boundaries had only just been printed in the *Herald* and we discovered that some of us were in

Marondera West and others in Seke, depending on where we'd registered to vote. I, and five of the workers, had registered at Waddilove School, four kilometres away and we were classed as Marondera West. The others had registered at the clinic, half a kilometre in the opposite direction and they were in the Seke constituency. So with this invisible line drawn across our farm, a line that hadn't been there in February when we'd voted in the referendum, I wanted to make sure that everyone knew where they could vote. We also discovered that polling stations, which had always been permanent before, had now suddenly been called "mobile" and would operate for six hours only in one location. I asked if anyone wanted a lift to the school and all said they did. Four kilometres was quite a walk, especially at dawn in the middle of winter. Those who were registered in the Seke constituency said they'd walk up to the clinic and I promised that if I arrived back in time, I'd run them up there. All the plans were set. I arranged to meet everyone outside the store at 6.15 on Saturday morning. Polling stations were due to open at 7am.

The talk in the store later that afternoon was about the newest piece of voter information being put out by the war veterans and their supporters. They had been standing around in the store for most of the day, asking people how old they were. Anyone who was under 30 was told they would not be allowed to vote so shouldn't even bother to try. Thirty-year-old people, the war veterans said, had been born free (had not lived through the war for Independence) and therefore did not have a right to say who should govern the country. I squashed this story immediately and my explanation caused much hilarity because they had their maths wrong. To be 'born free', would make you 20 years old, not 30. For weeks the war veterans and activists had been pedalling this nonsense that I was sure no one could possibly believe. They had said there were magic eye security cameras that could see you in the voting booth, that there was a number written on the back of the voting paper, which they could use to see whom you voted for, that the election observers were actually politicians in disguise and they would see your ballot paper. When the born free story had been squashed, we turned to much more serious news. The mob of singing youths who had run past the gate earlier, had gone to two farms a few kilometres down the road from us. On one farm they had pulled everyone out of their houses, searched the place for opposition t-shirts and membership cards and badly beaten two men. On the next farm they had told everyone that they were just waiting for the results to be announced. If they were in favour of MDC, the war would start immediately. With these stories fresh in my mind I went home from the store and was met at the gate by all the workers. They had decided they did not want to go to the polling station with me—they would find their own way. They had been warned by the war veterans that they should not be seen going with the whites as the whites would force them to vote for the MDC. I just laughed sadly and shook my head.

At 6.15 on Saturday, 24ᵗʰ June 2000, Ian and I set out for Waddilove. We pulled in at the store on the off chance that the workers had changed their minds but there wasn't a soul around. A little way down the road we met Emmanuel trudging in the freezing cold towards the school. He waved us on. Further along we saw Arthur, hands in his pockets. He turned away as if he didn't know us. Next we came across George and Anna. I rolled the window down a fraction.

'I don't know you,' I said, 'but would you like a lift down to Waddilove?'

George roared with laughter and they climbed into the back of the truck. Ian looked into the rearview mirror.

'Shall I go back?' he asked.

I turned and grinned. Running and shouting for us to wait was Arthur, and even further back, Emmanuel. When at last everyone was in the truck, we headed down the road, all determined to have a say in our future, all good patriotic Zimbabweans, black and white, men and women, employers and employees.

Richard's eighth birthday was celebrated in a much quieter fashion than normal on the second and final day of parliamentary elections. He had presents and balloons, chocolate cake and ice cream. The only difference was the number of children we invited to share this special day with him. Instead of the usual two dozen, screaming, over-excited kids wreaking havoc, this year we had three: Brian, Linnet and Simba. No one had thought it would be wise to come to a squatted farm. I couldn't guarantee their safety, couldn't promise that a mob of drunken war vets wouldn't try to gate crash the party. He had fun though. They ate too much cake, played and shouted and created enough mess to keep me busy for a few hours. Simba made us all laugh when it came time to cut the cake. He was the son of the district administrator and a bright, vivacious little boy who lived over the road from us. (DAs were very much in the forefront of organizing war vets, providing logistical support, deciding which farms should be squatted and, later, allocating plots of land on confiscated farms). It had seemed more than a little peculiar that his mother continued to send him over to us to play but I never said anything, never made Simba feel unwelcome or unwanted—he was after all, just another innocent witness to the destruction engulfing our lives. I don't know what, if anything, Simba's mum had told him, but when it was time to blow out the candles and cut the cake, he was as excited as the others. The cake, my special double-barrelled five-minute microwave marvel, was smothered in chocolate glacé icing and decorated with Smarties stuck into the topping. Four little faces watched very seriously as I cut huge chunks of the sticky brown cake, counting exactly how many Smarties each person received. Brian, Linnet and Richard started eating and Simba just sat staring at his slice.

'What's wrong Simba?' I asked. 'Eat your cake!'

'I don't eat shoclut cake,' he announced with an unusually small voice and a very pained look on his face.

'Oh dear! What would you like then?'

'Shoclut biscuits!' he declared. 'I eat schoclut biscuits. They are all right!'

Richard, Linnet and Brian rolled around in hysterics at Simba's pronouncement and I bit my lip as I went to fetch the biscuit tin.

When I took Richard to school on Monday morning, the roads were deserted and the number of children waiting to go into their classrooms seemed less than half of normal. I could only assume that everyone was doing what I would be doing shortly, sitting glued to television and radio sets waiting for the first results to come in. I couldn't remember the feeling in Zimbabwe having been this tense since the historic results of the 1980 elections when an era had ended. Perhaps now we were again going to start a new chapter in the history books. The day dragged and with Mum and Wiz compiling tables and graphs, pencils at the ready, I caught up on some of the reading. Finally, 17 weeks into the farm invasions, people were beginning to feel concerned about what was going to happen to all the farm workers who would be displaced by land redistribution. For weeks farmers had been asking what would be the fate of their workers if government confiscated their land. As always there were no answers but in a country with an estimated one million people working on commercial farms, the unions started to take note. Gapwuz (General Agricultural and Plantation Workers' Union) warned that half a million farm workers would lose their jobs, and their homes if the government went ahead with the confiscation of the 804 farms listed for take-over. Gapwuz's Secretary General, Philip Munyanyi said:

Our major concern is not the redistribution... We support fair and orderly land redistribution but we are worried that the programme excludes farm workers... We should not organize and disorganize at the same time. If we do that, we will only be repeating what was done in 1890 when settlers displaced villagers in order to establish their own settlements. Tomorrow these farm workers will tell the same story of displacement. They have a right to the land as much as anyone else. (Daily News).

There were two and a half million votes to count and by lunchtime no results had been announced at all. The interim report from the EU Election Observation Mission had just been released though and it was very worrying what Pierre Schori had found.

It is clear from the daily reports and weekly assessments made by EU observers in every part of the country that there were serious flaws and failures in the electoral process... The Office of the Registrar-General did not operate in an open and transparent manner... The Electoral Supervisory Commission was systematically rendered ineffective by both legal and administrative means... The EU Election Observation Mission reached the conclusion that this was not owing to administrative incompetence but to a deliberate attempt to reduce the effectiveness of independent monitoring of the election... High levels of violence, intimidation and coercion marred the election campaign. An assessment of violence and intimidation since February 2000 made by the EU Election Observation Mission, together with reports from EU observers operating throughout the country since early June, indicate that Zanu PF was responsible for the bulk of political violence. Zanu PF leaders seemed to sanction the use of violence and intimidation against political opponents and contributed significantly to the climate of fear... Overall, the conduct of the government has failed to uphold the rule of law and compromised law enforcement agencies. MDC supporters were also engaged in violence and intimidation, but the degree of their responsibility for such activities was far less. Moreover, MDC leaders were clearer in their condemnation of violence... In many rural areas, however, the levels of intimidation by Zanu PF were so intense as to make it virtually impossible for the opposition to campaign... Both the public broadcaster, the ZBC, and government-controlled newspapers were used as publicity vehicles for Zanu PF. The ZBC failed to ensure informed political debate. Propaganda crowded out the real issues of the campaign. Opposition parties have had to rely on commercial media only:... There were serious problems concerning the voters' roll and the number of intending voters who were unable to cast their ballots... The courts should deal with all cases of human rights abuses associated with the electoral process. This will be essential in helping to re-establish respect for the rule of law in Zimbabwe. (CFU).

And all this was being said before a single result had been announced. It was nothing that every Zimbabwean did not already know and the only comfort was that it gave credence to everything we had been saying for so many months. As every hour passed, there was only one word that screamed in my head: "rigging".

And still we waited. What better way to pass the time than watch again the BBC World interview of our president. Richard Dimbleby was asking the questions and the programme had been recorded just prior to the election. Dimbleby asked Mugabe if he had used land to reward government cronies.

The president laughed and shook his head, 'It is the whole population that is my crony.'

He asked if the referendum results and the sudden invasion of white farms by war veterans were connected.

'Yes ... on their own without instigation from us,' Mugabe said.

Dimbleby asked about the breakdown of law and order in Zimbabwe and about the government's refusal to obey High Court Orders.

'The law of the land must also work for moral justice,' Mugabe said. 'Law and order enshrines a vast area. This is just the little law of trespass. Elsewhere those who commit murder are being arrested... If they [the white farmers] suffer this little inconvenience of their land being occupied as against the inconvenience our people have suffered for decades...' Just the little law of trespass. I could not believe that my president would say anything as offensive and insensitive as that and thought once again that if I had any diesel to spare I would happily go and build a little shack on the lawn of State House and see how he'd like it. How insulting for one Zimbabwean to say that to another Zimbabwean. Richard Dimbleby then asked President Mugabe whether Zanu PF would work with the MDC if they won a majority of the seats in the parliamentary election. President Mugabe leaned forward slightly in his chair, as did I, and said: 'If the impossibility happened, I would regard it an impossibility. And impossibilities and improbabilities should not be entertained should they? I can never concede that they have the capacity to win. In dreamland perhaps...'

At 3.30pm, ZBC Television crossed live to a press conference with the registrar general, Tobaiwa Mudede and the commissioner of police, Augustine Chihuri. We all sat forward in our seats—here we go, we thought. Mudede said that there were no results to hand yet, not even one. In fact, he said, counting had only begun in two of the 120 constituencies. All other centres were still attempting to verify the number of ballot boxes. That little word now screamed at full volume in my head: "rigging". Even more peculiar was the statement then made by Chihuri, reported in the newspapers the following day.

I am appealing to those who will win that they must win gracefully and not target the losers for whatever reason. Those who lose, must accept the results with honour, so that they don't spark problems... (Daily News).

It was hard then not to think that they already knew something. Mum and Wiz and Ian and I sat up almost all night. Elated, depressed, elated again. By 10am the following morning the final counting was done. The Movement for Democratic Change had won 57 seats; Zanu Ndonga one; Zanu PF 61. Soon the analysis would begin, the stories would be told and I looked again at how Marondera had fared. Marondera West, where we were, had seen 11,221 votes for Zanu PF and 4,570 for the MDC. The results from Marondera East, which embraced the town itself, produced what was the most suspicious result of the entire election. Zanu PF won 10,692 votes, MDC polled 10,629. Perhaps I was paranoid but these figures, with the strangely identical digits were almost too coincidentally similar to be possible. Even Mudede had queried them as he read them out. If they were right though, I wondered how the whites and others who had run away for the weekend would feel when they returned home. There was only a difference of 63 votes!

The moment our telephone line was returned to us my weekly email letter was sent out to family, friends and strangers. I called it "Lobbying for Food".

The most frightening thing is what happens now. Even with the MDC having 57 seats in a 150-seat parliament, Mugabe and his old men continue to behave as if they are solely in charge. Every day since the results were announced, either he or one of his cronies has gabbled on about the farms. They still continue to say they will take not only the 804 designated farms, but as many as they need or want. They continue to refuse to call off the war vets; they continue to keep the police force away and we remain as helpless, powerless, and frankly, hopeless as we have been for the past four months (which now begins to feel like forever). If someone doesn't put a stop to this, and very soon, Zimbabwe is surely doomed. Crops will not be planted, vegetables will not be grown, cows will not be put to the bull.

I hope this doesn't all sound too melodramatic—it is the truth. How can any of us even consider continuing as farmers, fully cognizant that he may come and take everything, be it today, tomorrow, next week, next month? It is a truly desperate situation and can only lead to unprecedented food shortages in the short term and mass starvation in the long. More important than anything, Mr Mugabe must now leave us alone so that we can return to the business of producing food.

Across all the divides now encompassing Zimbabwe, everyone wanted to get on with their lives. A new chapter in our history had begun, a parliament, used to only one opposing voice, now had 58 to contend with. In a show of what many suggested was retribution and sour grapes, the army and police put on a spectacular show of strength. Into the bars and nightclubs they went with their batons, onto the streets of the high-density suburbs with their tear-gas and around the farms with their plot-marking pegs. People were beaten for no reason, arrested with no charges and subjected to a show of strength not publicly seen for a long time. On the farms, army and CIO (Central Intelligence Organization) officers openly claimed plots or even whole farms. Where was my policeman friend now? I wondered—the member in charge of Rural Affairs who had been so sure that four days after the elections all invaders would be moved off the farms. Squatters began moving back onto our farm, cutting thatching grass and roofing their huts. This went on for a few days and caused a great deal of amusement when one of the squatters arrived with a donkey. He openly cut trees in our gum plantation and then used the donkey to pull them to the hut he was building in the field above our dairy. Squatter and donkey slept together in the partially built hut at night and during the day my cattle grazed innocently all around his new complex. The squatter had marked out his new homestead with care—there were going to be three houses in a semicircle, a big shady tree behind and the whole plot a short walk away from a well. He worked at it tirelessly, felling the poles, dragging them to the complex and then cutting heaps of thatching grass, which he tied carefully onto the roof timbers. On a particularly foul, cold and wet day, our cattle, obviously not inclined to go far for food, ate a large section of the man's newly thatched roof. We all thought this was very funny and it gave us something to laugh about—a rare event on the farm these days.

The laughter died the next day though when a man came running down from the main Marondera road. All our cattle were on the tarred road, he said, heavily pregnant cows, tiny calves and weaners were dodging buses and speeding cars. When all the cattle had been rounded up, counted and bought home, we discovered that all five strands of our boundary fence had been cut, the poles and droppers removed and the fence deliberately opened. Again I phoned the police but nothing had changed, they wouldn't come out and speak to the man with the donkey and couldn't find a report book in which to record my complaint. The police in Marondera said they were busy keeping the peace and therefore could not attend to minor problems on the farms. The next day Ian and I found out what they were doing. On a trip to Murehwa we were stopped at a police roadblock. Ian was not asked to show his driving licence, nor his insurance disc. Instead the policeman asked to see his gun.

'I haven't got a gun,' Ian replied.

The policeman did not reply but looked at us closely. He told me to open the glove compartment and then, to our disbelief, he went to the front of Ian's truck and started running his hands under the fenders, looking for weapons. I wished they would show as much zealousness on the farms as they did at their endless roadblocks.

Ten days after the elections, Zimbabwe slipped back into a stupor of normality. People who had fled, returned, attendance at schools increased and a sort of tired resignation settled over the country. But on the farms the situation was deteriorating: cattle were being slaughtered, farmers were being given "eviction notices" by squatters and the lawlessness was worsening. The president of the CFU, Tim Henwood, issued a press statement, appealing again for a return to law and order.

The elections are now over and yet the extortion, destruction of property, theft and the threats continue largely unabated on farms. ... The situation is simply no longer tenable and farmers are frustrated and angry at their inability to farm their properties efficiently. Work stoppages continue, farmers are instructed to discontinue farm operations and demands are now being made that they immediately vacate their homes and farms as the war veterans are taking over their properties. (CFU).

Every day the situation report from the CFU told of the horrors and some days it ran to three, four, or even five pages. In the Save Valley, a world-renowned wildlife conservancy, war veterans were dealing the final blow to tourism and depriving Zimbabwe of millions of dollars of foreign currency. *The Farmer* told the story:

> *Using snares, nets or hunting dogs, "war veterans", most of them identified though no arrests were made, killed an estimated 81 different types of wildlife valued at $457,900. This does not include a potential daily rate paid by foreign clients and potential taxidermy fees, also paid in foreign currency. Among the animals killed were 60 impala, 12 warthog, six kudu, one bushbuck, one bush pig and unknown quantities of fish.*

One elephant was found dead, its tusk removed, another snared; then a rhino was also found trapped. Chairman of the Wildlife Producers' Association, John White, spoke at the annual general meeting.

> *'The situation is serious. On one property alone over 270 carcasses were found including impala, cheetah, elephant, zebra, leopard and, unfortunately, wild dog. It is estimated that over 3,000 animals have been lost with an estimated value of $11 million. In just one sweep of the area over 1,500 snares were found—most made from stolen telephone and fence wire,' said Mr White. (The Farmer).*

On 9th July, just over two weeks after the elections, I sent out my weekly letter. We had all been sure that the situation would have changed by then and depression was deepening.

I called my letter "The Rape of the Land".

> *Two weeks after the elections and the invasions continue. There are still demands for food, fuel, transport and, this week, forced evacuations. The incidents are occurring on both the 804 designated properties and any others, which the war veterans take a liking to. I don't know why any of us thought it would stop just like that because if it had then surely the whole world would have said, 'Ah so it was just electioneering.' As we were in the month before the elections, we are again a country in limbo; no cabinet has yet been appointed; parliament has still to be called. There is still no one giving orders, no one making policies and we remain a country without law and order. No one is answerable to anyone—yet. I can only speculate that the president is having some very sleepless nights*

wondering how on earth he is going to undo all the damage he has done without losing face. He has some serious back pedalling to do, and soon, if he's going to persuade any one of us farmers to plant even a single potato, let alone a saleable crop.

Morale amongst the farming community is now at its lowest ebb. Every day the conversation goes round and round, the same phrases dominate: "they shouldn't be allowed"; "when the police come"; "I don't know". None of us know what to do or whom to turn to for direction, guidance or even common sense. We don't know when or if a halt will ever be called to the invasion of our land. We don't know if we should wait another month or even another day and every day we hear of yet another farmer closing down and walking out. Perhaps Ian and I are being very stupid, naïve or just downright dumb as we both continue to believe that right will prevail. That said though, we aren't yet making any decisions. We don't know if we should buy a new bull to put to our remaining cows; if we should put the rams back in with the ewes; if we should restart our flock of layers. All the things we would normally be doing in winter are not being done. We are still unable to rotate the paddocks and ease the pressure on the land as every fence on the farm is down. We have not ploughed any fire breaks; have not done any of the usual repairs to the store; have not been able to clear any of the weed from the dams; have not bought in our usual tonnage of winter feed; have not sold any of our weaners. This dismally depressing story is being played out on every farm in the country. It is a very frustrating time and as every day passes we despair for the short- and long-term food security of the country. Basically, until we are given long-term guarantees that this is in fact our land, we cannot make any plans at all.

I went on, with the taste of bile fresh in my mouth, to describe what had happened on our own farm in the last week.

We've had a very strange week on the farm as, for the first time in four months, we went down onto the fields below the house where the temporarily absent war veterans have lived for the past 16 weeks. As our workers started on the mammoth task of re-erecting the first of many fences, Ian and I looked at what these bastards have done to our land. Everywhere there is litter: plastic bags, petroleum jelly bottles, cigarette boxes, shards of asbestos, beer cans and paper. I became angrier and angrier as I saw the unspeakable mess they have left in the field. When I reached the big tree under which their tent had been pitched, I had to swallow very hard to stop the vomit. An 18-inch square has been carved deeply into the bark, chipped out, and J A R has left his initials engraved into the wood. I ripped the political poster off another tree on our boundary fence and Ian closed the gate the squatters had liberated. We inspected two of their huts and were both shocked at how many trees had been felled to construct these crude structures. One house is about 12 foot by 12 foot and the walls are made entirely of poles, each one almost touching the next. Inside the hut we found a huge pile of poles, another of firewood and another of sheets of roofing tin... We just looked but did nothing although the temptation to drop a match was enormous.

Then we went down to our little dam and that was even more shocking. Once densely enclosed with trees, the surrounds are now sparse and a cold wind blew through the haven where our cattle used to drink. The dam wall has broken and water gushes out, with no sign that our liberators had even attempted to repair the breech. Great farmers they would be! The entire surface area of the dam is covered with thick, choking, red Azolla weed. Bloated and floating and in the water is a dead animal and at that sight I couldn't take any more and left Ian and the workers trying to remove it. Later I learn that it is a huge male Reedbuck that has a bullet hole through its shoulder. I am outraged at how these people, supposedly land-hungry peasants desperate to be farmers, have raped our land these past four months. Breaking down fences, burning poles and droppers, defacing trees, littering the fields, felling hundreds of trees, leaving exposed pit toilets—my God, my God.

All week we've kept working on one little fence, knowing we're being watched, wondering how long it will be before someone tries to stop us. As we've worked, I've bitterly resented every cent we've had to spend on new staples, poles and wire. The war veterans have continued to walk in and out at will to cut trees and collect firewood. They've pushed their cattle back in to graze and every day we've closed the gate and they've reopened it. It is a ridiculously insane situation, which surely cannot go on for much longer.

The response to my letter that week was enormous, but very depressing. "The writing's on the wall", some wrote. "I don't know how you cope!" "Isn't it time to leave now?" "Won't you consider starting a new life?" A cousin in America whom I hadn't seen for over two decades wrote:

I'm sorry to hear of your continuing plight. I can only hope that the horizon is still out there somewhere for you all. From the 1,000-foot level, my glimpse of your world looks as if it has completely fallen apart. The only news we receive now is that footballers are being shot at with tear-gas and that the Aids epidemic is rampant. The West seems to have lost its curiosity in its usual fickle way. I can only tell you that all of the friends we share your letters with are deeply moved by your words and courage.

Was this courage? I thought, attempting to hold on to what was ours, legally, constitutionally. I still had hope though and was convinced that an end was in sight. The footballers that my cousin had referred to had caused an outpouring of anger from all over the country. Forty thousand people had been in the sports stadium for an international football match. When the visiting team scored another goal and the crowd threw beer cans onto the pitch, Zimbabwe's usually inactive police shot tear-gas at them. Some exits were locked, others were blocked by the stampeding crowd of people trying to get out. Thirteen people were trampled to death. Two days later the Minister of Home Affairs, Dumiso Dabengwa, resigned saying he was old and tired and that the tragedy at the football match had nothing to do with his departure. It was not enough, though. Zimbabweans were outraged and called for the resignation of Police Commissioner Augustine Chihuri. But he did not resign. Instead President Mugabe turned this human tragedy into a political platform. He said that the only reason police had fired tear-gas into the crowd was that the supporters were trying to bait the police. They were, he said, making the open-handed symbol of the MDC. It was another national disgrace and I wept as I wrote to the father of Dean Fidesi, one of the children who had been trampled to death.

Dear Mr Fidesi
I am the mother of an eight-year-old boy and cannot begin to think of the anguish you must be going through.
*   Our deepest sympathy to you and your wife and family on the tragic loss of Dean. Our hearts ache for you. I hope you find the strength and courage to pick up the pieces and go on.*
*   We are farmers in Marondera and have been going through hell these past five months but nothing compared to your loss. I am so sorry.*

While the funerals were still continuing and before we even had time to dry our tears, the vice president made a statement that switched the spotlight back onto the farms, a spotlight that had become decidedly uncomfortable for our leaders. It was absurd, I know, but it seemed that whenever anything went wrong in the country, the way to placate dissenting voices was to shout: 'land—come and get it. Let's forget this latest tragedy and grab some more land.' Land was the cure for all ills, the tonic that assured vitality and prosperity, the one thing that would supposedly make everything all right again. Vice President Joseph Msika stood in front of the world's cameras and announced the commencement of "Fast Track" land redistribution. Coincidentally, suspiciously, the launch of this new plan took place three days before the opening of Zimbabwe's newly democratic parliament. The *Daily News* was among the many papers that covered the story:

> *Vice President Joseph Msika on Saturday launched the accelerated land reform and resettlement programme under which 200 white-owned commercial farms will be compulsorily acquired. There are about 20 farms identified in each province countrywide. Resettlement of the war veterans and landless people in the rural areas has already begun. Provision of infrastructure and other support systems on the 200 farms would not be provided immediately... Msika said, 'War veterans are not going to leave the occupied farms but government will use what it calls a shifting process to resettle war veterans. They shift from the occupied farms to where they have been allocated to go.' ... Msika said the government would carry out this programme alone as no donors have so far come up to contribute to the land reform programme. Then I saw Msika on television and listened carefully, trying to make sense of it: 'The whole process has been designed to ensure fair and equitable distribution of land to correct the racial imbalance in land apportionment... Those who cry foul of this programme do not have the interests of the country at heart.'* (BBC World Television).

Msika's shifting and shuffling plan was not acceptable, however, to Chenjerai Hunzvi. Two hours after Msika's statement, Hunzvi was on ZBC Television. He said that his supporters would not get off any properties, be they designated or not. Wearing a bright pink shirt and standing in front of a crowd of his supporters he shouted angrily, 'Land is going to be taken by the government. If the government is going to delay taking the land, we will take it.' (ZBC Television). He went on to give the government a two-week deadline to hand out the farms. The daily report from the CFU arrived to tell us that this really was about to happen—it had not all been a figment of my imagination.

> *...the situation is extremely volatile and President Tim Henwood asks all farmers to observe extreme caution over the next few days... At this time*

we do not have sight of the list of farms to be acquired… It seems unlikely that this is going to be a smooth and well-orchestrated event because at this time it is still covered in confusion. It seems, therefore, that war vets may take the situation into their own hands and this could be dangerous. (CFU).

I tried to explain this madness in my weekly letter and concluded by relating the happenings on our farm in the past few days:

On our own farm we've had another quiet week. Our war vets have been busy elsewhere. On the farm next door to us, owned and operated by a black Zimbabwean, the night guard was beaten up by two men with rocks and pangas, had his legs slashed, his wrists tied and was dumped in the maize field. The storekeeper was dragged out of her house, had her face and legs slashed, and was left unconscious. The attackers then broke into the store and stole cigarettes and a radio. They were tracked to the "war vets' headquarters" across the road from us, but no arrests have been made yet. We've spent the week repairing fences and again every day we've closed the gate on the main road, and the people have opened it and pushed their cattle in to graze. This went on every day until Thursday when I blew a fuse when about 20 communal cattle got into the tiny field where my dairy cows were grazing. We pushed the intruders out and have now wired the gate closed with rusty barbed wire. So far nothing's happened. The days ahead will tell. I'm sure it would be tempting fate to say that the worst of our problems are over. Someone's been busy on one of the huts that have been built below our house; the walls have been plastered with mud inside and out and a solid wooden door has been hung and locked. Whoever the builder is, he obviously thinks he's here to stay.

The Fast-Track plan was going ahead though and the government then announced that it had drawn up a budget of $1.3 billion for its implementation. This sum did not include, though, any money for the existing, rightful and legal owners of the land.

The $1.3 billion covers project costs for planning, implementation and the recurrent costs excluding land purchase. Land experts say the programme … was ill-conceived as it did not take into account logistical and technical shortcomings in the government departments tasked to implement the system. Ministry of Agriculture and Resettlement sources warned that the programme was bound to fail because of *manpower shortages at the ministry... According to the document the government's eventual goal is to resettle 48,000 families in 2001, 42,000 in 2002 and 30,000 in 2003... (Financial Gazette).*

When parliament finally opened on Thursday, 20th July, the country had very high hopes. Much damage had been done in the previous months and everyone wondered where these new men and women would begin. The usual colonial pomp and ceremony was there on that official opening, but so too was a lot of open support for our new democracy.

Africa Unity Square in Harare yesterday resounded to a deafening chorus of "Chinja!" from a sea of people as President Mugabe officially opened the Fifth Parliament. Thousands of people, some wearing t-shirts of the opposition Movement for Democratic Change (MDC) and flashing small plastic red cards, greeted the arrival of Mugabe and his wife, Grace, with the frenzied waving of open hands, shouting "Chinja" [change] as Mugabe proceeded to inspect a guard of honour outside parliament. Armed riot police in full combat gear cordoned off Nelson Mandela Avenue, but failed to dampen the exuberance of the crowd massed around parliament building from morning to midday. His face looking glum and downcast, Mugabe appeared shaken by the hostile reception as he delivered his speech in a sombre voice to a hushed parliament. The speech lasted 30 minutes. All 57 MDC MPs, led by Gibson Sibanda, wore black armbands in memory of the 33 people killed in politically motivated violence in the run-up to last month's parliamentary election... Apparently not wishing to be upstaged by the MDC, a handful of Zanu PF MPs, led by war veteran leader and MP for Chikomba, Chenjerai Hunzvi, started a war dance on Nelson Mandela Avenue, waving clenched fists. Police details enforcing the cordon allowed Hunzvi to approach the crowd in the park, triggering emotion-charged outbursts of "Chinja!" from the excited crowd who chanted "Zanu yawora!" [Zanu is now rotten!]. Stunned by the hostile reaction of the crowd, Hunzvi made an abrupt U-turn and beat a hasty retreat into parliament building. For the next 15 minutes, tension was high in Africa Unity Square as the crowd, joined by hundreds of workers from nearby offices and banks, some perched on balconies, danced and shouted... (Daily News Online).

Perhaps Zimbabwe's hopes would be justified.

My hopes, though, that the madness had ended on our farm, were dashed when a letter was handed to me through our gates:

Would you please let this woman pass with her trailer? She has a piece of land at your place. Thank you for your cooperation. Yours trully (sic) Comrade E. Mswaka. PS Her piece of land is along Watershed Road to Marondera.

Edward was back, albeit in a far less hostile way, but back nonetheless. Standing looking at me while I read the letter, were two elderly women, the owners of part of my farm. My letter that week was called "Tempting Fate".

Last Sunday, barely an hour after finishing my weekly letter, it was clear that I had tempted fate too far as our squatters came back. Twenty of them arrived and had a meeting outside our newly repaired fence. Later they dispersed and we held our breath. On Monday two women arrived with a letter from Edward. The letter asked that we open the fence and let these two women in with their scotch cart so that they could collect their poles (our poles) and start building their house as they'd bought a plot on our farm. I launched into a very lengthy monologue. I told them that our farm was not designated, that the government did not want our farm, that it was private property, that by cutting all my poles they were committing a crime. I told them that Edward had conned them. They had paid $20 for their plot. At the end of it all, amazingly enough, the women apologized profusely, thanked me for explaining it all so nicely and left! I felt really sorry for them.

Tuesday saw Edward and 70 others cut through our newly repaired boundary fence and invade the field again. They had a meeting, which went on for some hours and then left. We haven't seen them since but I'm not saying more for fear of tempting fate again!

While Ian and I were tolerating these comparatively minor abuses, other farmers were being evicted from their homes by impatient war veterans. The CFU report informed us that in a period of seven days, 70 unofficial eviction notices and death threats had been received by farmers. A statement was made by Tim Henwood:

Trouble in the Glendale Farmers' Association area, which has been simmering for some time, was bought to a head when the Farmers' Association chairman and his family were forced to leave their farm by a group of hostile invaders. The invaders who occupied the homestead yesterday evening, remain camped on the front lawn. Last night the CFU informed the police that the situation was untenable. At 12.40pm today the police arrived at the farm. They left at 14.30pm without taking any notable action. Because of this, the Farmers' Association has taken the decision to close down, believing that it is no longer possible to guarantee the safety of farmers or their workers. All farms in the area have complied with this decision. (CFU).

Forty farms, apparently employing 10,000 people among them *(Daily Telegraph)*, closed down in Glendale. Owners remained in their homes, workers did not report for duty in a united attempt to demand a return to the rule of law. Three hundred and fifty messages of support were received by one email activist. Letters came from England and America, Australia and New Zealand, from seven countries in Europe, even from Iceland. A lot of messages came from closer to home, from South Africa and Namibia, Mozambique, Kenya and Uganda. The bulk though, came from Zimbabweans with an equal proportion from blacks and whites. They were moving, very moving. It was wonderful to know that so many people supported farmers.

We salute you! Without the incredible courage displayed by people like you who are at the cutting edge, we will not be able to continue in the towns.

I support you 100 percent and I don't mind your skin colour!

Hang in there—somebody has to feed us next year. This anarchy will end. History proves that.

Thank goodness some farmers still have balls.

Eventually. A district has decided enough. Congratulations. Our area will follow your example, God willing.

Be strong. Africa is in our blood and in our thoughts every hour of every day.

Appeasement can only lead to further demands and threats.

It is about time that you resisted together.

Don't the war veterans realize they are ruining their own country?

If all commercial farmers followed this route it would give them massive bargaining power that the government would have to recognize.

It is our future as a nation that is at stake here.

The support was there; it gave hope and courage. But it made the new minister of Agriculture, Dr Joseph Made, angry. He told the *Herald*: 'We cannot have a few people threatening the majority because if they go ahead it will mean that everyone will go hungry.' I know that Dr Made had only just been appointed the minister of Agriculture, but I wondered if he'd been asleep for the last five months. War veterans, numbering fewer than 20,000, according to all reasonable estimates, had been holding the entire country of 13 million people to ransom for five months. It was regarded as fair for them to do it but not us? 'Anyone who feels threatened should go the police' *(Herald)*, he went on to say and I wanted to phone him then and there with his morning wake-up call. Murderers were still walking free on the streets, as were rapists, arsonists, petty thieves. Did Dr Made not know that there was a critical, country-wide shortage of police report books? Glendale farms closed down. Willem Botha, a farmer in his sixties, was murdered in front of his television at his home in Karoi when thieves broke in. Karoi farmers also went out on strike and the country teetered on the edge. Across Zimbabwe the word on everyone's lips was "strike". The people needed to stand together. Now was our chance, blacks and whites, bosses and workers, farmers and townies, professionals and street kids. Was it possible? Did our beaten, broken country have the courage and strength to do this?

ELEVEN ....
THE 3,000 "WISH LIST"

S trike!" "Stay-away!" Everywhere the words were being spoken. In some places they were being shouted, in others, whispered. The emails were flying backwards and forwards, as section by section, community by community the country tried to decide what to do and where it stood. An old family friend in New Zealand sent an email of political ideologies to try to cheer us up and it caused more hilarity than I'd had for a very long time.

Altruism: *You have two cows. You keep one and give the other to your neighbour.*

Communism: *You have two cows. The government takes both and shares the milk with you and your neighbour.*

Fascism: *You have two cows. You give the milk to the government and they sell it back to you.*

Capitalism: *You have two cows. You milk both and pour the lot down the drain to keep the price up.*

Sadism: *You have two cows. You shoot them both and drown yourself in the milk.*

Anarchism: *You have two cows. The cows shoot you and milk each other.*

Bureaucracy: *You have two cows. You fill in 17 forms in triplicate and don't have time to milk them.*

> *Idealism:*   You have two cows. You marry and your wife milks
> them.
> *Realism:*   You have two cows. You marry and you still milk them.
> *Common sense:* You have two cows. You sell one and buy a bull.
> *(Origin unknown).*

One wondered where Zimbabwe fitted in with her principles of governance.

Wherever it was though, the state-controlled media were having a field day with the farmers' strikes in Glendale and then Karoi. The only idea behind the farmers' strike was to draw the country's attention to the fact that anarchy still prevailed outside of the city limits. The strike was intended to ask for law and order, to ask police to do what our taxes paid them to do. To my knowledge, farmers were not running away from their farms during the strike, but simply not working. The *Herald*, however, believed otherwise. "Farmers flee to cities over fears for safety", the headline reporting on the Karoi situation asserted.

> *The potentially explosive situation in the commercial-farming sector has cast a deep, dark shadow on the future of the country's agriculture. Growing lawlessness on some farms has forced some farmers to flee to the cities for safety, leaving behind a frightened workforce with an uncertain future... They say the only way to guarantee their safety is to run. To the war veterans, seeing scared farmers leave their multi-million dollar investments behind means that their months of camping in the bush have not been in vain. But to some Zimbabweans, the latest development on farms spells disaster for the country.*

This was certainly neither the point nor the intention of the strike and soon there were calls for all farmers, civic leaders and businessmen to join the strike. A letter to the *Daily News* by a black Zimbabwean, said it all:

> *It has to be a disgrace and a matter of shame, that the business community has been so quiet about the plight of the farming community. The fact that the future viability and employment capacity of industry and commerce are threatened, equally as much as the future of the farmers and their workers, has not persuaded the business community to respond or show any sort of support for the commercial-agricultural sector... It is well past the time that all law-abiding citizens made it known that they require that the state perform its constitutional duty to provide law and order and protection to all people regardless of any other factors.*

Encouraged and buoyed by the knowledge that ordinary townsfolk were supportive, I sent one email to three different people and asked them to spread the message. Farmers in Marondera had now held a number of emergency meetings and agreed that we would all shut down for three days starting on Monday, 31st July. I was deeply shocked to see great blocks of my email reproduced verbatim on the front page of the *Herald* the next day. Paralyzed with shock for most of the morning, I thought about how far my letter had got but when I pulled myself together, I again switched on my computer and wrote to a friend in Harare.

> *... to think what I might have done to my family and what might happen in the next days—barricaded in, or out, or worse. But as a friend said to me yesterday—what more is there to lose? In five weeks Ian and I will no longer have any money left to pay wages or buy stock feed and will either have to walk out and declare bankruptcy or sell off the remaining cattle, live off the proceeds and hold out again—for what? In the past five months we've lost everything we've worked so hard for these past ten years and if we can't get this stopped it will all have been for nothing. Last night we phoned friends in Harare asking if they were going on strike on Monday. They're not—too afraid. So although everyone says how awful it must be for us, etc etc, when it comes to the crunch, number one comes first. Sorry, really down today. Keep plugging away though.*

On Friday 28th July, by 4.14pm, the Commercial Farmers' Union had still not given their members an exact directive on the proposed national strike. Instead they stated in their daily report: "With regard to the stay-away next week, CFU leaders are still in a national meeting of business leaders at the time of writing".

It was now close to the weekend and the situation was becoming very confusing. It worsened the next day though, when by midday on Saturday the ZCTU (Zimbabwe Congress of Trade Unions) came out of their meetings. They called for a national strike to run from Wednesday to Friday of the following week. Now no one knew if farmers were going on strike Monday and Tuesday and would be joined by the unions Wednesday, Thursday and Friday, or if we would cancel the first two days of the week and go out on strike for the last three days. What a mess it had all become. A people so fearful of being seen as ringleaders inciting civil action, that we couldn't even get a strike right—a strike that we'd been talking about for a fortnight! By the end of the day on Saturday, the CFU report told members that they supported the ZCTU call for a three-day strike beginning on Wednesday, but said nothing about the earlier part of the week. By Sunday, not knowing which way was up any more, the CFU sent out a special report.

CFU policy to shut down Farmers' Associations in which invaders continue to threaten evictions and cause work stoppages continues in place and should be used on Monday and Tuesday if necessary.

What a disaster. The strike was doomed to fail before it even began. On Monday morning some farms were closed; others were open, some shops were closed, others were open, some businesses were closed and others were open. The situation was the same on Tuesday until late in the afternoon when another announcement was made—the strike called by the ZCTU had now been shortened and would take place on one day only, Wednesday. What a wonderfully united, powerful country we were, I thought in disgust. Everyone said we couldn't do it and they were right. The fragmentation of the entire nation, which had been breeding since late February, had wormed its way into our society. Fear was our dictator and looking after personal interests had become the only priority.

Looking after our own affairs became my priority shortly after the disastrous strike when Edward reappeared yet again. Too bored or busy (or could it be ashamed?). Edward did not come and see me personally. Instead he went into the workers' compound at lunchtime and sent a message with George. Tell Mrs Buckle, he said, that we are moving in on Wednesday. "We" apparently referred to all the people he had sold plots to in the past five months, so it could be anything up to 300 or more people. The message went on to say that all the people coming to settle in on our farm would be accompanied by their wives, children and extended families, their household belongings and their livestock—goats, chickens and cows. I got in my truck immediately and went in person to Marondera Police Station, determined that I was not going to be fobbed off this time.

Eventually the two policemen at the desk had to find someone who would talk to me; they could see that I was not going to go away or shut up until they did. It had taken ten minutes of arguing and table-banging but at last I thought I was getting somewhere.

'Take a seat,' the sergeant said after I'd introduced myself. I did but was not at all comfortable with the other two people sitting against the wall behind me.

'Do you think we could talk in private?' I asked for the second time but the big man across the desk from me shook his head. I wished I knew him. He was new here and it looked as if I was going to have to start right at the beginning.

'It's all right, you can carry on,' he said with what I thought was a nervous smile.

I was already unnerved but had to start talking. The two men behind me had been in the office when I arrived. There had been a short and heated altercation between them and the sergeant. I did not know what it had been about but I had the distinct impression that I was not the only one who didn't want them there. I'd only had a quick look at them; perhaps in their middle thirties the men had long hair and were not smartly dressed. Were they war veterans? I wondered—or perhaps CIO? It took a good 15 minutes to explain the entire situation on our farm.

'But Sergeant, is there really nothing you can do? We are not even designated. Can't you at least try and do something? Can't you just come out to the farm tomorrow morning and be there when the squatters arrive? Can't you at least try and tell them that Stow Farm is not designated?' My questions and appeals poured out. My voice was thickening with emotion but I was beginning to realize that this visit had been a waste of time. The member in charge of Rural Affairs, the one who had come out to the farm when I'd been threatened by the gunman, had been sent on urgent leave.

'We have not had a directive, I am sorry,' was all he could say.

'Okay then, if you won't come out to my farm tomorrow, do I have your permission to tell these people myself that our farm is not designated? May I tell them that, at least? May I tell them that the police in Marondera have sent a message telling them not to move on with their children and animals and belongings? May I tell them that, Sergeant?'

'Mrs Buckle, you wait here. I will go and discuss this with my superiors.'

The sergeant left, followed by the two men, and they were gone for a very long time. I wandered around in the passageway while I waited. I greeted the policeman who ran the armoury, the woman traffic officer, the plain-clothes CID man. I knew them all and they knew me. Ten years in an area is a relatively long time and when you're on a farm, responsible for ten or 15 families, barely a month goes by when there isn't some matter or other needing police attention. I'd been here when our store had been broken into, when a man had pressed charges against his wife, when another had got into a fight, once when a child had gone missing, when a cow had disappeared, when I'd charged people for stealing fencing wire. I'd been here on one awful occasion when a passer-by had dumped her newborn baby into our public toilet near the store. And when a petrol tanker had missed the turning and crashed into our trees and we'd had to get the fire brigade out at dawn to cut the driver out. Once, to my shame, I'd been here to pay a fine for not stopping at a stop street—the stop street right outside our store! The police too had been out to me often enough, to take details of a stolen water pump, a break-in, a routine patrol, an undercover investigation. They all knew who I was, but that day as I stood in the courtyard they all spoke to me with downcast eyes, embarrassed, shuffling and all had one word engraved onto their foreheads: shame.

After half an hour the sergeant reappeared, without his followers. He called me back into his office and half closed the door behind us.

'I am very sorry, very sorry,' he said quietly, not looking in my eyes. 'We cannot help you. But,' he said, making eye contact now, 'please Mrs Buckle, do not try and stop them. Please do not do this. It could be very dangerous. Just leave them. Do not go to that place. Do not talk to them. Do not get into a dialogue. Just let them do what they are going to do.'

I spoke quietly too, coldly. 'Let them do what they are going to do, Sergeant? Do you know what you, a policeman, are saying to me? Let them take over my property. Let them cut down my trees? Let them bring their livestock? Let them live on land I have paid for? Let them take down all my fences—poles and wire that have cost thousands and thousands of dollars? Let them dig pit toilets in the grazing land? Let them cultivate in the vleis and springs? Let them have what the law says is mine? What must I do then, Sergeant, and my husband, my son? What about all the people that work for me, and their families? What must we all do? Where should we all go? How should we survive? How should we make a living then? Do you think that if all these people take over my farm tomorrow that they have the money needed to run that farm? Do you think that they will produce 50 litres of milk a day? Or eggs—will they produce eggs for your breakfast? Steak for your lunch? Lamb? Poles for construction, firewood to heat a country without fuel? Can they employ people? Can they pay Zesa and rates and stock feed companies? Do you think this should be allowed Sergeant? Will you be next? Will they come and squat on your property tomorrow or the day after? Will you still say then: let them do what they want?' I was angry and the questions poured out. At last they came to an end and the man across the desk from me said nothing. He too had "shame" emblazoned across his forehead. For a time I just sat looking at him, willing him to wave his magic wand.

'Do you think you'll get a directive soon?' I asked eventually.

'I am sure it will be soon now,' the sergeant said and then did something totally unexpected. He leant across the desk and put his hand on my arm. 'We do understand. We really do. It is becoming very serious now and we too are suffering. There will be a directive soon, we are sure. The best is to stay quiet and wait. If you try and do something or say something, there will be blood. We know who they are,' he went on, 'the ones troubling you, and all the others. We know them.'

I stared at this sergeant. What was he saying to me? He knew how bad things were. He knew that the impact on the country was going to be phenomenal. He knew that lots of people were going to suffer but he was just not able to do anything. Until the police had a directive from their superiors they could do nothing. For the first time I felt the tiniest bit of sympathy for the police. Their hands were tied. They too had wives and children to feed; they desperately needed to keep their jobs. Principles and morals had not kicked in yet.

When I returned to the farm, another group of war veterans had claimed our farm. They had written and left a letter for me:

Dear Mrs Buckle
We came here looking for you but we heard you have gone to Marondera.
We will come to see you sometime.
We have decided to come and share the land with you. We are not taking almost everything.
Thank You.
War Veterans.

The letter had a return address, was dated and signed. The names of the three writers were printed in block capitals and underneath were their war veteran numbers. I simply showed the letter to Ian and added it to the others.

Zimbabwe staggered into August still shaking her head in disbelief that the rule of the country by war veterans had been going on for five months. Perhaps August would be the month when something would happen to change this rapid descent of the slippery slope. There had been a couple of hopeful signs in the last days of July, one of which was another scandal in the war veterans' company. A Harare based accounting firm released their findings from an audit of Zexcom (a company formed and run by ex combatants).

> *The audit revealed that $10 744 679.18 was withdrawn in three days in April last year, among entries in the Zexcom cashbook which did not specify the details of the payment or the beneficiaries. (Daily News).*

Bill Saidi, a regular columnist for the *Daily News*, spoke out frankly and explicitly about the damage to Zimbabwe's national pride. How sad it was that people who had once saved the country, now seemed intent on destroying it.

> *Few people could say they have no relatives, however distant, who either died, were maimed or are surviving war veterans. They could be getting stinking drunk on stolen vodka or skinning a duiker on the more than 1,500 commercial farms they have occupied since February... Others could be happily married, sporadically terrorized by horrible nightmares from their days in the bush, still happy most of the time... Hunzvi's international image as a rabid racist has probably cost the government as much international goodwill as its reputation as one of the most corrupt in the world... Today, the "good" war veteran is the exception. Those who despise the laggards preying on white housewives and their children on the commercial farms are to be admired... (Daily News).*

Another positive sign was the growing condemnation of the takeover of peri-urban farms surrounding Harare. This time criticism came from the Harare City Council.

> *The officials, who preferred to remain anonymous, accused the government of allowing the illegal settlements to take shape and said the local authority would absolve itself from all future health hazards caused by the unauthorized developments. 'The only authority which can approve the allocation of stands in areas of the city is Harare City Council and the Council will not accept responsibility for any potential health hazards that may arise from the activities of the war veterans,' said one senior council official. (Financial Gazette).*

Yet more hope came when Nathan Shamuyarira, a senior Zanu PF spokesman, called on war veterans to stop disrupting farm operations. He did not go as far as to tell the war veterans to leave occupied farms, but it seemed as if he too could see the long-term implications on the economy of the country. Shamuyarira was now the fourth senior and veteran Zanu PF politician to speak out, his voice joining those of Msika, Nkomo and Dabengwa. Even more positive, was the fact that a few people who had perpetrated violence in the election period were being arrested. These weren't thieves, arsonists, rapists or murderers but at least it seemed to be a start, perhaps placatory. Two men, accused and found guilty of public violence, were given suspended gaol sentences. Another notorious war veteran, who liked to be called "Black Jesus", was given a five-month gaol sentence for breaking a court order barring him from entering a farm in Masvingo.

> *Unmoved by the judgement, Zimuto shouted the slogan, 'Pamberi nevhu' [Long live land] as Mrs Mukondiwa finished handing down sentence. He added: 'I am Black Jesus, the saviour of the land of his people. I am the first one to invade a farm in Zimbabwe.' But the magistrate retorted, 'You will also be the first one to go to gaol for land.' (Herald).*

The costs of the damages inflicted by war veterans though, were just beginning to be publicized and they were costs that hardly seemed appropriate to the suspended or paltry gaol terms that were being handed down to a very few. The CFU conducted a survey, which covered only the period from the start of the invasions in late February to the elections—four months. Fifteen hundred and twenty-five farms had been surveyed and over $400 million had been lost on commercial farms. Losses recorded were for cancelled farm and hunting safaris, damage to property, loss and theft of crops, damage to permanent structures and from demands acceded to by farmers under threat.

Any positive signs that had been seen at the end of July, were soon shattered though as the new minister of local government, Ignatius Chombo, announced that 3,000 farms were now going to be confiscated from white owners. In another suspiciously timed coincidence, the announcement came just days after the country's farmers had attempted to unite and go on strike. Vice President Joseph Msika made a statement:

> *Government has identified an additional 2,237 properties to yield a total of 3,041 farms measuring just above five million hectares (19,000 square miles) which are now at various advanced stages of processing for gazetting, acquisition and resettlement. (Daily Telegraph Online).*

Speaking of people's lives and livelihoods as if they were bags of maize being added to this harvest of destruction. Three thousand farms—dear God, poor Zimbabwe! Could she really survive? Could the remaining farms really grow enough food to sustain the country? How long would it take, if ever, for previously landless peasants, to reach the point of producing surplus food for sale on the open market? Landless peasants with no capital and no title deeds to use as collateral. Landless peasants, like those on my own farm, who had candidly admitted to reporters from the *Zimbabwe Independent*, that they had no capital at all and would have to look to the state for every one of their needs. Three thousand farms represented a staggering 67 percent of all commercial farms in Zimbabwe and with this latest announcement, morale, or what was left of it, plummeted. The minister did not say which the 3,000 farms would be, the Commercial Farmers' Union were not told either. Farms would be gazetted, bit by bit, as and when the government was ready. The most unnerving part of the waiting game had begun in earnest.

The announcement of the 3,000 farms attracted world attention, briefly, and then Zimbabwe slipped into oblivion again. The local newspapers were full of the announcement though, and were obviously as bewildered as we farmers were about exactly how many farms the government was taking. Was it 3,000 or 3,041? No one knew. The numbers had become too high. Individual casualties were being lost in the overall chaos. The *Zimbabwe Independent* tried to make sense of the confusion:

> *The government is resettling people on the 804 farms gazetted in June and not on the 2,237 farms that politicians have recently been touting, the Zimbabwe Independent established yesterday. There has been uncertainty among commercial farmers after government announced last weekend that it had identified 2,237 farms for resettlement before the onset of the rains. This at the moment is a wish-list as the farms involved have to be assessed by experts to see if they fit the requirements of the resettlement programme.*

Whatever the number was though, and when they were actually going to be confiscated, was of minor importance at the moment. What was important was that it was August, winter had come to an end and now was the time to start preparing the ground for the next crop. It was almost the time to start putting the bulls back in with the cows and it was past time to start preparing budgets, cash flow projections and balance sheets for the coming season. Was any of this possible with so much uncertainty?

A brief moment of hope came with the arrival in Zimbabwe of President Thabo Mbeki. President Mugabe promised his South African counterpart that he was about to move all war veterans and squatters from invaded farms.

> *President Mugabe told a joint press conference with South African President Thabo Mbeki that acquisition of land in accordance with the law was in progress, following which the landless will be moved to these farms. 'We will be consulting those who are in need of land: both those in the farms and those who have not done so, identifying the farms where we will resettle them. In this regard we will be removing all war veterans in the rest of the farms but the time frame I cannot be exact although it should be within the next month,' said President Mugabe. (Herald).*

Our moment of hope increased to a minute when the new minister of Home Affairs, John Nkomo, supported the words of President Mugabe.

> *New minister of Home Affairs, John Nkomo, told the Financial Gazette that police were now ready to deal forcefully with rogue elements within the independence war veterans' fraternity flagrantly ignoring orders to vacate farms they have occupied since February... 'Past police inaction,' said Nkomo, 'had been caused by different statements emanating from various government departments on the land invasions.' (Financial Gazette).*

But it was double talk, again. The president had said one thing to Mbeki and moments after the leader left Zimbabwean soil, he changed his mind. The writer of the editorial in the *Daily News* was as incensed as we were. In a scathing editorial entitled: "Mugabe's dangerous flip-flops on the land", he wrote:

> *At last President Mugabe himself has revealed a plan to remove the war veterans from the commercial farms they have occupied since February.*
> *This was how today's editorial comment started, before we received the shocking news that Mugabe had done another flip-flop; nothing has changed.*
> *The war veterans would not be moved off the farms until they could be resettled on other farms. The donors could keep their money and*

> Zimbabwe was going ahead with its seizure of the farms, increased from
> 804 to 3,000.
>
> On Wednesday, as thousands watched him on TV, Mugabe spoke
> clearly and distinctly; he did not have a time frame for the removal of war
> veterans from the farms, but it would be "within this month". We all
> heard him say that, not in deep Zezuru or Korekore, but in plain English
> in the presence of the South African President, Thabo Mbeki.
>
> Yesterday, 24 hours after the two had gone public with what people
> thought was the essence of their five-hour discussion in Harare, Mugabe
> repudiated everything they seemed to have agreed on. (Daily News).

All this furore was another example of our president's habit of
changing his tune according to whom he was addressing. He had been
speaking to delegates attending the AGM of the Zimbabwe Farmers'
Union in Bindura and had said:

> I didn't say war veterans should be removed... Our roots are in the soil
> and not in the factories. We can never allow a return to racial oppression.
> Our land is to us first. The donors can stay with their money. We will not
> give up our land because of what the donors say. (Daily News).

Of the two conflicting messages being sent out by President Mugabe,
on the farms it was clear that the war veterans were abiding by the
latter and were not moving. Army personnel were suddenly being
seen on the farms, asking peculiar questions, saying only that they
were collecting data for land reform.

> Farmers said the army arrived at their properties in combat gear and
> armed with assault rifles. 'They came in green Mazda 323 military cars.
> They had assault rifles and communication radios. They were in full
> camouflage and were very aggressive in their approach,' said another
> farmer. 'My family was very scared by their unexpected visit.' (Zimbabwe
> Independent).

How could so much be happening all at once? I thought. In the space of
three days, war veterans were going to be told to get off, then to stay,
uniformed army personnel were "collecting data" and then, suddenly,
17 farmers were held hostage by war veterans in Mazowe, one of them
being a woman.

The first we knew of this crisis was when we read of it in the
newspapers; the CFU's email system had collapsed—no reports had

been issued for some days and the shock of both the news and the confusing information was frightening. According to reports in *The Farmer*, war veterans assaulted workers at a farm they had been squatting on for some time. The police were called but left shortly afterwards when the squatters became hostile. The war veterans then began harassing the farmer, stopped him from working on his cattle and when he retreated to the safety of his own home, the squatters followed him and started banging on the door. The farmer called his neighbours for assistance. They responded immediately and when they arrived, the war veterans became even more aggressive. They told all the farmers to leave, without their vehicles. When the farmers refused, the war veterans held them hostage overnight and senior police officers managed to resolve the situation the following day. I did not hear any more details but the pictures on the front page of the *Daily News* said more than enough; two large pictures, one of a 25-year-old farmer in tears after the ordeal, the other of a 55-year-old man and his wife, shocked, holding on to each other. I cried with them and for them and I am sure that thousands of other Zimbabweans did likewise as we again tried to prepare for another Zimbabwean school holiday and making decisions about the immediate safety of our children.

Richard was quite talkative on the way home from school one afternoon towards the end of term. This was very unusual. He often climbed in the car and said nothing all the way home. It was a long day for a little boy. He left home at seven in the morning and only returned at about five. If we did have a conversation in the car it would be very one-sided with me asking all the questions and getting mumbled one- or two-word answers. A typical conversation sounded like this:

'Hi Rich!'

'Hi.'

'How are you?'

'Okay.' (Shoes and socks are being stripped off).

'Have you had a good day?'

'Mmm hmm.' (As thumb goes in mouth).

'What did you do today?'

'Don't know.' (Almost inaudible between sucks).

'Did you have something nice for lunch at school?'

'Ya.'

'What was it Rich? What did you have for lunch, and pudding?'

'Don't know.'

Some days he would be so tired, especially if they'd been doing cricket or cross-country, that he'd fall asleep on the way back to the farm. It wasn't a particularly stimulating time of day for me or him but every now and then there would be a little jewel and today was to be one of those days.

'We were in trouble today Mum!'

'Oh! Why? What happened?'

'Mrs S (the acting head) was very cross with us and she said if we didn't say who did it then we would all stay in all week. But it wasn't us Mum. It wasn't even us. We can't even reach there and anyway we can't even spell that. It's not fair. And Mrs S says if we don't say who did it she's going to take the doors off and then everyone can see. It's not fair!'

The end of the story was poured out in a long stream and I had no idea what he was talking about.

'Why is Mrs S so cross Rich? What's the problem?'

'Someone wrote something in the toilets. But Mum it's not fair. It wasn't us. It's not fair.'

'What did they write in the toilets Rich?'

Richard's eyes shone and he put his hand to the side of his mouth to let me know that this was a secret and not to be overheard. 'Fuck you war vets,' he said and then giggled at his open use of the swear word.

I looked out of the window so he wouldn't see what was happening on my face and he carried on talking.

'Mrs S says if we don't say who did it she's going to take off the toilet doors Mum. That's not fair. Then everyone can see us, it's not fair.'

Richard went to a junior school where the oldest child was possibly 12. It was a co-ed government school where teachers and students were made up of about 65 percent black, and 35 percent white Zimbabweans. It was impossible to tell which of the 220 children had written that on the inside of a toilet door and it was sad, very sad that these children, the future doctors, lawyers and politicians of Zimbabwe felt as angry as the rest of Zimbabwe. They too understood that our world had been turned upside down; they knew that a handful of bad people had changed their lives.

Pre-pubescent children were not alone in their disdain for people who had been heroes, people who were honoured once a year on 11th August, a public holiday in Zimbabwe called Heroes Day. In the very apt leader page of the *Daily News* on Heroes Day, the editor echoed the words written on the toilet door in a junior school.

Some misguided and criminally inclined elements among the surviving heroes have progressively turned villain. Over the years they have soiled and betrayed the whole concept of heroism upon which the nation based its respect for them. Brick by brick, line by line they have been busy demolishing from its 1980 foundation the freedom edifice before it had the chance to reach even roof level. The destruction and reversal by our erstwhile heroes of everything they fought for began in earnest in 1997 when they made it clear they expected to be treated as a special class of citizens by making all manner of demands upon their so-called patron, President Mugabe. They demanded lump sum payments, pensions, a special quota from all land acquired for resettlement and much more… Out of gratitude for the surviving heroes' great sacrifices to bring about independence, the people of Zimbabwe tolerated those demands. We did so fully aware they were responsible, through the crash of the dollar, for the acute downturn of the economy that is causing so much suffering.

However, we had to draw a bold and solid line to indicate precisely where our tolerance of freedom fighters' unreasonableness and abuse of privilege ended. And it ended in February when they signed their evil pact with Mugabe to keep Zanu PF in power at any cost in return for money and then launched a campaign to break the law with impunity. Since entering into that unholy alliance, they have not only become a law unto themselves but have also undergone a complete transformation from being our liberators to becoming our oppressors. By turning against the people, maiming, raping, robbing and murdering them, they have become outlaws, hated and despised by most citizens and disowned by true heroes. That should give no one any cause to celebrate. (Daily News).

Worse though, than the popular discontent for Zimbabwe's heroes, were the calls from newly appointed opposition MPs to impeach President Mugabe. The ideals of a nation, the beliefs, "ologies" and "isms" were collapsing like a house of cards. On a BBC World Television programme, Morgan Tsvangirai was interviewed by John Simpson shortly after the June elections. Tsvangirai spoke for us all when he said of Mugabe, 'I would have died for the man in 1980.'

If I close my eyes, even now, 20 years later, I can still see that day so clearly, can feel my heart racing—the day the results of the 1980 elections were announced. I was at university then and was on my bicycle riding home from lectures. As I approached central Harare, there was a sea of people—a tidal wave of humanity. Men and women, running, shouting, roaring their joy at the announcement of freedom. I'm not ashamed to admit that I was afraid. I'd never seen anything like it in my life before. I'm not ashamed to say that I didn't join the stream of people pouring down the streets. I was just 20 and theirs was an angry joy. At last they had rid themselves of white rule and I was white.

I too had fought for an end to racism. I shared their beliefs and their joy. Now I could walk out with pride with my black university friends; I could greet them in the street; we could go into a coffee bar and sit together. Now the world was ours. Later I was stoned as I cycled home—a group of youngsters threw gravel at my bare legs. It stung and drew blood as they shouted after me, 'Whites get out.'

Were those youngsters the ones who were now squatting on my farm or were they the MPs sitting in parliament calling for the impeachment of the man they had so adored in 1980?

Whoever these war veterans and their supporters were, whatever their beliefs, they chose this time to move in a little closer to their claim on our farm. Immediately behind our dairy and in full view of the driveway, a man arrived and walked into the gum plantation. He started chopping trees from the plantation, 10, 20, 50, 100. In three days he felled nearly 200 prime gum trees. We went there and told him to stop. He shouted and threw stones at us, threatened to come back in the night and burn the workers' houses down. He said that this was his plot; he had paid for it and would do whatever he wanted. I phoned the police and again they did not come. The man proceeded to build a house right there below the dairy and as we drove in and out of our driveway he stood watching us, hands on hips.

Next was a group of youngsters who came through the fields nearest the house, the last fields left where the cattle and sheep could graze, the only fields that had not yet been liberated. There were six young men in a group and with them a pack of five hunting dogs. They were out on a hunt to roust out the last duiker, hares or guinea fowl that had escaped previous raids. The men were obviously not afraid of being seen as they came towards the house in broad daylight. They shouted and whistled to one another and their dogs; the cattle scattered, calves bellowing as they were separated from their mothers. The men laughed at the chaos their dogs were creating and moved into the next paddock where my sheep and their three-month-old lambs were. Ewes called frantically for their babies that answered with equally terrified cries. The men finished their little hunt by parading with their yapping dogs along the security fence that surrounded the house, daring me to try to stop them. They called out to me, shouting that it was past time for whites to leave. This was their farm now. When they had finally gone, I was shaking with anger. They were barely adults and yet no one dared stop them. They were cocky and arrogant and filled with their own self-importance.

The following evening six men arrived at the locked gate to our yard. It was just after 5pm and Ian went out to see them. They demanded to know from Ian who had been building huts right behind our dairy. They were in charge of allocating plots on this farm, they said. Who had we allowed to build over here? They insisted that Ian go to the field behind the dairy so that they could confront whoever it was building houses there. Ian came into the house looking for the gate keys, which for months had been permanently in my pocket. Ian asked me for the keys to the gate but I wouldn't give them to him. Only three days before a farmer had been ambushed under exactly these circumstances. War veterans had called the farmer out and when he was alone and exposed a group of them had jumped him, attacking him with sticks and axes. I was terrified that something was going to happen and refused to give Ian the keys. I followed him back outside and together we stood at the gate in front of these six men.

'I'm sorry, it's nearly dark; we are not coming out now,' I said.

They all roared with laughter and then the one wearing a black leather jacket and black cap spoke: 'You think we are going to catch him and beat him?'

'Yes,' I answered quietly.

Again they all laughed and the heat and adrenalin that I was generating would have lit up a Christmas tree.

'This side of the farm is ours,' leather man said. 'You must not allow others to build here. This side it is ours.'

'Who are you?'

'Motsi, I am Motsi. I am in charge of this farm. No one can build here without seeing me.'

And so it went on. I couldn't listen any more, I had heard it too many times before and I left Ian standing in the twilight having this ridiculous, one-sided conversation. Again I phoned the police and again they didn't come. How many people had now claimed they were in charge of this farm? I had lost count.

By the middle of August I had reached crisis point. I had to decide where I stood, how much more I could take, how much more I could put my son through. How much longer Ian and I could survive this psychological war that had been going on for almost half a year.

TWELVE...

ETHNIC CLEANSING

For 171 days our farm had been under invasion, our every move watched. For 171 days we had been living behind permanently locked gates, sleeping with car keys under the pillow. For 171 days we had not been able to farm the land that was ours, had made no plans for the coming season, had made no money and had lived off the capital realized from sold assets. For 171 days not a single person, country or organization had intervened successfully in the invasion of Zimbabwean farms. Five and a half months down the road and the police were doing nothing. Optimism and hope began to fade. Yes, the world had told our story, the IMF and World Bank had withdrawn financial support and almost all donor countries had suspended aid, but still nothing changed. It seemed the more local and international condemnation there was, the harder the government dug their toes in, the more determined they became. But still we held on, convinced the madness would stop, convinced right would prevail, convinced that the courts and the country would force an end to farm invasions. A deafening silence though, had fallen over the vast majority of Zimbabwe. Yes, the newspapers were still telling our story but we needed so much more. We needed people on the streets, in their thousands, demanding an end to it; we needed our MPs banging the tables in parliament every day. More than anything else, we needed a return to law and order. Time was running out. With every day that passed, the temperature crept up another degree on the thermometer, summer was approaching. The rains were only two months away. Fear though, was the only real ruler of Zimbabwe. Fear of tear-gas, of bullets, of truncheons, of sticks and stones, of 20-year-old war veterans. The editor of the *Zimbabwe Independent* tried again to rouse the national conscience:

> *If as a nation we are not shocked by the events of the past few weeks then nothing will ever move us. In a supposedly democratic country that respects the rule of law ... we have farmers being abducted and held hostage in broad daylight while law enforcement agencies stand by and watch.*
>
> *School children, some as young as 13 years old, are abducted and molested. All this for no other reason than being on a commercial farm which Mugabe is determined to grab to fulfil his own political ambitions. And the rest of us sit helplessly by and watch as this madness plays out.*
>
> *We can ill-afford the funereal silence over this issue. We have paid a heavy price for choosing to do nothing as Mugabe launches a one-man assault on the economy and the quality of our lives...* (Trevor Ncube, Zimbabwe Independent).

Far from waking up though, it appeared that everyone in the country had only one thing on the agenda—self-survival—and in the light of what happened next, it wasn't really surprising. On the front page of the *Daily News* was a report that war veterans had begun invading residential properties.

> *In Kambuzuma, scores of war veterans invaded residential stands belonging to members of the Wadzanai Cooperative who hold title deeds to their properties. They allegedly started digging foundations right in the middle of homesteads in preparation for the construction of houses.*

A 63-year-old retired teacher was one of those whose backyard had been invaded.

> *He said upon noticing the ex-fighters, he tried to persuade them to understand that: 'I am not a white man and I bought the stand, which they were now invading. They just would not comply.' (Daily News).*

That article made me almost angrier than when I was facing drunk invaders at my own gate. I was horrified that small, domestic properties were the new target of war veterans. I could not, however, believe that a school teacher, an educated professional, would be saying things like: "I am not a white man and I bought that stand". What did that mean? Did it mean that because I was white it was all right? Did it mean that money he'd used to buy his land was okay and money that I'd used was not? Did it mean that because his skin was black he had rights? Because mine was white, I didn't? Did it mean that even though his mother and mine both went into labour and gave birth to a child in Zimbabwe, he should be protected by law and I shouldn't? I saw clearly, I think for the first time, the mentality of a generation of Zimbabweans who still saw only one right in Zimbabwe: skin colour. How ashamed I was, as a white, for having kept quiet for the past 20 years. His words, which had translated into my thoughts and shame, were then echoed by Morgan Tsvangirai who was commenting on the latest move by the Commercial Farmers' Union. They had withdrawn all charges in the courts against Mugabe, Chihuri and Hunzvi—without our knowledge, consent or approval.

"Tsvangirai attacks commercial farmers", was the headline in the *Daily News*.

> He said, 'As far as support for political parties, they should be clear. This is not a question of sitting on the fence. They should make a choice as Zimbabweans. They cannot become opportunists. I think that all the whites who have remained in Zimbabwe are committed Zimbabweans.' Commenting on reports that the Commercial Farmers' Union (CFU) had withdrawn all the litigation that it had instituted in the law courts against President Mugabe, Police Commissioner Augustine Chihuri and the leader of the war veterans, Chenjerai Hunzvi, Tsvangirai said, 'Commercial farmers want to sup with the devil with the hope that they can buy time. There is no buying time here. The white commercial farmers are so evasive and it is their evasiveness that is going to expose the membership of the CFU.' (Daily News).

Morgan Tsvangirai was right. There was no time left to buy and if, as farmers, we chose to continue sitting on the fence, we were going to fall off.

Dropping the litigation against the government was to prove to be a very bad mistake. It showed the government we had no strength; it showed the country that we were in a state of terrified paralysis; it showed the war veterans and their supporters that yes, they could get away with this if they held out a little longer. The newspapers were full of it and the condemnation strong. *The Farmer*, not owned, run or edited by the Commercial Farmers' Union had, of late, taken to writing some appropriately analytical articles. When news came that the litigation had been dropped, the Leader article attempted to give both sides of the story:

> *No one can deny that there are a lot of angry people in Zimbabwe, or that a lot of the anger is being directed at the Commercial Farmers' Union. Almost every newspaper has criticized the union's decision to withdraw its litigation… They've also criticized the union's decision to withhold a court challenge on the use of Presidential Powers to acquire land.*
>
> *But it's not just the press. The Movement for Democratic Change (MDC) also joined the chorus of despondent disapproval. So have farmers themselves, often staunch union members.*
>
> *Well it's not quite as simple as everyone thinks.*
>
> *The CFU's alleged allies in its fight for law and order, not to mention the even more important fight for a common-sense approach to land redistribution, have been sitting on the sidelines. Everyone has advice, but no one has helped. And that includes the MDC.*
>
> *A handful of greedy, uncompromising men are leading the murderous rabble on Zimbabwe's farms. They have made farming an unworkable, unprofitable and dangerous pastime. And it has to be a pastime. It is no longer much of a business, still less an occupation. But for all the involvement farmers have had from their urban cousins, the fight on the farms may as well be in another country…* (The Farmer).

A group of 13 farmers went public with their feelings about the leaders of the Commercial Farmers' Union. Their letter was published in *The Farmer*:

> *We … are all members of the CFU and intend to remain so. But we do have serious misgivings about the way the CFU is conducting itself. The CFU is a union of farmers with a mandate to act in its members' best interests… We are a group that asks the CFU to recommit itself to working within the laws of Zimbabwe and with those who are determined to respect the rule of law. The CFU must align itself with the majority of Zimbabweans who want an orderly land resettlement programme, which is done peacefully and lawfully, denounce and refuse to deal with a government that is using state machinery to endorse terror and lawlessness. We call on the CFU to be a lobbying group with the interests of our nation at heart.* (The Farmer).

Signed by well-known, respected farmers and leaders in our community, they spoke for many of us.

I too spoke out, not in public though but in my weekly letter. I related the various numbers that were being spouted daily about farms to be confiscated and continued:

> *Our leaders in the Commercial Farmers' Union have gone deafeningly quiet, have not offered any of us any advice, have not managed to get hold of these huge lists of farms to be taken and in fact, have said absolutely nothing. So those farmers who were still clinging on to the CFU have realized, as we did four months ago, that this is now a case of every man for himself. Perhaps the really big players in agriculture in Zim will survive, but for the rest of us, the tumble has started.*

The leaders in the Commercial Farmers' Union took offence at my words; someone had shown them my weekly letter. One of the directors sent me an email that read:

> *I have just read your rather emotional email to your family and friends about your predicament and my heart goes out to you.*
>
> *However there are some aspects of your letter that I find very difficult and I quote: "CFU have gone deafeningly quiet, have not offered any of us any advice, have not managed to get hold of those huge lists of farms to be taken and have said absolutely nothing". All of this is quite untrue and therefore very misleading.*
>
> *Clearly you do not attend Farmers' Association meetings, do not read the daily sit-rep, do not read the independent papers (particularly the Financial Gazette), do not watch TV, have no contact with your regional representative or his office, do not read overseas newspapers (even Reader's Digest, Time, Newsweek, the Economist, to name a few of the more widely distributed papers), do not watch BBC or CNN or listen to SABC and have not attended any of the special meetings called by the Commercial Farmers' Union...*
>
> *If none of these messages reached you I can only assume your head has been buried deep in the sand, and while this may be so, I believe your accusations against us are totally uncalled for and, if you are a member, there are more constructive ways of addressing our shortcomings...*
>
> *You may be interested to know that part of the "deafening silence" has included the expenditure of over $1 500 000 on legal fees on your behalf.*

I did not know if this director who clearly had taken offence, spoke for the entire union but so had I, and I replied immediately:

Thank you for your letter this afternoon and I am sorry it has caused you such obvious and angry distress. Allow me to answer some of your comments.

Firstly, I am a registered member of the CFU...

We were invaded on 28th February and so for six months and two days we have endured and endured and endured. Our farm is a war vets' headquarters so for six months we have been the location of political meetings with 100 – 300 people from the nearby communal land converging on the fields 200 metres below our house every single Saturday. Poaching is rife, war vets openly hunt the wild game left on our farm with packs of hunting dogs. Upward of 3,000 gum trees have been felled and countless cords of wood hacked from the indigenous trees and carted off our land. Our boundary fence lies almost in shreds on the road—poles pulled out, droppers gone and many hundreds of metres of wire stolen. The WVs claimed all our grazing and three stock dams months ago and we have had to sell almost all our cattle. The farm is littered with plastic, bottles, paper and a dozen or so huts in various states of disrepair. Five different factions have shouted at us through locked gates. One lot have demanded money and vehicles. One lot have pulled a gun on me and threatened to kill me. One lot started ploughing and burning. One lot burned one of my employees on her upper lip with a hot steel bar—etc. I am sure these tales are nothing new to you but day after day for six months this insanity goes on and on and on.

What have I as an individual done? I'm not as ignorant as you seem to believe. I am on email, have read and kept every sitrep and CFU announcement since this began. I have printed out copies for all my neighbours. I read and occasionally write to the Independent. I buy the Daily News whenever I can find a copy. I bring the Daily News up on the Internet whenever I miss a day. I buy and read the Fingaz every Thursday, the Independent every Friday, the Standard every Sunday. I listen to ZBC news at least twice a day, SABC, BBC and CNN the same. I have six three-hour video tapes crammed with news reports. I have been writing a weekly letter to family and friends about the situation for six months. My mailing list, which started at 12 names, now goes from my computer to 93 names, who in turn put it out to upwards of 6,000 others. From day one I have actively lobbied contacts in the British government. I correspond directly with journalists in New Zealand, Australia, South Africa, America and Britain. I put out upwards of 500 personal letters

every week to people on four continents in 15 different countries. I have
personally appealed for intervention from eight foreign embassies based
in Harare. I have weekly contact with The Catholic Commission for
Justice and Peace in Harare. I have direct contact with one of the
country's top lawyers…

   My main criticism of the CFU is that you never tell us anything. Yes
we get a sitrep every day but it never tells us anything we don't know.
You never tell us what happens at these meetings. A sitrep will say that a
meeting is planned for a certain date but we are never told what was
discussed, what the outcome was. At no point, until last week, have we,
the members been asked what we think should be done. No questionnaire
has gone out. We were not consulted about the "deal with Hunzvi" all
those months ago. We were not consulted about the dropping of the
litigation…

My letter did not receive a reply from the director who had been
offended by my words.

   Land redistribution began and with it some serious doubts about the
recipients. Mashonaland West Governor, Peter Chanetsa, presided at
the first official handing-over ceremony.

   We chose this farm for our official launching ceremony as it is on the
boundary of two districts, Makonde and Hurungwe, and it's going to see
97 people getting plots. Twenty percent is reserved for the war veterans.
(Daily News).

A black Zimbabwean wrote a letter to the newspaper. He said that
while 14 families had been moved onto a 2,000 hectare ranch, 15
families and the farmer and his production, had been displaced. He
seriously doubted the credentials too, of the people being resettled.

   At least two of the settled people are not from the land-hungry masses in
the overcrowded rural areas. They have homes and jobs in Gweru. Why
are they being given land intended for the overcrowded rural masses?
One settler … described himself as an auto electrician from Gweru. He
said: 'I want this land as a money spinner. I have no cattle but I will work
hard.' …Without cattle they will be able to make use of only a tiny
fraction of the land where crops can survive. Msipa [Midlands governor]
admitted that most of the ranch would be unused unless cattle were
donated. He called for help from international donors. (Daily News).

On our farm we too doubted the credentials and land hunger of the next person to claim our property. I had contracted a timber company to come and fell some of the enormous gum trees that lined our driveway. The income from the sale of this timber would possibly keep us financially afloat for another few weeks. They started work early in the morning because they had had firsthand experience of war veterans on other farms. I smiled and waved to them as I left the farm on my weekly trip into Marondera town. When I returned, I slowed down to turn into our gate and then slammed the brakes on very hard. Someone had erected a signboard on the tree at the gate. I got out and read it. Printed neatly in black letters on a circle of sawn timber was: "Mr T. Maingehama". The tree-fellers came over to where I stood, hands over my face, battling to deal with rage and tears—again. They had seen the man who had put the sign there. He had arrived in a car, they said, got out and nailed the sign onto the tree and then left. The tree-fellers knew him. They said he owned a little shoe repair business in Marondera and a nice little house in one of the high-density suburbs. I listened as they told me the story, listened as they said I should just ignore it, listened as they said how terrible it all was, listened as they said I should leave the sign there and just wait. I was so very tired of it all, day after day, week after week, month after month. I hated coming home to this place I called "home" now.

I tried every possible thing I could think of to get hold of this 3000 list, even to see it, but to no avail. In desperation, Ian and I went into Marondera town. I was determined to see the whole list of 3000 farms. I could not bear this agonizing waiting. Why the government did not publish the entire list was a mystery. Not knowing had become unbearable and I was sure this too was a part of the psychological master plan. We started at the CFU offices in Marondera. They did not have the lists. We then went to the offices of the Town Planner. They did not have the lists. We continued to the Governor's Office. The governor was not available; I couldn't help myself and tears started filling my eyes. The man we had persuaded to talk to us, took pity on our plight and left us sitting in a plush, carpeted office. He returned with a large, ring-bound book. Beautifully printed on glossy paper, this was The List. The man would not let us hold the book but he looked through it on our behalf. He looked for every possible name that we might have been listed under: Farm, Subdivision, Company, Personal. We were not listed. I could not believe it and sat back in the chair not knowing whether to laugh or cry. We were not listed.

'What do you suggest we do?' I asked this man who had been so helpful. 'We have had war veterans on our farm for over six months. A number of different factions have claimed ownership. They have taken all our grazing, destroyed most of our fences; we are on the verge of financial ruin. We cannot farm. What should we do?'

The man did not answer but a door behind him opened and his superior stood there looking at us. Clearly he had heard the entire conversation. I knew who he was, everybody did.

'Just hang on,' he said quietly. 'It is nearly over.'

This very public man told us it was nearly over with confidence and conviction. A very senior policeman had told me the same thing, two months before. Did they really know? I wondered.

That night I wrote to friends in Harare relating the story and ended my letter with the daunting truth I had begun to face:

So where do we go from here? It's awful but I'd actually prayed that we'd be on the bloody lists somewhere so that we could get on with our lives, try and start again. Just thought you'd like to know. Ian's trying to encourage me to hold on again, stand up for what's ours, but I don't know where to look for the fighting spirit any more.

I sent that email and read the new ones that had arrived. The daily report from the CFU began with a summary of events that had occurred on farms in the past seven days.

Invasions (new and revisits)	34
Work stoppages (mainly tobacco)	89
Unofficial eviction notices	8
Poaching incidences on farms	2
Animals killed (livestock and game)	69
Cases of theft on farms	16
Properties with hut-building	43
Properties with tree-cutting	57
Cases of abductions on farms	3
Assaults on farms	14
Veld fires on farms	11
Intimidation or threats on farms	28

Since the elections 680 properties have been affected by farm occupations. (CFU).

Three hundred and sixty-one offences in seven days and we had been told to hold on! Who was mad here?

As a mother I was trying to raise my son to have principles, to love his fellow man, tell the truth, help people when they were in trouble. I didn't set a very good example though, when squatters occupying our farm got into trouble and we didn't help. They had begun clearing land around the huts they had built on our farm in preparation for planting maize. This was hard going. The land they had chosen had not been ploughed for the decade we had been here. The ground was rock hard, full of stones and covered in tall grass. They decided the only way to clear the ground was to burn it. Burning was my forte on the farm. I loved it. The challenge of burning a firebreak, gauging the speed and direction of the wind, the dryness of the grass and the timing of it was an intricate job. You didn't just go down into the fields and drop a match. You ploughed two strips on either side of the grass you wanted to burn; then you cleared the plough lines of any overhanging vegetation. When the conditions were right, the grass dry enough, the wind blowing in the right direction and at the right speed, then, late in the afternoon, you burned in between the two plough lines. I never went without at least five men to help me and we always had at least two knapsack sprayers, 50 or more litres of water and five fire-beating batons. These were made from stout gum poles that had hessian sacks tied firmly on their ends. The sacks, dipped in water, were extremely effective at smothering flames and hung permanently at the ready in our yard.

The squatters on our farm did none of the groundwork: they didn't clear a fire break; didn't call their friends to help them; didn't prepare tools with which to fight the fire; didn't have anything to extinguish the fire; didn't even wait till late in the afternoon. They just dropped a match. The result was, of course, an enormous fire, which was totally out of control in a matter of minutes. We saw the smoke from the house but did nothing. So many times in the past six months the squatters had told me to keep off their parts of the farm, so I did just that. I watched as the bottom part of our farm burnt down. Even though I wasn't there, I could smell the smoke in my head. I could feel it burning in my throat; could sense it stinging my eyes; could almost touch the tears streaming down my cheeks as they did when I was out burning. I could feel the heat burning against my legs; could smell the singeing of the hairs on my arms; could hear the swizzing of the locusts as they hopped out of the way. I could see the hares running from the flames; the drongoes and eagles swooping and diving into the fire to pick off fleeing insects. I could hear the voices of the workers shouting to one another across the fire; I could hear their laughing and joking as we worked together as a team to save the last of the grass for the cattle. But I wasn't there. This was no longer my job or responsibility and I just sat on the veranda of the house watching the great clouds of smoke obliterating the horizon, wondering if I would ever go burning on my own farm again. Richard came and stood next to me.

'Aren't we going to the fire Mum?'

'Not this time Rich,' I said with a catch in my throat. 'It'll go out by itself.'

Yet again the intimidation was being stepped up. Clouds of smoke rose up across the country and the sky was filled with ash-laden haze. The farms bounding Harare City were back in the spotlight and for a moment we thought the end had arrived. These farms, so close to hugely populated areas, had had more than their fair share of trouble. In early August a group of school children had been abducted by squatters and taken to a war veterans' base camp situated on Stoneridge Estate. Attempting to rescue their children, parents had then also been detained and the incident received national coverage. The war veterans on these peri-urban farms had gone a lot further than their counterparts out in the countryside. Their shelters were not plastic shacks or pole-and-thatch huts like those on our farm. They were made of bricks and cement with sawn timber roof trusses and asbestos sheeting. It was on these farms that there was a sudden flurry of police activity. The *Daily News* told the story:

> Police yesterday burnt and destroyed all structures erected by war veterans and Zanu PF supporters at Stoneridge Estate, along the new Chitungwiza Road. The demolition comes a week after the Minister of Home Affairs, John Nkomo, said the government would start evicting the invaders from commercial farms they have occupied since February. Smoke was still billowing when the Daily News crew arrived at the scene. About 18 police vehicles and 200 policemen were deployed on the farm... Scores of homeless war veterans streamed down the Chitungwiza Road saying they were going to look for alternative accommodation.

The following day the police action continued on neighbouring properties with equal vigour:

> Harare police yesterday continued their blitz against the illegal construction of houses on stands allocated by war veterans and Zanu PF supporters in Kambuzuma extension... The officer commanding Harare province, Senior Assistant Commissioner Emmanuel Chimwanda,

yesterday said the government had ordered the demolitions. He said police in Harare would be evicting all invaders from council land, once they were identified. Yesterday, hundreds of Kambuzuma residents cheered the police as they went into action… About 500 policemen and 20 vehicles were deployed at the industrial land near Kambuzuma, which belongs to Rothmans of Pall Mall. Police officers, armed with baton sticks and tear-gas canister launchers, provided security… Police were still knocking down the shacks and houses, mostly built with cement bricks, using logs and sledge hammers when the Daily News arrived.

At last there was hope, a pinprick of light at the end of this oh so long tunnel. At last we had something good to talk about; at last the police were showing their mettle; showing us that they could very easily do their job, given the right instructions. All the papers were full of it and their headlines were as hopeful as our spirits. "Cops finally get guts to tame war vets—police torch illegal houses as govt makes U-turn on its supporters", said the *Financial Gazette* as yet another Harare farm was cleared. Reporters spoke to some of the people being evicted:

'This is what we get for taking the advice of the war veterans and President Robert Mugabe to take back our land,' said one.

'The war veterans have deserted us but they are the ones who recruited us from Chitungwiza to come and settle here…' said another.

The evicted people must have done some serious table-banging though, because two days later the government was to get a taste of the beast they had unleashed.

About 200 war veterans from Harare province gathered outside President Mugabe's offices at Munhumutapa Building along Samora Machel Avenue in Harare yesterday, to protest against the destruction of unauthorized houses they had built on occupied land. They displayed placards denouncing John Nkomo, the minister of Home Affairs and Zanu PF national chairman. The group sat at the entrance to the building, chanting Zanu PF slogans and singing war songs. The former freedom fighters, who were in a hostile mood, harassed a journalist from Reuters News Agency, threatening to take away his camera… A delegation of war veterans met Vice President Simon Muzenda who allegedly concurred with them that the police action was improper. The delegation consisted of Douglas Mahiya, chairman of Harare province, and other war veterans… 'We are going back to the farms. The police have to pay for the buildings they demolished. They have to rebuild them.'

Someone was going to have to back down to placate all these angry people and it was those who were apparently least in control who did the retreating.

Information Minister Jonathan Moyo told the Financial Gazette that a Cabinet meeting yesterday had decided to stop all police action against the squatters and war veterans who have invaded hundreds of white commercial farms across the country, precipitating a crisis. 'What was done was wrong. The way they approached the issue was wrong,' Moyo said. 'We are looking at ways to redress the situation immediately and compensating the victims and taking corrective measures…' Efforts to get comment from Nkomo [minister of Home Affairs] on the Cabinet's action, which dramatically clipped his authority, were fruitless up to last night… (Financial Gazette).

The commissioner of police was also not saying anything: Chihuri yesterday flatly refused to discuss the issue. 'I do not want to talk to you journalists,' he said. (Zimbabwe Independent).

Depression returned and the short-lived speck of light went out. It had been a very interesting week though and in the post-mortem of these amazing events, Zimbabwe saw again who was in control. President Mugabe had been out of the country on a visit to Mozambique when Home Affairs Minister John Nkomo had ordered police to remove squatters and demolish their buildings. The moment the president returned, everything regressed again. Had the minister of Home Affairs really acted without the knowledge of the president? On whose authority were these squatters now going to be compensated? Perhaps though, the whole exercise had been staged for the benefit of representatives of the International Monetary Fund who had just arrived in Zimbabwe. Would the IMF really be fooled?

On Friday, 25th August 2000, as Harare lay shrouded in the smoke and dust of demolished squatters' dwellings, the *Herald* listed a further 509 farms which were to be compulsorily acquired by the Zimbabwe government. As with the last list, this one too defied understanding and again left Zimbabweans speechless. Included in this latest list was land owned by the Cold Storage Commission—land on which cattle were penned and fattened prior to slaughter and export to the EU. On the list was Liebigs, a top vegetable exporter. Three mines were to be confiscated: Union, Sunbird and New Barrier Mines. Chishawasha Mission was on the list, a seminary training both black- and white-skinned Catholic priests. The 13,000 hectare Hippo Valley Estate was on this list—the largest citrus producer and exporter in the country. Hunyani Agri-Forestry was on the list—one of the country's largest producers of poles and timber for construction. Sixteen black Zimbabweans had their properties listed for acquisition. Closer to home, 38 properties in Marondera were on this new list. One of these 38 was that of our immediate neighbour—the farm on our bottom boundary.

On Monday morning, Philip Munyanyi, secretary general of GAPWUZ (General Agricultural and Plantation Workers' Union of Zimbabwe) again tried to make his voice heard.

'The fast-track programme has displaced over 15,000 people in Mashonaland Central and West. Affected families are being told to seek places to live elsewhere. This is happening every day so the figure may have since risen.' ... Munyanyi said selection [of people to be resettled] criteria sidelined farm workers. 'At our last count only 50 out of more than 700 farm families had been resettled in Centenary and Shamva. War veterans are asking for party cards in their vetting exercise and some farm workers are being punished for having supported the MDC in the June election,' Munyanyi said. 'What we need is not speed and figures. We need a fair land resettlement policy, which caters for everyone regardless of their political affiliation.' ... (Daily News).

No one was listening though, not to Mr Munyanyi, not to farmers, not to civil rights leaders, not to the condemnation from the world. Was I being melodramatic now, when I thought that thousands of Zimbabweans would soon be starving.

Decision time, a time that had been drawing ever closer, arrived for me when news came of the death of the newly appointed MP for Marondera West. Rufaro Gwanzura, the Zanu PF member of parliament, was killed in a car crash and a by-election would have to be conducted to replace him. It was about to start all over again. I related our decision in my weekly letter, which I called "Ethnic Cleansing".

...We have now very reluctantly made the final decision to leave our farm and will spend the next few weeks (assuming we have that long) selling all the remaining livestock, disposing of mountains of farm-related bits

and pieces which have accumulated to alarming proportions, and generally close our operation down. This has been an incredibly painful decision but perhaps for the best as the future of commercial agriculture in Zimbabwe seems to be drawing to a close. Sadly, we are not alone in our decision. Our immediate neighbour has already left his farm; another plans to leave within the next few months and a third has started winding down his operation as well. It seems without doubt that this was the ultimate aim of the "war veterans"—simply wear us down, cripple our operations, drive us to the edge of bankruptcy until we gave up. And now they have won...

Our squatters are now living permanently on the property, driving vehicles across the fields and felling the timber, stripping the bark and piling up heaps of prime gum poles. We are helpless and I find it hard to describe the feelings that churn in my gut as I see trees that I planted with my own hands, pruned over the years, weeded and protected for all this time, simply taken.

Last Saturday a crowd of people gathered in our fields and waited for the arrival of the Zanu PF MP for Marondera West to arrive. The esteemed gentleman had apparently sent word that he would himself be sharing out our farm on that day but as the day wore on and he didn't arrive, people became restless. Finally a messenger came to say that the MP wouldn't be coming. He had rolled his brand-new government 4x4 five times a few kilometres from here and was dead.

It took the locals a couple of days to work out the implications before they realized that this now means a by-election—back to square one with the intimidation, the rallies, the beatings and finally the voting. Three days after the death of our MP, the youngster who pulled a gun on me some weeks ago, moved onto our neighbour's land, started felling trees on their 300-acre plot and building himself a hut in their cattle paddock. Until now largely untouched by the war veterans, our neighbours, in their 70s, have to endure the rape of their land for the third time. They lost everything in the Mau Mau uprising in Kenya; lost everything again in Nyanga in the Zim war in 1980 and now it starts all over again.

We all begin to feel more than a little like the Jews who were stripped of their human rights, their property rights and then their lives in Nazi Germany. We can only hope and pray that, for us, we can leave our land with our lives and can remain in the country of our birth and try to rebuild. Ethnic cleansing—such a strange term. How terrifying to be the victims of it.

So now, for the first time in ten years I need to find a job—a frightening prospect after having been an employer for a decade. Even

more frightening is the thought of living in a little box in town. After
these six months of hell, however, even a smallholding has lost its appeal
as perhaps those little pieces of land will be next on the WV's list.

For Zimbabwe I weep. What is to become of her and her people when,
by this time next year it won't be only diesel and paraffin we are queuing
for but bread, sugar, maize meal, etc. There are now many farmers doing
what we are doing. Agriculture has become untenable. There is no end in
sight. There is no one that seems able to quell this insanity. How very sad
that it has come to this.

The decision was made. That was the easy part. Implementing it was
another thing altogether. I called the workers together under the
Muhacha tree in the yard. They all stood looking at me. The fear was in
their eyes—they knew exactly what was coming. I looked at the
ground and cleared my throat, trying to start on the words I had so
carefully prepared and rehearsed in my mind. The moment I looked
up, I could feel the tears stinging and turned away. The chicken house
we stood next to was empty and quiet. For ten years it had been filled
with the incessant pecking, scratching and gossiping of our layers. It
was so quiet now that I could hear myself swallowing and turned back
to the men who had stood by us so faithfully.

'I am so very sorry,' I said, 'but we have decided to leave the farm
and I have to give you all a month's notice.' I couldn't say any more, not
yet. The tears had welled up and were running down my cheeks. I tried
not to look at them, tried not to see the despair on their faces, tried to
stop the tears. I had never cried in front of these men before. For ten
years I had never shown them such raw emotion. When the big ram hit
me so hard behind the knees that I fell flat on the ground and put two
discs in my neck out of line, I hadn't cried. I'd cursed and groaned,
begged for someone to help me, but I hadn't cried. When number
eight, the maddest cow in Marondera, had charged me, knocked me
face down onto a concrete path and butted me around the dairy, I
hadn't cried. When the electricity lines collapsed and started a huge
fire in the ostrich pen, I'd got caught in the blaze and lost all the hairs on
my arms and legs; eyebrows and eyelashes singed. I hadn't cried then
either. When the weaner had kicked me in the dipping race and I lost
all the skin on my knees and elbows, I hadn't cried. Oh God, so many
times I had found the strength but now it had gone—it had all gone.

Arthur, the big, loud, burly night guard put his hand out, touched
my arm. 'Don't cry,' he said quietly. 'We know this is the right thing; we
understand.'

Arthur's words broke me and I stood and sobbed uncontrollably in front of them all. I cried for myself and for the farm. I cried for Zimbabwe. Mostly I cried for all these people in front of me: for Arthur, his wife and their six children; for George and his wife and their four children; for Wilfred and his wife and their six children; for Emmanuel and his wife; for Jane and her husband and their two children; for Isaya, his pregnant wife and their two children; for Clemence and his new young wife. Thirty-four people had put their trust in me. Thirty-four people depended on me for a roof over their heads, clothes on their backs, food in their stomachs and I had betrayed them. I had let them down.

TAWANDA

The inbox of my computer's email was overflowing in the days that followed my letter announcing our decision to leave Stow Farm. People from Zimbabwe and all over the world, most of whom I had not met, offered words of support and comfort, of encouragement and love. Their words gave me the strength to face this last month on the land that was ours; to deal with the pain and anguish that was still to come; to tolerate the final round of insults, obscenities and atrocities from the war veterans; to keep my sanity. I doubted I would ever be able to repay their kindness but kept all their letters in case I ever queried the goodness of ordinary people. There were so many letters, each one treasured. Some of them read:

> *This will be one of many, many letters flooding in to you. You've become somewhat of a symbol of everything that is happening—and today's letter from you was certainly one of the saddest I've received.*
>
> *I'm sure it's a wise decision, and I'm sure it's one of the hardest you will ever have to make. Your lives, your welfare, your health are of the most importance now—and all are at risk on the farm, for no benefit and just daily gut-wrenching heartbreak. Take care of yourselves, you brave people.*

Oh Cathy, Cathy, Cathy. After your last communication we were so saddened by the news that you have been forced to make the decision to get out of farming. All you have been through, the heartache of seeing your home, family and workers being treated in such a vile way, with no way of retaliating and with the powers that be so helpless (or seemingly so) to assist. I feel so frustrated for you and if only I were nearer I would give you a shoulder to cry on. All we can do is give our moral support, and hope that in the end you will find peace of mind in whatever you decide to do. You, with all the other farming families in Zimbabwe have experienced terrible humiliation and grief, which the likes of us cannot contemplate. Please, be careful now and try to come out of this without too many scars (mental and physical). It will take some doing but you have shown you have the strength to face the future, whatever it holds...

I am so very sad it has come to this. Platitudes are inappropriate at this point—but I believe you will find it easier having made the decision. Inaction, or having to be reactive, is ultimately the cancer that saps at your roots...

Your last email was so full of the pain of your decision it made me weep. However, I still think it is the right decision. Your safety—physical and emotional—is of paramount importance. I am thinking of you and send all my love. You have been so brave through this whole torture...

Thank you for today's message, and for all the others you have sent in the past... Your words today have touched us here like little else we have read over the last few months...

Your latest email has left me speechless! I am shattered for you and indeed all other people in your situation. I don't know what to say...

We are so sorry that you have been pushed and harried and terrorized into your decision to leave your farm... We understand why you have changed your mind about a smallholding. Anything can happen, it seems, when even a small parcel of land is involved...

I am so distressed for you and your farming neighbours and Zim as a whole. The mind boggles at the stupidity of it all...

Our hearts have gone out to you so much in these past few weeks where you have expressed feeling the lack of hope in terms of a future for yourselves and the workers and their families on your farm. You have been courageous and positive even in the depths of depression. Our only encouragement comes from knowing that you will still be in Zimbabwe and you will always be an asset to this country… We are still with you. All the best to you both as you work out your future…

You don't know me but I feel that I know you. I am on M's mailing list and have been closely following your trials and tribulations. On reading that you and your husband had decided to give up your farm, I wept… I live in Bulawayo and have no concept of what you must be going through. To say that I, and many of my friends and acquaintances, feel helpless amid the chaos and madness in our beloved country, is a gross understatement. Our hearts go out to you and all the farmers and farm workers in the country…

To be honest, I don't know what to say. I certainly admire your fortitude but was relieved to hear you have decided to move off your farm. I'm sure it was a difficult decision to make given all the hard work you've put into making it a place to call home. My feeling of relief only comes on the assumption that you and yours will be safer once you leave. Good folks are impossible to replace and I know you are among the finest. I have taken the liberty of showing a few of your letters to Dave and his reaction is much the same as mine. Having never been in your situation, we can only imagine how trying it must be to have your work destroyed by lawless, ignorant bandits especially when there is no recourse. As I'm sure you know, I'm by no means the most religious guy on earth but believe me when I tell you, you and yours are the subject of my rare, but hopefully effective prayers…

We ache with you in your terrible situation, particularly the last scenario when you and your husband have had to work through the business of leaving the farm. What a trauma. We are so sorry that you have had to make such a decision…

What can I say after your letter … the power of the written word in the form of your emails is very great. Your name even came up at our Harare South Farmers' meeting this week where we discussed how effective you were in starting the stay-away—not that it proved popular with the CFU that rolled over again. However, so as not to confuse or change your decisions, I do believe there is something on the horizon worth waiting for…

    I recently took 14 kids from a remedial school to Mana Pools [a wildlife, wilderness area on the banks of the Zambezi River]… We rattled into

Mana, the kids got out at our campsite and sort of befuddled around. Then one came up to me and asked where we would be staying and I replied, 'On this dusty patch of ground and our camp will be built under that tree.' So this little thing—the oldest was 12—found a stick, made a peg and waltzing up to a patch of ground claimed in her loudest voice: 'I am nooooow peeeeging thizzzz ppplot!' It really struck me how we have to keep our sanity and keep focused on what is important: faith and family…

I've just read your latest email… There is nothing I can say from here to express how sad I feel that all your hard work on the farm and amazing strength in putting up with all that you have is coming to an end. It must have been a very difficult decision to make but I think that now the time has come to try to salvage what you can from this disaster…

I read your email the other day with a heavy heart. I am glad to note that you are not leaving for overseas and are going to try to make a go of it in town. At the end of the day I still believe we will pull through this terrible time…

I just wanted to say how very sad—and also angry—I was to hear that you have finally been forced to give in to the unequal struggle. I think you fought on way beyond the point at which most people would have given up. In the end there's nothing else you could have done, but that doesn't make it any less heartbreaking. You must be desolate… I hope at least that you are able to leave the farm with some dignity. I will always remember it as I saw it on that last day when I was over last summer (your spring), with everything looking so good in the sunshine…

Ethnic cleansing it is indeed. Our hearts go out to you—to have built up so much and now see it all destroyed before your eyes is tragic…

"The last thing we know about ourselves is the effect we have on others". I do not know who wrote those words, or where I read them but in the hundreds of emails I received, I began to appreciate the effect I had had on other people. I was humbled.

While I began to make a start on the mammoth task of packing up ten years of our lives, there was a storm brewing in Harare. In an unexpected move, the War Veterans' Association held an emergency meeting and voted for the removal of Chenjerai Hunzvi as their chairman. This development made local and international news. For a moment it looked as if the instigator of eight months of instability might be losing his grip. Hunzvi himself had not been at the meeting and there were accusations and counter-accusations. Some accused Hunzvi of making and implementing decisions without consulting them; others said he had siphoned off large sums of money from the association. Those making the claims were then accused of being puppets of whites but in a few days the whole rift was sorted out. Chenjerai Hunzvi refused to step down from the chairmanship of the War Veterans' Association; threats were made; there were whisperings, mutterings, mumblings and then it all became suspiciously quiet.

September 1st was a bad day. It began with the *Herald* and more lists of farms to be acquired. In one section of the newspaper was a list of 183 properties to be taken by government; in another section, a list of 410. Amongst these combined 593 properties that had been gazetted for compulsory acquisition were many that made no sense at all. Thirty-one black Zimbabweans had their properties listed and with disgust I saw that one of these was registered as belonging to James Dambaza Chikerema. Chikerema was the elderly war veteran, friend and mentor of Robert Mugabe for 50 years—the same man who had dared voice his opinions about the president a few months ago. The price he now paid for having told the truth was to see his name on a list. Also there were more bastions of Zimbabwe's tottering economy: The Wattle Company, Suncrest Chickens, 55 hectares belonging to Bata Shoe Company, the biggest wheat grower in the country and the biggest fruit juice exporter. Also there was Compensation Farm, the property owned by murdered farmer Martin Olds. Hope Fountain Mission was listed for confiscation and so was a property owned and run by the Quakers' Trust. Ten more properties in Marondera were on the list. I found it increasingly difficult to see the logic behind the gazetting of many of these properties. Was the minister of Agriculture playing a game of Russian Roulette with the lives of 13 million Zimbabweans or was this all about hate, or racism, or vengeance? It defied logic, understanding or even plain common sense.

The comment in the *Zimbabwe Independent* on that same day, shouted it out, loudly and clearly:

Disaster looms as fast-track scheme uproots thousands. There is a land crisis in Zimbabwe. Not the artificial one created by Zanu PF in recent months but one that is about to overwhelm us. Over half the two million people who live on commercial farms could soon be dispossessed. No thought for their welfare has been given in the fast-track resettlement "programme". They will almost overnight become destitute in the country of their birth... Under the current fast-track approach there is no supporting investment. The resettled farmers will be abandoned to their fate... The pattern to date has been instructive. More people have been displaced on farms than resettled. Despite repeated assurances that it sought to acquire five million hectares, or half the commercial farmland available, government has now moved to seize 60%. This is likely to make over 300,000 people redundant at a time when the economy is only able to create 30,000 jobs a year. A human tragedy will result with thousands squatting on rural land or drifting into the towns. The government is apparently indifferent to the social and economic cost of its breakneck rush to satisfy its followers. There has been no planning, no attempt to anticipate the consequences of resettling 500,000 families on farms that are often very far removed from their home areas with no resources to actually undertake farming.

Farmers and farm workers were far from being the only ones who were bound to lose in this fast-track scheme, which gathered increasing momentum as every day passed. The rain clouds that began to gather and that should renew pastures and provide another year of life, seemed set to bring only misery and turbulence to Zimbabwe. In our little country town of Marondera, the effects were already being felt. Eighty-nine farms in Marondera had now been listed for compulsory acquisition. That meant that 89 farmers were not buying anything from the shops or businesses in the town. Eighty-nine farmers were no longer paying telephone bills, electricity bills, rates, licences, levies and taxes. Eighty-nine farmers no longer bought seed, fertilizer, chemicals, machinery, equipment, stock feed. Eighty-nine farmers would no longer be paying people to work for them and those people in turn, would not be buying anything from the shops and businesses in Marondera town. This was devastating for Marondera, for Zimbabwe.

By chance I met the Marondera town planner. We were old friends. I had tried to support her when her partner had died a year before. She had tried to support me when she heard our farm had been invaded. What hope was there? I asked this black, highly qualified, professional woman. She shook her head sadly and said this was a learning curve without a curve; it was a line on a graph going straight up (or was it straight down). She said that no one had looked ahead to the repercussions for the town and its services. On the fingers of both hands, she listed the businesses she knew that were on the brink of collapse in Marondera. We parted, both shaking our heads, and when we met again two months later, my friend had been forced out of her job, replaced by someone who was more appreciative of fast-track thinking. My friend, like so many others, was leaving the country.

I had an email from a contact in Bulawayo and wanted to paste his words in huge capital letters on the walls of our little town to try to stop these wonderful, intelligent people from leaving the country.

> ...*Don't give up on your country now! Don't make hasty judgements during a period of abnormality. It's not the time to make a decision about your future when thought is clouded by emotion and negative thinking. Don't make a mistake that you will regret. There will be a resolution... My family and I are not going anywhere. I belong and, like others, must solve the problems that we all helped create, largely through apathy and lack of principle when it came to standing up for what is right and condemning what was wrong. That's history. It is the future that counts now and it is up to us, not "the others" to do our bit...*

While Zimbabweans, both black and white, started packing their belongings to leave the country of their birth, I too was packing, to leave our squatted, broken farm. All the workers on the farm, whether they were on duty or not, lent a willing and voluntary hand. During glorious, sun-drenched September days, we hauled out sheets of tin and asbestos, window frames, door frames, security fencing and other building materials—materials that had been bought, salvaged and saved for the improvements we had planned for the years ahead. We worked together in the sun, wiping off cobwebs and rust, measuring and pricing. Everything was to be sold; nothing could be taken to the small one-acre property we were to rent in Marondera town.

The conversation went round and round. Mostly it was sad and filled with reminiscences. Sometimes it was happy as we laughed together over a particular memory. Often though it was angry. Our farm was not even on the list. Everyone knew it was not a cropping farm, the infrastructure was poor. There were not miles of that rich red soil so highly sought after. The anger was there though, very real and palpable because we all knew that these squatters were not going to go away. They would not leave us alone. Perhaps we were not on any of the lists so far, but what about next week, next month, next year, or 2002 when the presidential elections would be held? There was not a man, woman or child on our farm who thought that we were making the wrong decision—a decision that would also change their lives forever but a decision that they helped to implement. As all these "things" were dragged out of storerooms and workshops I watched the faces of these men I had grown to know and care for. A feeling of deep loneliness grew within me and I realized how very much I would miss them all. To each person I gave as much as I could—not junk, but things that would help them make a new start, things I hoped they would be able to use to support themselves in what could only be the hard times that were undoubtedly coming. Some wanted roofing, others fencing; yet others wire or furniture or tools. Ten years was a long time and there was a great deal to do in the few precious weeks we had left.

Richard too was packing and I can't remember when I had loved him as much as I did then. He stripped his bedroom and piled everything onto the floor: toys, books, clothes, magazines and all those weird little things that were once treasures but were now junk. He divided his possessions into piles: one pile was for things he couldn't bear to part with and would take with him to our new house. Another pile was for Linnet and a third for Brian. Every now and then I would pop my head round his door and see how he was getting on, ask if needed any help. Always he kept telling me what he was doing, which pile was for whom and asking if I thought his friends would like what he was giving them. In his mind he perhaps thought he was going to another country, another continent. I kept telling him, with a choke in my voice, that I knew they would be delighted with whatever he gave them, if for no other reason than that they had been given with such love. On one of these packing days I took Richard with me to the house we were planning to rent in Marondera. He needed to see exactly how much space he was going to have; exactly where he could put his toys; how much of a driveway there was for him to ride his bicycle; which sandy little corner of the garden he could have to play with his dinkie cars and if, when he felt the urge, there was anywhere he could just dig in the mud.

The people whose house we were renting in the town were also farmers. They too had made their final decision and were emigrating. They knew how painful this move was for my family and me. I had no conception of how they were going to cope with their own move to England—another country, another continent. I was leaving behind a part of what had been safe and familiar. They were leaving behind everything. Seeing their anguish was good for me—it put my own into perspective. Our new landlady opened her house to us and Richie and I walked, hand in hand around every room of their partially packed house and then every corner of the garden. He was quiet, and hardly said a word until we were in the car and driving back to the farm.

'So, what do you think Rich?' I asked as we drove.

'It's okay,' he said.

'Do you like it?'

'It's okay,' he repeated.

Something was bothering him and I waited until he found the right words.

'There's just one thing Mum. I wish we could take our own dogs to that other house.'

'Of course we'll take our dogs there Rich. We'll take all our things there.'

'You mean we won't have to keep their dogs?'

Richard had obviously thought that we would move into someone else's house and take on all their possessions, furniture and animals. When I told him that his beloved Casper, the hair-brained white Boxer would be coming with us, and the other dogs and the cat, the questions streamed out.

'You mean I can take my own bed? My pictures? What about my little red train carpet and my curtains?'

Once Richie had it clear in his mind, he started singing again, those wonderful songs that only children can sing, the ones that go on forever and the words and the tune are made up as they progress.

As Richard sang his way through the packing and sorting and piling, and played from before dawn until well after dusk with Brian and Linnet, Ian and I tried to come to terms with leaving the farm. The war veterans continued to make their presence known and felt every day. They and their followers were around all the time, brazenly walking across the fields, fishing in our little dams, collecting firewood and cutting down yet more trees. Every morning they herded 50 or more cattle onto our fields. Every weekend they held their meetings. One Saturday night someone came into the last paddock we had thought was still safe and slaughtered one of the two oxen we used to pull the scotch cart.

The animal's name was Headman and he was a beautiful red ox, named, reared and trained by an old man in our neighbouring communal land. Headman, the old man had told me when I'd bought him five years before, was the leader in the yoke. Headman was taller than his ploughing partner German, who was jet black and had a feisty temper. Headman would walk in the furrows and German atop the ridges and together they made a perfect pair. Of late the two hadn't done much work but had served us very well over the years. They ploughed a maize field for the workers, pulled a cultivator, dragged long poles in from the timber plantations and trudged along with endless scotch cart loads of both firewood and poles. From time to time their cargo was not wood but giggling, bouncing, raucous children and they carried that cargo with great care. The last few months, thanks to the war veterans, Headman and German had been having a well-earned rest. I had found a good home for them and while they waited to be re-located they had spent their days idly grazing with the other cattle in the last paddock right in front of the house.

Shortly after dawn on Sunday morning, Isaya and Clemence came to the house to report that they could not find Headman. He was not in the paddock with the other cattle and they had found pools of blood in the grass. Ian went with the two workers and they followed the blood spoor through the paddock and down towards the little dam. The pools of blood were filled with big bubbles, a sure sign that the fluid had come from a punctured lung. The splatters in the grass clearly pointed the direction the perpetrators had taken with the stabbed animal. Ian, Clemence and Isaya soon discovered the remains of Headman and pieced together what must have taken place the night before. Headman had been killed near the little dam, his intestines removed, head chopped off. The meat had been hacked into chunks and carried across two other fields and deposited under the tree where the war veterans' tent had been. The fresh footprints of a number of people, possibly six, were fresh in the dust under the tree. The meat had then been loaded into a car or truck as that too had left clear signs on the ground. The only thing left of Headman, lying in the sun and covered in a million flies, was his head, hooves and intestines.

I phoned the Marondera police before 8am on that miserable Sunday morning and they promised they would be out at the farm shortly. Ten hours later, as dusk fell, a police Land Rover arrived at our gate. They took statements from Ian, Isaya and Clemence and then asked to be taken to the scene. Armed with torches and headlights on high beam, they drove down to the little dam. All the footprints and other tracks had been obliterated by a day of trespassers, war veterans and 50 communal cattle. Any footprints or vehicle tracks that may have remained had disappeared into the darkness. Poking at Headman's head with a stick, the policeman said he would like to have it, not as evidence, but to eat, and the two officers loaded it into their Land Rover and left.

I had nothing to say. There were no more adjectives and no new swear words that could describe my rage at this crime or my disgust at the supposed protectors of life and property.

Trying not to take my anger out on anyone, I buried my head in Friday's *Herald* that lay, still unopened, on the coffee table. In what had now become a weekly serial, another 150 farms had been listed for compulsory acquisition. This time Marondera had been spared. Not so fortunate though were three black Zimbabweans, another property owned by Hunyani Agri Forestry, a citrus Estate in Chinoyi, land owned by the Cotton Corporation and, a ludicrous four-hectare plot belonging to the Forestry Commission in Mutare. Two huge horticultural producers had been listed—one was Eskbank, possibly the biggest grower of export vegetables in the country. Land registered as having been bought by an aid organization, Danida, was listed, the name on the title deed being "Development aid from people to people". As this list appeared in the newspaper, the CFU announced that it was going to re-introduce legislation against the government. The *Financial Gazette* reported it under the heading: "Farmers sue Mugabe again".

> *Commercial farmers yesterday abandoned their soft approach to the government's seizure of farms and unanimously agreed to take President Robert Mugabe to court again over the 3,000 farms gazetted for takeover in the new fast-track land resettlement programme… The CFU's decision to withdraw litigation against Mugabe and some of his top lieutenants had created a huge rift in the farming community with most farmers threatening to dump its top leadership at a union congress that began in Harare yesterday. CFU director David Hasluck said yesterday his union would now challenge the acquisition of 3,000 farms without compensation as well as the validity of temporary presidential powers used in the process to seize them. 'We are going back to the courts to challenge the acquisition of all 3,000 farms, which have already been issued with notices as well as press the need to restore the rule of law on the farms,' Hasluck told the Financial Gazette yesterday.*

It was 8th September. Farm invasions had been going on since the last week of February. Seven months had passed. The damage was already done and with every day came new reports of major devastation. Surely now it was already too late? The ravages of seven months of anarchy, even if stopped tomorrow, would take decades to repair.

All the newspapers in Zimbabwe, even those owned by the government, reported again on the continuing devastation in the Save Conservancy. Where two months ago, poaching figures were of 60 impala, now it was over 600. So serious was it, that even the new minster of Mines, Environment and Tourism, Francis Nhema, finally went to see for himself.

Poachers reportedly killed over 1,600 animals worth about $23 million in the Save Valley Conservancy during the past six months, prompting the national parks department, police and conservancy game guards to step up patrols in the area. The stepped-up operations follow a tour of the game park by the minister of Mines, Environment and Tourism. Among the recovered carcasses and skins were those of 600 impala, 300 kudu, seven buffalo, two elephants and a lion. The animals were either shot or snared. Also recovered in the conservancy were over 10,000 snares used by poachers. 'What I saw pains me. My heart bleeds,' said Cde Nhema soon after viewing some decapitated carcasses... Horrified by what he saw, Cde Nhema fired questions at both the war veterans and farmers. 'I have no clue as to what is taking place here. What is the problem? What are you doing to this country? What are you doing to my animals?' (Herald).

Perhaps all of those questions should have been asked of Francis Nhema and those above him who pulled the strings. But particularly, why had it taken him so long to see the truth for himself?—whether it was the comparatively miniscule devastation on Stow Farm or the extermination of an entire area. This was his portfolio after all, to protect the natural resources of the country, to ensure the well-being of what he himself called "my animals". How dare he admit, publicly, that he "had no clue" about what was happening? Where had he, and ministers in other relevant departments, been for the last seven months? Mars?

Regardless of Francis Nhema's outrage at what he saw in the Save Conservancy, the war veterans were not impressed either by his visit, his anger or his words. Again, we were to see who was in charge and it certainly did not appear to be the Honourable Nhema.

Their leader [the war veterans'] in Chiredzi, Munyaradzi Mhike, said over the weekend the veterans who have cleared land in the 340,000-hectare conservancy, would plant crops this year. Mhike said, 'The problem is that since we have been here, the farmers have not offered us anything. We want to benefit directly from the conservancy.' ... The war veterans have declared part of the conservancy a "No Go" area, forcing patrol units to leave. The war veterans have disarmed, intimidated and assaulted ranch scouts and prevented them from carrying out their duties... (Daily News).

Perhaps the only advice Comrade Mhike would benefit from would be that at the rate he and his followers were going, there would be nothing left for the farmers to share with him. The farmers had, though, already initiated programmes, which saw the local Rural District Councils in the area benefiting from the conservancy, but the governor of the province denied any knowledge of this. There was so much double-talk going on that it was becoming very difficult to believe anything that any of our newly elected Zanu PF ministers or provincial governors said. Or even if they believed what they were saying themselves.

Professor Jonathan Moyo, a master at the art of double talk, became very flustered when in early September it was reported that President Robert Mugabe had been sued. Maria Stevens, the widow of murdered Macheke farmer, David Stevens, had done what others so feared doing. She went to America with three other Zimbabweans and filed a lawsuit against Zimbabwe's president. The matter was first reported in America's *Washington Post*:

> *Robert Mugabe, the president of Zimbabwe who was in New York this week for a UN summit of world leaders, was served with a civil lawsuit Thursday, accusing him and two associates of human rights abuses against political enemies. The lawsuit was filed under the Alien Tort Claims Act, a 211-year-old US law originally meant to combat piracy. The act gives foreigners the right to file civil suits in US courts for injuries suffered in violation of international law. Last month, a jury in New York ordered Bosnian Serb leader Radovan Karadzic to pay $745 million to a group of women who accused him of killings and other atrocities. The suit against Mugabe seeks nearly $400 million in damages, though plaintiffs in the past have had great difficulty collecting judgements in such cases. ... In light of the US government's position, a judge instructed the plaintiffs to get the court papers to Mugabe on their own. They did so without incident Thursday night, as he was entering a church in Harlem to give a speech. (Washington Post).*

The next morning the news was carried in England, in the *Sunday Times*. On Monday morning it was the only story on the front page of the *Daily News* in Zimbabwe. Professor Jonathan Moyo was furious. He was on national television that night, huffing and puffing. It took him more than five minutes to tell Zimbabwe that it was all lies, utter lies. No one was suing the country's president, he said, it was all lies. Time would tell.

Sadly, the next list of farms to appear for compulsory acquisition, on Friday, 15th September, was apparently not lies. This time there were no farms listed in Marondera. Most were safari and game ranches and amongst the 57 listed properties were those belonging to the Anglo American Corporation. As each Friday came, and with it the black-edged list, I could not understand why our farm was not there. In my weekly letter I updated our situation, expressing my confusion.

Since my last letter, a further 207 farms have been gazetted and published in a local newspaper for compulsory acquisition. The total now stands at 2,159… Amazingly, I don't know what the odds are. We have escaped every list so far and cannot understand why. With over 50% of the country's commercial farms taken, why have we been spared? We are immediately opposite an overcrowded communal land and, if anything, our not being listed shows how haphazard this whole land resettlement thing is…

The air seems permanently filled with a smoky haze around here and according to the CFU, over 10,000 hectares have been burnt by invaders this week on various farms. For cattle farmers this is a disaster and we hear daily of people desperately looking for grazing for their animals. To compound this problem is the current critical shortage of stock feed. When I tried to order four tonnes of cattle feed last week to maintain our remaining cattle, the local stock feed company eventually agreed to let me have one ton. There is a shortage of stock feed throughout the country because there is no foreign currency to buy the imported ingredients of the feed and no diesel for the trucks to collect feed from the railways.

Since the slaughter of our ox outside our fence a couple of weeks ago, we have not heard a word from the police—no follow ups, no suspects, no arrests. … As a result of the slaughter of the ox, we have bought all our cattle into the small dairy next to the house and I wake up every morning to look out on the remnants of our lives. The sun rises directly outside my study window and at this time of year it is a great red ball, so spectacular, that even after ten years, I still sit and stare at it in wonder every morning. I can hardly believe that in 13 days' time this part of my life will be over. I'm filled with a huge sense of relief that we've got out of this alive but so sad that what we thought was the security of our old age and a legacy for our son, is gone. I've my Mum staying with me at the moment and this week she asked me if it was okay to walk down to her favourite grove of Masasa trees on the farm. I had to say no—not on her own. With that knowledge in mind, I know we have made the right decision to leave the farm. •

Amazingly we have found a tenant to lease our farm … and contracts were signed and exchanged yesterday. I fought really hard to persuade him to keep on our workers and although I definitely secured a job for Jane, I didn't do so well for the others. Eventually he agreed to keep on three of the others for at least a month but after that could not make any promises. All farmers have just been told of a compulsory 46% wage increase for their workers so those that have managed to keep their jobs through the invasions, squatters and war vets, now have to fight again to survive as the remaining farmers downsize their operations because of the crippled economy. The workers are the real losers at the end of this nightmare but the strange thing is that instead of becoming really, really angry at a government that has ignored their needs and rights, they say nothing and accept their fate—for now…

Going out to my workers early this morning, carrying the buckets for milking, I was greeted by a beaming Isaya. The proud father announced that his wife had last night given birth to their third child, a son, whom they are going to call Tawanda—it means "we are plenty". To Tawanda I dedicate this letter. He is our hope, our future. God help him.

Our farm had seen a few babies arrive in the world. Aside from Richard, all three of Isaya's children had been born here, as had ten others, to workers who had come and gone, made their contribution and their mark on this land. Tawanda was the only one I would not get to know, the only one who would not play with Richard. It had taken Ian and me 12 years of marriage to find the courage to become parents. Our arrival on Stow Farm had been the point in our lives when we finally found what we thought was the place where a child could grow up free and wild, happy and safe. The place where I could park a pram under a big shady tree and not worry, where I could trundle a pushchair down bumpy, dusty tracks and let a baby breathe this wonderful, quiet, fresh country air. This was the place where we could build a tree house for all the children to have their adventures, where we could teach them to fish for bream and barbel in the little dams. This was the place where they could be Robin Hood or Superman; they could run and squeal, build forts and hide-aways, climb trees and discover the wonders of nature.

As it neared the end now and Richard's little piles of treasures were shared out, we were left with his little pair of gumboots. They were navy blue with crimson soles and had once had stickers of Paddington Bear on the sides. These little boots had done a lot of walking on the farm. They'd sploshed through endless puddles, squelched through soggy vleis, paddled in the shallows of the dam on tadpole-collecting expeditions. They'd stomped on dying embers on a firebreak, squashed huge baboon spiders, been hurled at snakes and been sucked, sniffed and chewed by all seven puppies of our Border Collie. The decision was, whom would Richard give the Wellington Boots to? They were too small for Brian or Linnet and we agreed to give them to Isaya's daughter, Cecilia. They were scrubbed and polished till they shone and then I carried them up to the little girl. Her eyes were huge as I held out the boots. Bending down I called Cecilia to come closer. She put her little hand on my shoulder as I lifted and dusted off her toes and she slipped one, and then the other foot into the boots. Solemnly she shook my hand in thanks and turned to run to her mother. A little big for her, Cecilia had to lift her feet high so as not to trip. Standing next to her mother she marched and stomped in delight. In Shona she called out excitedly: 'I'm ready to go to work with Dad now,' and then she was gone, marching off to show her treasure to the others. I walked back very slowly to the house and, again, could not stop the tears that were now always running down my face. So many painful partings lay ahead in the 13 days to come and I didn't know where I was going to find the strength.

Fourteen..

Siya

W hen people asked me if I regretted having made the decision to leave our farm, I didn't really know the answer. In many ways, now that the decision was made and being implemented, I felt relief. Relief that I wouldn't personally have to deal with the problems every day, wouldn't have to see the war veterans all the time and watch them destroying everything we had worked very hard for. Wouldn't have to keep getting forced into these ridiculously one-sided conversations where they claimed, by virtue of their skin colour, everything that was mine. Relief that we were alive and had found a tenant who actually wanted to try to run our farm. Relief that there was now a time in the foreseeable future when I wouldn't be permanently afraid and that Richard could go back to being a happy, carefree little boy again.

On the other hand, I was overwhelmed with sadness at everything that we had been through, at everyone we were leaving behind. Sadness that we wouldn't be here to see all the indigenous trees that Ian had so lovingly planted and tended. Sadness that I would not harvest the fruits from the dozens of trees I had planted over the years: peaches, plums, oranges, litchis, bananas, nectarines. And that Richard would not see the first avocado on the tree he had grown from a pip, rooted as it hung on three matchsticks atop a jar of water. Sadness that we could no longer open the gate and watch our four dogs go racing across the fields, flushing hares and guinea fowl or endlessly trying to catch the wattled plovers who scolded angrily and led them away from their nests. Sadness that I would no longer be able to go out and quietly pull the weeds from the grave of Queenie, my much-loved Border Collie. Sadness that the sight of frolicking lambs at dawn and calves cavorting around their mothers at feeding time, was to be a thing of the past. Sadness at all the breathtaking beauty of nature that would not be on my doorstep any more. Flocks of 300-strong Abdims Storks squabbling and fidgeting every evening from October to March in the gum trees in the garden. The tireless nest building of the weaver birds in the peach tree outside my study window; the owls leaving their roosts at dusk and patrolling low over the fields. The barbel in their dozens, flapping and squirming in the grass as they migrated from one dam to another in the height of the rainy seasons. There was so much, but the greatest sadness, was how unnecessary this all was. If only all the ordinary people, the many hundreds of ordinary black people (from professionals to peasants) in Zimbabwe that I had spoken to in the months since February, had found the courage to say something, do something. The war veterans rampaging through the country represented less than a half of one percent of the population of Zimbabwe and yet we were all silent, powerless pawns.

If I was having regrets about leaving our farm, events in the following days, both on our farm and in the country, made me shut my mouth and count my blessings. Farm workers were beginning to see the reality and starting to fight back. It began on a farm in Ruwa, on the outskirts of Harare City.

> ...the farm manager said about 20 ex-fighters arrived at the farm, wielding grenades, revolvers and assorted weaponry... The workers, who have lived with the war veterans on the farm since April, said they simply could not take it any more. They moved onto the group and allegedly attacked them with hoes, sticks and bricks, kicking and punching them... Police arrested 23 farm workers and shielded some of the war veterans who fled in terror from the farm. ...When the Daily News arrived, the situation was tense with hundreds of farm workers gathered outside the farmhouse. They said the war veterans were disrupting their life and farming operations. (Daily News).

The trouble soon spread and was reported the next day to be in Beatrice.

Hundreds of rampaging farm workers ... in Beatrice on Friday razed to the ground dwellings built by war veterans and Zanu PF supporters with some of the occupants fleeing to Chitungwiza... The senior foreman at the farm said the workers decided on Thursday night to evict invaders from the farm to protect their jobs. 'These people are occupying land on which we are supposed to grow tobacco ... if we stop working on this land we have no reason to be here. We agreed not to beat up anyone but simply to remove them so that we can save our families from poverty.' (Daily News).

On another two farms near Harare, 400 workers joined together and attempted to make their voices heard by going on a protest march into the capital city. These were two of the farms, which had previously had war veterans' shacks broken down and burned by police.

Riot police yesterday stopped scores of Stoneridge and Blackfordby farm workers from marching to the Zanu PF headquarters to demonstrate against the reoccupation of the farms by war veterans and Zanu PF supporters. (Daily News).

A few days later, the police returned in force and again evicted squatters and burnt-down huts.

Armed police yesterday destroyed shacks and evicted hundreds of land occupiers from five farms in Ruwa and on the outskirts of Harare and Chitungwiza... The occupiers at all the farms accused police of being sympathizers of the MDC. (Herald).

Again, one step forward had been taken but was immediately followed by two steps backwards.

War veterans' leader Dr Chenjerai Hunzvi, however, said he was "shocked" that police had evicted landless people in an "inhuman manner". ...'It is unfortunate and unbelievable. It is now loud and clear that these police officers are loyal to MDC and should all be fired ...' said Dr Hunzvi. (Herald).

As farms around Harare burned, again, Friday approached and with it the weekly list of farms the government had decided it wanted. There were 29 this time, mostly near to or on the outskirts of Harare. On the same day of the list of 29, more details were emerging of the private deal that had been incensing me all week. The deputy chairman of the Anglo American Corporation, Nicholas Oppenheimer, had asked for, and been granted, an audience with President Mugabe in connection with the acquisition of some of the 960,000 hectares of their land that had been listed. All the newspapers covered the story, which showed without a doubt that my fears were right: anyone with enough power, influence and money, would have their land spared. Mr Oppenheimer, on behalf of his family and the Anglo American Corporation, offered 40,000 hectares of land to the government in exchange for the remaining 920,000 hectares being de-listed. This might have sounded like a huge piece of land they were sacrificing, but in fact amounted to less than five percent of their holdings. Five percent of their holdings was equivalent to 39,550 more hectares of land than Ian and I owned. To sweeten the deal, a trust fund was also proposed whereby Anglo American would put up $10 million for loaning to people to be resettled.

> *Mr Oppenheimer, who is also the chairman of the world's leading diamond mining company, De Beers, said the government would deliberate on the proposal.* (Herald).

I did not hear any more details on the offer, or if it had been accepted. This had become, more than ever before, a case of every man for himself. Whilst I was glad that, if Mr Oppenheimer's proposal was accepted by Mugabe, hundreds of jobs would be saved and a part of the economy spared, I was incensed that farmers had lost all remnants of unity.

While Mr Oppenheimer and his delegation left State House to fly back to their homes in South Africa and Britain, I called the workers and we loaded sheep into the back of my pickup truck. The dispersal of my flock had been carefully worked out. Sixty percent of my ewes were destined for slaughter and would go, in a number of loads, to the abattoir. With George, Clemence, Isaya and Emmanuel, I helped load the first batch into the truck, trying very hard not to dwell on what I was doing. I knew each ewe by sight, had reams of pages in my files on every aspect of their lives, every injection I'd given them, every abscess I'd lanced, every lamb that had been born. I lovingly stroked the brown ewe known as Y105 before pushing her in with the others.

Y105 had been what I called a "lamb lamb". Her mother had deserted her at birth and I had become her surrogate parent. When she was just a day old, I had caught and milked colostrum from her mother and fed it to the tiny lamb from a little brown medicine bottle. From then on, six times a day, I would go out and feed the lamb. Arriving at the edge of the field where the flock was grazing, I would sit down in the grass and call out, again and again, "lamb lamb", until the little thing heard me and came running for its milk. As the lamb grew stronger, the brown medicine bottle was replaced with a large plastic baby bottle and a much bigger teat. The feeds were cut down to four times a day but still it was the shrill calling of "lamb, lamb" that brought it bounding across the fields. When I was sure the lamb was strong enough, I would let Richard, Linnet and Brian do the feeding. They loved this job and would race off arguing about whose turn it was, who would hold the bottle first and it was always accompanied by a great deal of giggling and laughter. The bigger the lamb became, the more boisterous the feeding, and the bottle would be drained in fewer than two minutes. Wanting, but not needing more, the lamb would then suck on fingers, hands, my skirt, anything it could get its mouth around. Lamb lamb would follow me wherever I went, once even coming past four outraged dogs right into the kitchen. Y105, once a lamb lamb, was now a mother, having successfully reared four lambs of her own and I hastily turned away as I pushed her into the truck. She was the last of many lamb lambs I had reared over the years. That day I went backwards and forwards with my ewes to the abattoir, hot, tired and very depressed that because of a few cocky louts, I had been forced into this. The last load reduced me to tears as I could delay no longer and had to part with Big Mac.

Big Mac was a magnificent, enormous, purebred Wiltiper Ram. I had bought him from a dear friend and farmer in Ruwa. Big Mac, weighing in at well over 100 kilograms when we bought him, had a thing about me. When we met with a fence between us, he was an angel, rubbing his head against my hand, closing his eyes with the delight of a hard scratch on his nose and between his ears. When I went to his side of the fence though, Big Mac turned instantly from angel to terrorist. He would toss his head menacingly, leaving me in no doubt that he wasn't happy about my presence and wished me to leave. If I didn't, Big Mac would paw at the ground, snort, grunt and then come at me. Often a bellow would stop him in mid rush. Sometimes I would have to beat a hasty retreat over the nearest wall or fence. Sometimes it would take all four of the farm workers to turn him away. When he tired of this game, Big Mac thought of a far more devious way of bringing me down to his level. I would go in to the field or pen and he would completely ignore me, carry on grazing, not even looking up. As I continued with whatever I was doing, I would forget about him and only remember when I heard someone shout out a warning to me. Big Mac would approach from behind and then butt me very hard in the back of the knees. If I didn't get out of the way in time, I would be pushed face first into the dirt where the ram, deed done, would leave me and amble innocently away. Once I'd been bending over, dosing the ewes, and Big Mac hadn't bothered me at all. The first I knew of his presence was an agonizing wrench of my hair. The ram had a chunk of my hair in his mouth and seemed determined to pull it out. It took all the workers to get him off me—and he pulled out a lot of my hair with him. The strangest thing about Big Mac though, was that he never ever tried any of his nonsense on either Ian or Richard. There was obviously something about me, and only when I was on his side of the fence, that drove him wild. Big Mac had sired many hundreds of lambs on our farm and, even with his quirky personality, it broke my heart to see him go. I rationalized the pain though. He was getting on a bit, I told myself, his teeth were becoming a bit thin. This day would have come eventually.

As I drove in and out of our farm gate with my truck continually loaded with one thing or another, I was constantly watched. The infant war veterans stood, day after day, hour after hour on the corner opposite our store. How they knew to keep their distance from me I don't know, but they did and I was glad because my temper was volatile, my rage immense. Once in a while, as I drove past them, they would raise an arm with a clenched fist and my hatred was palpable. Richard had gone back to school now and I was glad that he didn't have to see the anguish of these last days, which became indescribably busy and never seemed to have enough hours in them. I had resorted to getting up at 3am to try to deal with the paperwork in order to leave the daylight hours free for all the carrying that still had to be done. My Mum had again put her entire life on hold and stayed on the farm packing and labelling endless boxes. At first she would consult me about what to pack and where to put it but when she too received the short end of my tongue, she just carried on anyway. I behaved abominably, like a spoilt brat whose favourite toy was lost as I tried to deal with this pain. Mum knew though. She understood, and I am sure that my pain was hers too.

The remaining adult sheep on the farm had been split into two groups. One, of five ewes and a young ram, was going to a smallholding in Bromley; the other, of 20 ewes and a ram, to a smallholding on the other side of Marondera. Again I trundled backwards and forwards, in between sitting in two-hour long queues for the precious diesel that kept me mobile. George and I spent our days loading and unloading sheep, saying the last sad farewells to all these animals we knew so well. Often there were tears on his cheeks too. My last trip was to Ruwa with 40 lambs and Mum came with me this time. Following the truck and trailer of the farmer who had so kindly agreed to take my little three- and four-month-old lambs, we were mostly quiet as we drove. There was almost nothing left to say any more as we passed other farms whose fences were also falling down and fields dotted with the abominable shacks of war veterans. We could only wonder if these farmers, like me, had reached the end of their financial and emotional tether. We were not being told, though, how many farmers were closing down. The papers' headlines were not reporting this. They were still telling us what Hunzvi was saying, what war veterans were doing, how many farm workers were being arrested, what police were doing on that day and undoing the next. In a five-kilometre radius around our farm, we were the third to go. It must be happening all over the country but no one was publicizing it. We were, after all, only the white racist commercial farmers who had stolen all this land from the ancestors of "true" Zimbabweans.

With the last of my sheep gone, I turned now to the cattle. First to go were the dairy cows. Superb, pedigree Holsteins from imported semen with names as long as short stories, they were walked to a small dairy farm nearby. For the first time in ten years we had no fresh milk in the house or in the store. For the first time in ten years there were no large plastic containers filled with souring milk on every possible surface in my kitchen. For the first time in ten years all of the workers went off for mid morning break to have black tea as I could not give them their customary daily litre each. I think that on that day, it sank in for us all. The end was very near.

With little over a week to go before we moved off the farm, something amazing happened. Just before dark one evening, a police Land Rover arrived at the gate and hooted a couple of times.

'Good evening. May I help you?' I asked through the locked gate.

Two uniformed policemen got out. One I recognized immediately.

'Ah Mrs Buckle,' this one said. 'How are you these days?'

'Good, thanks,' I replied. I knew he hadn't meant "How are you?" as in the genuine inquiry, but was following the customary Shona way of greeting. He knew too, that I didn't mean "Good, thanks" as in "Yes, I'm fine, the farm's fine and everything's great".

'What can I do for you?' I asked.

'We've bought your engine back!' he announced delightedly and waved his arm vaguely towards the back of the vehicle. Engine, I thought, what engine? I unlocked the gate and went to peer in the rear window. There was certainly no engine that I could see, only an enormous pile of firewood.

I turned to him with a frown. 'Engine?' I queried.

'Yes, don't you remember, it was stolen from your place some time back?'

I peered at the paperwork, signed where I had to sign and read the docket. They were returning a small blue electric motor that had been stolen from the farm over two and a half years ago. I smiled and quietly shook my head as the two policemen then proceeded to unload all the firewood in the back of the vehicle. The electric motor was underneath it all. It took them almost 15 minutes to get to what had once been a small blue electric motor and was now a rusted heap of seized, useless machinery. It was heavy though and they dropped it under the nearby Msasa tree for me.

'Thank you very much,' I said when they had finished reloading the wood into their vehicle. There was no point in asking them what had happened, why I had never been called to court to give evidence against the man who had stolen the engine. The man who I had not only caught carrying the engine away in a wheelbarrow, but had then driven to the police station in Dema. There was no point in asking them why, when I had arrested the man, charged him and delivered him into their custody, it had taken over two and half years to have my property returned to me.

'We are just clearing our backlog,' the policeman said after I had thanked him.

Was this an indication of what lay ahead perhaps for war veterans? If it had taken two and a half years to deal with a small blue electric motor though, how long might it take for a few thousand war veterans on over 2,000 farms to be dealt with? And their crimes were far more serious than little blue engines. Theirs were crimes of malicious damage, of poaching, looting and torture, of rape, arson and murder. Would the police ever get to them in the months or years to come? Would they ever be made to stand in front of a judge and answer the charges that would be laid against them? And how, I wondered, would they answer these charges? Would they say it had all been only a "peaceful demonstration"? Or perhaps they would argue that it was "just the little law of trespass"?

Eight days before we left our farm, I trudged out to my overworked truck early in the morning and got in with a very heavy heart. Today was the day I had dreaded, perhaps more than any other. Today the last cattle on the farm, 23 cows and 22 calves were to be loaded onto a truck and taken away. After today there could be no turning back. Loading 23 cows that weighed between 450 and 650 kilograms each onto a truck, was not the easiest of jobs at the best of times. When those cows though, still had calves at foot, it was a recipe for the farmers' worst nightmare. The 22 calves ranged in age from one week to five months. All were still suckling and all were very nervous at this sudden, frightening change in their normal, carefree routine. It had been carefully planned—a truck and trailer were to come to the farm over the road where there were no war veterans, and the loading ramp was in good condition. This was the third time I had attempted to load the cattle. The first time the truck hadn't arrived at all—they had no diesel. The second time, the truck came but without a trailer. I was not prepared to load tiny calves in the same compartment with huge cows and it was sent away. Today, hopefully, everything would go according to plan. Micky and Myrtle had cleared their calendar for the morning and they, and all their workers, were there to help. We would load all the calves first, in the truck with one or two of the younger, quieter cows, to keep them calm. The mothers, seeing their babies ahead of them, hearing their calls, would be anxious to follow. The driver would then move forward a few metres and we would load the cows into the trailer. Or that was the plan!

None of it worked the way we'd planned. The driver would not load the cows into the trailer, saying the balance would be wrong. He said he couldn't load the calves before their mothers because the calves would have to go into the trailer and he couldn't reverse with the trailer. Neither could he turn the truck around because of the position of the loading gates. Tempers flared, swear words rang out, but eventually Micky and the driver made another plan. The calves would be loaded onto the trailer, the trailer would be towed, turned and lined up, the truck would be turned and reversed and… I gave up listening after a while, it was all too confusing and I was so exhausted that I would gladly have gone home to bed, pulled the blankets very firmly over my head and never woken up again. Already I was sniffing and snivelling, my eyes were burning, I'd smoked more than a dozen cigarettes and felt weak and dizzy. It was as bad as I had thought it would be. The calves bellowed and cried, turned back and escaped. The mothers kicked and smashed poles and bellowed even louder. The eight workers shouted and swore at one another and everyone seemed to have cuts and scratches, grazes and bruises. But at last it was done.

All were loaded. The moment the last gate was closed and the final bolt secured, I wanted to leave, to run. I couldn't bear to see the lifeblood of our farm in the huge truck. Myrtle put her arms around me and I sobbed. It was over. Now there was nothing of the essence of our farm left.

Still hung-over and exhausted from my excessive indulgence in emotion, I woke up feeling sick and empty the next morning. I didn't want to go to my study, the heart of the house, because I knew that when I opened the curtains, I would see nothing. My view of the dairy and 45 cattle was gone. All I would see was dust and manure. Dust and shit, dust and shit. The words went round in my head as I sat in the lounge and stared at nothing. Here too there was almost nothing. The pictures had been removed from the walls, dusty squares on the paint offering their final silhouette. The ornaments were packed, their contours, colours and memories wrapped in the newspapers that described this year from hell. The bookcases stood naked, filmed with dust, their contents never again to be revealed in this house. The cold concrete floor was no more covered with the brightly patterned Persian carpet. The carpet held many more stories than could ever be told. It had belonged to my parents, was over 30 years old and had always graced their living room as I was growing up. The carpet had carried the feet of thousands of people. On it and around it people had sat and discussed the antics of Rhodesian politicians, of those involved in the making of Zimbabwe-Rhodesia, and then of Zimbabwe itself. It had seen racism and oppression, freedom and democracy, nationalists and dictators. The bright red Persian carpet had seen five children being reared during my childhood. It had been soiled with food and drink, with cigarette ash and baby vomit. If carpets could talk, this Persian would fill many volumes. Now it was rolled up and waiting to move again. Worst though, was the echoing that filled this room, and the others, through the old farmhouse. Gone were the sounds of laughter and contentment and happiness. My voice came back to me now as it bounced off the bare walls and it was a sad, broken and exhausted one. This wasn't home any more—just a dirty, empty house.

The last people to come to our home in this final week were the worlds' reporters. And they came from Sudan, Nigeria, South Africa, Britain and Zimbabwe. The journalists came to record the remaining fragments of our farm. They were doing their jobs, I knew that, but they wanted me to go right back to the beginning, to 28th February, to the day when seven people came to the gate and declared war as they shouted: 'Hondo, Hondo, Hondo.' Their pencils flew across the pages of their notebooks; the flashes from the cameras the only thing brightening the tale. They didn't ask many questions but the ones they did, were repetitions of my words and already told the story. You mean you were born in Zimbabwe? You were educated in Zimbabwe? You did not inherit this farm? You bought the farm ten years after Independence? You got a Certificate of No Interest from the Zimbabwe Government? This farm is not designated? You have not been listed for acquisition? Your property has not been gazetted for confiscation? The police will not remove the war veterans? And so it went on, two hours to tell of ten years. As each group of reporters left, they wished us well, offered their condolences, empathized with our pain. There were black and white reporters and, as we did, just shook their heads sadly.

Five days before the end of the month, the war veterans made their presence known to me again. Perhaps it was a final act of defiance, or possibly they wanted to make sure I would not change my mind. Coming back from the store, I saw a cloud of smoke rising from the other side of the little dam. Even though it was late in the afternoon, the grass was tinder dry and there was a strong wind pulling the fire towards the house. The house with its boxed contents was all we had left now so I called all the workers and we went out together to see what could be done. The way the fire was racing across the field, I knew we would never be able to stop it, so we immediately planned and lit a wide firebreak in front of the house. Working in a steady line, and with the help of a neighbour and his workers, we burnt all around the house and then the dairy, finishing as night fell. We were filthy, covered in soot, ash and sweat and stood together in the driveway watching as the wild fire on the field below us lit up the night. By now the wind had changed and the flames were streaming away from us and towards the two plantations of gum trees planted on our side of the boundary. One of the plantations was of mature trees ready to be felled; the other of 10,000 saplings I had planted three years before. Even from where we were, we could see the heat intensifying as the fire reached the trees, the smoke thickening and the visibility reducing. As we stood watching yet more of our work going up in smoke, another neighbouring farmer arrived to help and so we replenished all the knapsack sprayers and went down to try to control it. I was too exhausted even to walk, so sat with a neighbour in the truck and watched as the workers did what they could. It took over an hour for them to put one side of the fire out and by that time it was completely dark. All traces of the sun had disappeared and the first stars were beginning to appear. The only light came from the burning trees and the glowing red embers in the accumulated leaf litter below. I could hear the men calling out to one another in the dark, could hear their voices coming closer, knew they were on the way back to the truck. I stood outside in the cool night air, next to the truck, waiting for the men when I suddenly heard a rustle in the grass behind me. Out of the smoke appeared one of the men who called himself a war veteran. He was an enormously tall man, well over six foot, and the sight of him, his glistening face inches away from mine, scared the life out of me.

'Good evening. May I help you?' I whispered, one foot already in the car, my hand on the door.

'Siya!' he said, quietly the first time and then, louder and with more emphasis: 'SIYA.'

It meant "leave". I knew it did and before he could say another word, I was in the truck and locking the door. When I was safe, I turned and looked but the man had disappeared, back into the smoke, as silently and swiftly as he had appeared. Minutes later the exhausted workers returned to the truck and we all returned home, leaving the fire to blaze down the farm where it would eventually go of its own accord. I stumbled into the house and collapsed, shaking from both the nearness of this latest encounter and from exhaustion.

The man who had come out of the smoke and told me to leave did not have to try very hard to convince me. That same day it was reported in the papers that the murderer of David Stevens had been in court in Marondera. Facing a charge of murder and backed up by an eyewitness account of the killing, the man had not been asked to plead but remanded out of custody, allowed to go home until a later date.

Also on that same day, war veterans attacked a farmer in Karoi with a machete, in broad daylight, in front of all his workers. Horrific pictures of a huge man, his face covered in blood, appeared on the front page of the *Daily News* the next morning.

Karoi farmer, Marshall Roper, was seriously injured yesterday morning after being brutally assaulted by war veterans and Zanu PF supporters occupying his farm. Roper, of Peveril Farm, was struck in the face with a machete after resisting demands by the invaders to stop planting tobacco… A neighbour said, 'Roper sustained serious facial injuries. His nose was sliced in half and he sustained a ten-inch gash across his face.' Roper was rushed to Karoi Hospital, moved to Chinoyi Hospital before being finally transferred to the Avenues Clinic in Harare. The incident immediately triggered a demonstration by farm workers. Hundreds of farm workers gathered at Karoi Police Station to protest against the assault. (Daily News).

On the second last day of September as the country reeled in shock at renewed attacks on the people that fed them, the war veterans were again rewarded for their deeds. "War vets to be paid again" was the front-page headline in the *Zimbabwe Independent*. The Ministry of Defence announced that war veterans were to be re-trained and would become a reserve force attached to the Zimbabwe National Army. Once trained, the veterans would be called into active duty as and when needed. Zimbabwe already had an army of over 30,000 people and even though a third of them were fighting in Africa's forgotten war in the Congo, we all wondered if we actually needed a reserve force. Frankly, the implications behind this latest move were worrying. Were the men serving on this reserve force really going to be the same ones that had been terrorizing the country for the past year? What were the entry qualifications for this reserve force—murder, rape, arson, looting, torture?

On the second last day of September 2000, a list of 80 farms to be compulsorily acquired by government was published in the *Herald*. I glanced at it briefly. There were another 14 properties in Marondera. Adding this list to the growing pile, I turned my attention to the last things waiting to be done. This was to be the last working day for everyone on the farm, the last day the store would be open and there was a great deal to be done. I loaded the truck with the final things for the store, mostly farm tools I hadn't been able to dispose of until now as they were still in use. Things I would have no use for in a little urban garden: a dozen hoes and grass slashers, sickles, axes, picks, shovels, chain and wire strainers, cane cutters and hay forks. Also in the truck were the last things that didn't fit into any of the sealed and stacked boxes that lay in every room of the house. Baby blankets and an old alarm clock, excess pots and pans, those hideous things that had been inherited from strange people over the years and really had no place to go. A peculiar green china dog flower vase, a strange black string jersey, a radio that only ever spoke in Japanese. There was a lot and Jane conducted her own one-man auction throughout the day, dropping the price once at teatime, again at lunch and probably ended up by paying people to take the stuff away by mid afternoon.

The store was always full of people these days, people who were curious to see what was going on; people who were hanging around for handouts and people who were waiting around to say goodbye. Amongst the latter was the man who grew peas, beautiful, sweet green peas and sold them to me by the sack load through winter, knowing that I shelled and froze them in huge quantities to keep me going through the summer months. Then there was the very elderly woman who always bought half a loaf of bread and a cup of milk on her way home from work. She was a primary school teacher and we had spent many hours discussing the principles of reading and writing. She too came to say goodbye, to wish me well, to say that she would miss our little chats together. There was, of course, the gang of kids that hawked bananas and hard-boiled eggs on the road outside the store. They came to get the big boxes of magazines I had promised them and see if there was any chance of a last free bubble gum or toffee, sucker or frozen cold drink. The ET drivers (Emergency Taxis) came also, to say goodbye, and they made the tears start again when I popped into the store later in the afternoon. Their vehicles lined the road outside the store and formed a rank of fairly decrepit but very familiar vehicles: three Peugeot 404s, a VW Golf, an ancient pickup truck of an unknown, long-forgotten make, and a station wagon. All the men were waiting for me in the store and with much pomp and laughter bought me a coke, a bun and one cigarette. Standing in my filthy, ragged shorts, stretched t-shirt and black tackies with holes in the toes, I passed the time of day with them. I knew them all well. For ten years we'd shared our laughs and tears, ups and downs, successes and failures. I was humbled that they'd got together, planned this little farewell drink and we talked about where we were going in this beloved country of ours that was in tatters around us.

Into the midst of our final conversation came two strangers, one after the other. The first was a man in his thirties who had had his entire business destroyed by war veterans just before the elections. He had lost everything. All the windows of his store and butchery smashed; all his stock looted; all the tables and equipment broken; his wall and fence destroyed. Friends, relatives and well-wishers came to his aid and he was starting again. This man led me outside onto the veranda and begged me not to leave the farm. 'This will end,' he said. 'Don't give in.' After some minutes though, he agreed that because the colour of my skin was a lighter shade than his, my chances of survival were far smaller than his. We shook hands and wished each other well. The next stranger was a middle-aged woman in a very fancy car with government number plates. She too wanted to know what was going on, why I was closing down, why all these people were saying goodbye to me, where I was going. She admitted that all the happenings of the past seven months were "not good" but when I told her the farm was on the edge of bankruptcy, she did not believe me. 'Ah, you whites,' she said, 'you always have plenty of money.' I think perhaps my appearance put paid to her belief though. I tried to explain for a few minutes, but her well-dressed children were getting restless in their plush seats in the air-conditioned government car and she had to go. She shook my hand and wished me well as she left and, I might be wrong, but was sure that the look on her face was one of both shame and embarrassment.

If only they knew, I thought, if only all these government people really knew what they had done to the commercial farmers of Zimbabwe. They had broken our spirit, left us feeling unwanted and unneeded, left us feeling like strangers, aliens, in our own country. If only, I thought, more government people like this woman had taken the time actually to come and see for themselves, to talk to us, to discover that we too were human beings. But they were like the minister of Tourism who had said only weeks before: 'I have no clue as to what is going on here.' Someone at the top, had unleashed the war veterans on us and no one dared come and see what effect seven months of terror and intimidation had had. Perhaps they didn't care, or perhaps they were too ashamed. I felt very sorry for this government woman, and the thousands of others like her. What would she tell her children in the years ahead? How would she explain what had happened on the farms? Would she ever be able to look a white person in the face again without shame and embarrassment? Would she be able to say, with pride and conviction, that yes she helped chase all white Zimbabweans from land that was legally theirs? But that it was good because our grandfathers had stolen the land from their grandfathers and someone had to pay for those sins. God's judgement and punishment would not have been sufficient. Oh shame on you, I thought. Shame on you.

Everyone gathered around my grossly overloaded truck to say goodbye to Clemence and his very young wife that day. All his worldly goods were packed into the truck and I prepared to take him to his new job and new home. Unsure of his job security on our farm with an unknown employer who had only been able to guarantee one month's work, Clemence had found another job on a smallholding 30 kilometres away. He was nervous, tired and excited and warmly shook hands and had one last laugh with all the workers that had been his friends and neighbours for his short working life. I could hardly bear to watch these goodbyes and we both had tears in our eyes as I slipped the truck into gear and we finally got away. We didn't talk on the journey and I drove quite slowly so that Clemence could get his bearings, see where the nearest shops would be, the nearest bus stop.

He was certainly in for quite a different way of life. His new employer was not only a black Zimbabwean but also a man. I, white and a woman, was the only thing that Clemence had ever known in the world of work as he had come to the farm straight from school. I was sure though, that Clemence's new employer would treat him well, look after him and be sensitive to his needs. His new employer was a good friend of ours, an honest, hard-working Zimbabwean that saw a future in the country and was working day and night to be a part of it. I couldn't bear to hang around once the truck had been unloaded and drove home wondering where all these bloody tears kept coming from.

If the partings so far had been painful, it was nothing compared to the anguish of saying goodbye to the people who had so faithfully worked with and for me over the last decade. Each person received a large envelope and in it was everything that I was required by law to give them, as well as whatever else I could spare. The proceeds from the sale of all the bits and pieces sold in the store had been shared out, as had the money from the sheep that had been slaughtered. It was a sizeable amount on its own, not much though, when split eight ways. Each person had to find a way to budget this little windfall, to make it last until better times came their way, to try to save some of it, invest it for the education of their children. I spoke to each person in turn, thanking them for everything, wishing them luck and health and happiness in whatever the future held for them, wherever they might be. I would not forget them—not for a very long time. We had shared so much, joy and pain. I was no longer ashamed to let them see my tears.

There was nothing gracious or dignified about our departure from Stow Farm. The "removals" truck, which was actually a cattle truck, did not arrive until past three in the afternoon. The driver was most apologetic—he had been double booked and moving bricks all day. His truck was inches deep in rubble and brick dust. We arrived at our new house in the dead of night. The truck would not fit through the gateway. Furniture and boxes stood jumbled in the darkness. The dogs barked and the cat yowled all night. The glare from the streetlight outside shone directly into the bedroom.

And so, for me, it was over.

Postscript

Three months after we left our farm and one week before the end of the year, Ian and Richard and I embarked on a 400-kilometre journey that took us across the boundaries of Mashonaland East, up into the Eastern Highlands and then plunging down to the edges of Zimbabwe's lowveld. Having so recently been a farmer, I took a particular interest in the view from the window. What I saw was unbelievably depressing.

The three promises made by our government for the last 20 years were uppermost in my mind: Health for all by the year 2000; Housing for all by the year 2000 and, Education for all by the year 2000. Zimbabwe had chosen to make her entry into this new millennium in a drastic, dramatic and very destructive way. At least that's how it looked from my window. How wonderful it would have been if all of Zimbabwe's 13 million people had a decent home, good health care and schooling for their children by the year 2000. How wonderful it would have been if Zimbabwe's Zanu PF government had been able to fulfil even one of its election promises.

We left Marondera town behind us, its snaking, 200-car queues for petrol and diesel the sole sign of life in the town. At the only filling station in the town where paraffin was available, there was a crowd of perhaps 150 people. All carried containers into which they could put this precious fluid. Some had small glass bottles, others 20-litre plastic containers. They were not in a quiet, orderly line. Someone at the pump head was being given too much and everyone was shouting and jostling as armed police arrived. On the verges of the roads, outside the shops and factories sat crowds of young men, in their twenties and thirties, unemployed, bored and with nothing to do except sit and stare. At the bus stops on the outskirts of town stood dozens of people waiting for transport, transport that would only arrive if their chosen vehicle ever made it to the front of the queues at the petrol stations. On the main road, less than half a kilometre from the town of Marondera we passed the official Tip, the site where all the town's garbage is deposited every day. In a huge, unfenced, uncovered and unprotected gully lies a sea of plastic and paper, of rusting tin and broken glass, of rotting vegetation. From this abomination, rise a million flies each time a child or woman bends down to rescue a scrap upon which to survive.

Outside the town are the farms that until recently have produced everything that Zimbabwe needs to survive. Farms that once grew vast fields of maize, which should now be standing almost two metres tall and sprouting golden silks. Farms that were once covered with mile after mile of tobacco, which should now be almost ready to reap, its huge leaves drooping heavily, waiting to be taken to the barns for curing, waiting to drop US dollars into the country's coffers. Farms that had once sported fields of soya beans, the hot dark green leaves folding and turning in the gentle breeze. Farms whose fields were once covered with miles of black shadenetting to protect the vegetables and flowers in the carefully tended soil below. Farms where once hundreds of cows had grazed with their calves.

That is not what we saw.

Instead we saw farms that had been "liberated" by war veterans. We did not see these war veterans or even landless peasants carefully tending their new fields. We did not see Zimbabwe's "new" farmers weeding and cultivating. We did not see healthy, flourishing crops. On every "liberated" farm we saw perhaps three or four shacks constructed by the war veterans—shacks whose pole walls were collapsing, whose half-thatched roofs lay open to the weather. We saw rags tied onto decrepit fences—the signboards of the new owners. In hundred-acre fields we saw little squares of one, sometimes two acres of weed-infested, yellowing maize. In between the maize, rogue tobacco plants stood tall and arrogant, a small reminder of what had once been there. It was a hot day but I shivered as the reality struck home. What I saw from the window was the crop that was to feed 13 million Zimbabweans in 2001.

Mile after mile, the view from the window was the same: a few broken-down shacks, a patch of yellowing squares of maize. It is true that every now and again there were fields of tobacco or maize being tended by dozens of commercial farm workers in overalls, on tractors. Even these fields had not been ignored by the war veterans. On the edge, or in a couple of cases, right in the middle of thriving tobacco lands, would be a broken-down shack. Our journey covered only a fraction of Zimbabwe's farming land but I knew this picture was the same all over the country. If we had seen "liberated" farms bursting with maize or vegetables, it would all have seemed almost worthwhile.

That is not what we saw.

The war veterans had claimed the farms and were unable or unwilling to tend them. Perhaps they did not have the resources, or perhaps they simply did not care. Perhaps they wanted the land so that they could say "We have won, we have chased the whites away, we have taken back what they stole from our ancestors".

As we drove slowly through Rusape town, we sensed the tense and angry atmosphere. On every street were police reservists, all carrying AK rifles. The entire town was at a standstill, every road lined with cars queuing for petrol and diesel. At the tiny filling station of Nyazura Bridge, ten kilometres from Rusape and seemingly in the middle of nowhere, there was also a very long line of vehicles waiting for fuel. At the pump head an angry mob had gathered. Something had happened because there were riot police with batons and facemasks. We drove on. A feeling of disorientation and confusion filled my senses. This is not the country I know and love. These scenes of angry mobs, of armed police, of endless fuel queues do not happen in Zimbabwe. In Nigeria perhaps, or the Congo, but in Zimbabwe? My God, what is happening to us? How can we ever sort this out?

On our gradual ascent into the mountains surrounding Mutare, the picture was slightly different. Here stood the orchards of peach, plum, apple and other fruit trees. The soil here was not suitable for maize but the war veterans wanted this land too—their huts were there, their rags and bags tied onto the fences. Climbing up Christmas Pass, we entered Mutare on its main road, which is called Robert Mugabe Avenue. We zigzagged along this highway, dodging the potholes, passing vandalized public telephone booths, the verges decorated with plastic bags and wind-blown litter caught in the waist high, uncut grass. On every street corner was a woman, her children playing under her feet, selling her wares from a rickety table: bags of popcorn, frozen drinks, bananas, tomatoes. On every square of land that didn't have a house on it was maize, not the yellowing little squares we had seen in the middle of vast fields, but enormous green plants, keenly tended by city dwellers. The maize was everywhere we looked: alongside the railway line, on the edges of silted rivers, under trees, on anthills. There were no fuel queues here—the pumps were all empty. There was no fuel here. We turned and headed out of the town and followed the rusting road signs, still decorated with political slogans, towards the Birchenough Bridge road. Leaving the built-up suburbs of the city of Mutare, to our astonishment, we saw the unbelievable squalor that stands alongside the main highway. A huge plastic town sprawled along the roadside, looking like a child's gaudy drawing. I could hardly believe that people lived there, operated their businesses from there, under these multi-coloured plastic stalls. Stalls in which you could buy anything from a wardrobe to clothing, from a red Dralon lounge suite to a cabbage. Stalls whose owners live day and night, week in week out, right next to the goods they sell because this overcrowded city has not managed to fulfil the promise of "Housing for all by the year 2000". Mutare, like Marondera has grown massively in the past two decades but the services have not grown in proportion. I turned in my seat to read the big signboard: "Welcome to Mutare: the jewel of the east".

Outside the car the temperature rose as we began our descent into the lowveld. I handed out warm cold drinks and we drank as we drove. There was nowhere we felt we wanted to stop. The lay-byes in the year 2000 were not attractive. In most of them the big shady trees had been reduced to scarred shadows of their former glory, branches hacked off for firewood. In almost all of them the concrete tables had either gone altogether or were in pieces; the benches underneath were the same. In all of them the hanging, wire dustbins were not emptied anymore and the litter lay piled up in smelly, fly-laden heaps. From the car window, the view now was of the vast communal lands that lie in the valleys below Mutare. These are overcrowded villages where people struggle to survive on over-grazed land where the trees have all gone and only thorny shrubs offer small patches of shade for the desperately thin cattle. These people have no title deeds for their land in the communal areas, no collateral to offer to a bank manager, no money to develop, no incentive to improve. Here are the very people we would expect to see tilling the empty "liberated" fields we had so recently passed. The truth is that neither here nor on liberated land, would they ever be given title deeds. Everyone knows it.

The houses in these communal lands were from another era. Muddied, cracked walls, roofs covered with pieces of rusty tin held down by dozens of stones and rocks. Windows covered with yellow fertilizer bags; fences made of old car fenders. The occupants look tired, hot and ragged. Women in wafer-thin dresses carry mounds of firewood on their heads and barefooted children push decrepit wheelbarrows filled with water containers. And the men sit crowded on the verandas of the bottle stores, their hands curled around the brown plastic scuds, the beer whose price the minister of Finance had reduced in his new budget. Every second store was a bottle store: "Come Again Bottle Store", "The Castle Cannibal", "The Blue Desert Bottle Store", "Star Bar". The hanging road sign, one post missing, told of an approaching health facility. We drove slowly past the clinic, its peeling, faded paint proclaiming another broken promise: Health for all by the year 2000. On the veranda of the clinic one bench leans against the wall with at least 20 people on it. The rest are on the floor, some on the ground, waiting to be seen by a nurse who has only Chloroquin and Paracetemol and perhaps, if they are lucky, a few strips of contraceptive pills. As in Marondera, she has no disposable gloves, no bandages, no medicine for diarrhoea or vomiting, no condoms, nothing to ease the suffering of her patients. But tiredly, faithfully, she sees each patient, faithfully records the problem in their little exercise book, faithfully refers them to the nearest hospital, 40 kilometres away in Mutare.

Through every city and town we pass there are hordes of street children. The survivors, the ones whose parents have died of Aids, the ones who have never seen the inside of a classroom, the ones who spend their days begging and their nights huddled under cardboard boxes in drains or shop doorways. The children who are the same age as my son and who have neither heard of nor seen the benefits of Health, Housing and Education for all by the year 2000. The only thing they saw at the end of the year 2000 was what I too saw, headlines in a newspaper. Finally, the Ministry of Health admits that 2,000 people a week are now dying of Aids in Zimbabwe.

Across the country war veterans are squabbling over little squares of land they say was stolen by the whites from their ancestors while 2000 of their own children die of Aids every week. I wonder if the war veterans cannot see what they are doing to their own people, their brothers and sisters, aunts and uncles, sons and daughters. I wonder if they know of the massive new squatter camps forming all over the country, filling daily with farm workers who have lost everything in this insane land grab. I wonder if they have not read about what is happening at Chiwiti, in the Makonde communal area. I wonder if they have visited the 40,000 farm workers now squatting there. Have they seen how those former workers are coping with unemployment, hunger and destitution? Are the war veterans not aware that they have been used for political purposes? Do they care? Perhaps they do. Perhaps they just have a different view from their window.

I, and many hundreds of other white farmers, may have lost everything in this new so-called Agrarian Revolution. I may have been brought to my knees, may have been made to pay for the sins of my ancestors, may have been made to feel shame at the colour of my skin. But will my loss benefit all these struggling, suffering people? Will my loss be their gain? Or will all these people, like me shed hot African tears?

I did not want to look out of the window any more. I closed my eyes and thought of everything that had happened in Zimbabwe in the three short months since we had left our farm. There was so much, so very much.

Our personal nightmare was over but what had begun in February 2000 as a land question affecting only a tiny white minority, had blazed across the entire country, spreading like an uncontrolled bushfire to every facet of Zimbabwean life.

October 2000
- 4th October: Armed police raid Capital Radio studios in Harare, confiscate equipment, dismantle aerials and search shareholders' homes. (*Daily News*).
- 5th October: European Union imposes an arms embargo on Zimbabwe. (*Financial Gazette*).
- 6th October: Government gazettes new broadcasting regulations using Presidential Powers to ensure that 75 percent of all programming should have Zimbabwean content. Regulations exempt state-owned ZBC and ZTV. (*Zimbabwe Independent*).
- 6th October: 77 farms gazetted for compulsory acquisition. (*Herald*).
- 6th October: A Karoi court messenger is given a death threat after serving eviction notices on squatters and war veterans. (CFU report).
- 6th October: Macheke farmer, Alan Don, is attacked by war veterans. He is hospitalized with head injuries, a gunshot wound in his leg, three broken teeth, extracted fingernails, ruptured eardrum and severe bruising. (*Daily News*).
- 6th October: President Mugabe proclaims an amnesty for political prisoners. Clemency Order No 1 of 2000 grants a free pardon to

every person liable to prosecution for politically motivated crimes committed between 1st January and 31st July 2000. (*Daily News*).

- 12th October: Noczim (National Oil Company of Zimbabwe) debt to suppliers rises to Z$11 billion. (*Financial Gazette*).
- 16th October: Karoi's Superintendent Mabunda is transferred to Harare after repeated accusations of biased policing. (CFU report).
- 16th October: The war veteran accused of murdering opposition supporters in Kariba during the elections is released on the grounds of "insufficient evidence". The war veteran proceeds to a farm in Karoi, evicts the owners and moves into the homestead. The owner, Mr Slim Botha, dies of a heart attack days after being forced off his property. (CFU report).
- 17th October: Bread riots break out in Harare after a 30 percent price rise is implemented. (*Daily News*).
- 18th October: Bread riots spread to more suburbs in Harare. (*Daily News*).
- 18th October: Armed police assault an opposition member of parliament and his family accusing them of inciting food riots. (*Daily News*).
- 18th October: Army and police assault four South African journalists covering the food riots. Forced to lie on the ground, the four are beaten with batons and electric cables. (*Daily News*).
- 19th October: A 14-year-old schoolboy is hospitalized with two bullets in his ankle after being shot by riot police in the aftermath of the bread riots. (*Daily News*).
- 19th October: The Matabeleland Chamber of Industries states that 50 percent of its members face closure at the end of the year owing to the harsh economic climate. Analysts estimate 200,000 jobs will be lost. (*Financial Gazette*).
- 20th October: The Harare High Court orders that Zanu PF is not to disburse $30 million it obtained under the Political Parties Finance Act. The money should by law be given to the opposition. (*Daily News*).
- 20th October: 108 farms are gazetted for compulsory acquisition. (*Herald*).
- 20th October: A maize shortage is imminent as planting is down by 40 – 60 percent. (*Zimbabwe Independent*).
- 22nd October: Bindura farm manager, Keith McGaw, is severely assaulted by war veterans. Beaten with axes, pick handles and sticks, Mr McGaw has a fractured skull requiring 18 stitches and widespread bruising and lacerations. (CFU report).

- 23rd October: President Mugabe refers to white Zimbabweans as "cheats" and "crooks" in a BBC radio programme. (*Standard*).
- 23rd October: On farms in Trelawney and Darwendale, convoys of government vehicles arrive and start distributing plots of land on unlisted properties. On one farm a convoy of 14 vehicles arrives, including army, air force, police and other government vehicles. (CFU report).
- 24th October: Victims of political violence are forced to flee their homes after being harassed and threatened by their assailants, pardoned by President Mugabe. (*Daily News*).
- 24th October: Food riots in Mutare. 40 youths arrested. (*Daily News*).
- 26th October: The opposition tables a motion in parliament to impeach President Mugabe. (*Daily News*).
- 26th October: South African President Thabo Mbeki publicly condemns Zimbabwe's land grab for the first time. (*Daily News*).
- 26th October: President Mugabe threatens to revoke the policy of reconciliation and prosecute whites for war crimes during the fight for Independence. (*Financial Gazette*).
- 30th October: Macheke farmer, Herman van Duren, is hospitalized with head wounds after being attacked and robbed by armed assailants. (CFU report).
- 30th October: An air force helicopter circles tobacco seed beds on a farm in Norton to check that the owners had complied with their order not to plant. (CFU report).
- 30th October: 97 prisoners have now been released under the Presidential Amnesty. 89 of the beneficiaries had already been convicted and were serving sentences in prison. (*Daily News*).
- 31st October: Shamva farmer, Guy French, and five of his workers are attacked by war veterans with sticks and nail-studded clubs when they try to plant their ploughed field. Mr French is hospitalized with severe concussion, bruising and lacerations; his workers are admitted to Shamva Hospital.

November 2000
- 1st November: Fuel prices increase for the second time in three months. (*Daily News*).
- 1st November: Information Minister, Jonathan Moyo, calls for the removal of Chief Justice Anthony Gubbay. (*Financial Gazette*).
- 1st November: Karoi's Superintendent Mabunda returns to Karoi and visits all war veterans' bases on farms in the area. Increased violations are reported throughout the area that weekend including

work stoppages, threats and a bull slaughtered. Farmers are laughed at by police in Karoi when they report the incidences. (CFU report).

- 6th November: University of Zimbabwe students hold a demonstration in support of striking lecturers. Riot police arrive and shoot tear-gas throughout the campus including in the hostels and UZ Clinic. Students are forced off the campus and the institution closes the following morning. (*Daily News*).
- 6th November: A High Court Judge in Harare reserves judgement in the fraud case against Chenjerai Hunzvi. Hunzvi, accused of fabricating medical records, claimed a 118 percent disability from the War Victims' Compensation Fund. (*Daily News*).
- 8th November: The continuing illegal movement of cattle from communal to commercial farms by war veterans leads to an outbreak of anthrax in Makoni North. Two people and 32 cattle die. (*Daily News*).
- 9th November: Z$25 million worth of export beef is found rotten at the CSC factory in Gweru because of a faulty vacuum-packaging machine. (*Financial Gazette*).
- 10th November: The Supreme Court signs an Order by Consent declaring Fast-Track Resettlement unlawful. The commissioner of police is ordered to remove all squatters from farms that have been "fast-tracked". (CFU report).
- 12th November: Municipal police in Mutare shoot and kill a 13-month-old baby whilst chasing unlicensed vendors at a bus stop. (*Daily News*).
- 13th November: Mazoe farmer, Robin Marshall, in the presence of police, is attacked by war veterans and hospitalized with head injuries. (*Daily News*).
- 14th November: War veterans begin rebuilding shacks on farms near Harare. (*Daily News*).
- 17th November: President Mugabe's sister, Sabina, arrives at a farm in Norton in a Mercedes. She instructs 40 villagers to allocate land to themselves on a commercial farm that produces almost half of the country's seed maize. (*Daily News*).
- 17th November: 23 farms are gazetted for compulsory acquisition. (*Herald*).
- 17th November: Finance Minister Simba Makoni presents the 2001 budget to parliament. Income and corporate taxes are reduced as is duty on beer and bicycles. (*Daily News*).
- 21st November: Anthrax spreads to Makonde where three pigs and 17 cattle die and six people are hospitalized after eating contaminated meat. (*Daily News*).

- 21st November: Police fire live bullets at students protesting over catering at Hillside Teachers' Training College in Bulawayo. (*Daily News*).
- 21st November: High Court Judge Chidyuasiku issues a Provisional Order preventing implementation of the Supreme Court Order to remove "fast-tracked" squatters. (*Daily News*).
- 23rd November: Leading pharmaceutical company, Johnson and Johnson, relocate their manufacturing division to South Africa owing to continuing economic instability. (*Daily News*).
- 24th November: The Supreme Court overrules the High Court's Provisional Order saying it has no jurisdiction in the matter. The original Supreme Court Order stands. (CFU report and *Daily News*).
- 27th November: Zanu PF wins the Marondera West by-election. The campaign was violent with numerous clashes and the death of one man. Out of 37,000 registered voters, only 12,000 go to the polls. (*Zimbabwe Independent*).
- 27th November: Army and police are put on full alert to deter mass action threatened by the opposition. (*Daily News*).
- 28th November: Nigeria's President Obasanjo says that whilst he is willing to be a mediator in Zimbabwe's land crisis, the laws of the country must be followed. (*Daily News*).
- 30th November: Minister of Information, Jonathan Moyo says government will not be removing squatters and war veterans from farms grabbed during "fast-track" resettlement. Minister Moyo says the Supreme Court Order is not a blanket eviction notice and that the government has not been acting unlawfully. (*Daily News*).
- 30th November: Farmers in Bindura name three top government officials (two of whom are government ministers) involved in master-minding violence in the area. (*Financial Gazette*).
- 30th November: The CZI (Confederation of Zimbabwe Industries) announces that 23 percent of local manufacturing companies are to disinvest from Zimbabwe owing to economic decline. (*Financial Gazette*).
- 30th November: Telephone calls from Zimbabwe to Britain may be barred because the local PTC has failed to service its debt of Z$870 million to British Telecom. (*Financial Gazette*).

December 2000
- 1st December: Bert Gardener, a Chinoyi farmer in his mid seventies is attacked in bed where his assailants attempt to strangle and suffocate him. (CFU report).

- 5th December: The state withdraws all charges against the war veteran suspected of murdering Macheke farmer David Stevens. According to the public prosecutor, charges are withdrawn owing to "lack of evidence". (*Daily News*).
- 6th December: A Nyabira farmer is abducted by war veterans and forced to drive to State House for an audience with President Mugabe. Guards at State House refuse the war veterans entry and police are called in to defuse the situation. (*Daily News*).
- 8th December: The Electoral Modification Act is promulgated. This Act nullifies all electoral petitions filed by the MDC challenging the result of the June election in 40 constituencies. (*Daily News*).
- 11th December: Ndabaningi Sithole, born in 1920 in Nyamandhlovu, dies aged 80. Sithole, a veteran nationalist, was the founder and president of Zanu with Robert Mugabe as secretary general.
- 12th December: Henry Elsworth aged 70, a former MP in both the Smith and Mugabe governments, is shot dead in an ambush on his farm. Mr Elsworth's son, Ian, is shot five times in the same incident and rushed to hospital. (*Financial Gazette*).
- 14th December: High Court Judges confirm that they have been informed that war veterans intend to attack them in their homes. The Police Protection Unit says they are on full alert. (*Daily News*).
- 14th December: A Karoi farmer is attacked by 40 war veterans and receives severe bruising. (CFU report).
- 14th December: The MDC files an urgent application with the Supreme Court challenging the Electoral Modification Act. (*Daily News*).
- 15th December: Addressing delegates to the annual Zanu PF congress, President Mugabe accuses whites of destroying the economy. He says, 'Our party must continue to strike fear in the heart of the white man. They must tremble …'(*Daily News*).
- 15th December: The anthrax outbreak in Makonde spreads. Thirteen people are hospitalized and 21 cattle have died. (*Daily News*).
- 15th December: The French Ambassador to Zimbabwe announces that France will not fund Zimbabwe's land reform programme as it is not being done within the law. (*Daily News*).
- 16th December: Police in Harare shoot and kill a woman vegetable vendor whilst chasing a bus driver. (*Daily News*).
- 16th December: A policeman is stabbed and killed by people angered at the shooting of a vegetable vendor. Riot police use tear-gas to control mobs that stone and burn police vehicles. (*Daily News*).
- 18th December: Chenjerai Hunzvi threatens to "deal with" police whom he accuses of not supporting land resettlement. (*Daily News*).

- 18th December: A farmer in Bulawayo receives a written death threat from war veterans. The letter refers to the murder in April of farmer Martin Olds and reads: "Your friend Martin was our breakfast for Independence Day, so you are going to be our breakfast for Christmas". (*Daily News*).
- 19th December: 50 people are injured in political violence in Bikita ahead of parliamentary by-elections to be held in three weeks' time. (*Daily News*).
- 19th December: Zanu PF Politiburo announces that Ndabaningi Sithole (founder of Zanu in 1963) is not to be given hero status and will not be buried at Heroes Acre. (*Herald*).
- 19th December: Anthrax spreads to Mashonaland East. Five cattle die in Chiota. (CFU report).
- 20th December: A Harare South farmer is assaulted by war veterans, beaten with chains and bitten. (CFU report).
- 21st December: President Mugabe is heckled and booed in parliament as he makes his annual State of the Nation address. (*Daily News*).
- 21st December: The United Nations Development Programme administrator, Mark Mallock Brown, submits his report on land reform to the government. The UN restates its position that the government should drop the "fast-track" resettlement programme. (*Zimbabwe Independent*).
- 21st December: The Supreme Court declares that the rule of law has been persistently violated in commercial farming areas and that the people in those areas have suffered discrimination in contravention of the constitution. The Court further states that the people in those areas have been denied the protection of the law and had their rights of assembly and association infringed. The Court orders the minister of Home Affairs and the commissioner of police to restore the rule of law in commercial farming areas by no later than July 1st 2001. (CFU report).

Source list

Books

Austin, Reg (1975) *Racism and apartheid in Southern Africa*. Paris: Unesco Press.

Bhebe, N. & Ranger, T. (1995) *Society in Zimbabwe's liberation war Vol 2* Harare: University of Zimbabwe Publications.

Frederikse, Julie (1982) *None but ourselves – masses vs media in the making of Zimbabwe*. Harare: Zimbabwe Publishing House.

McLaughlin, Janice (1996) *On the frontline*. Harare: Baobab Books.

Mitchell, Diana (1980) *Who's who. African nationalist leaders in Zimbabwe*. Harare: Books of Rhodesia.

Loney, Martin (1975) *Racism and imperial response*. London: Penguin Books.

Martin, David & Johnson, Phyllis (1981) *The Struggle for Zimbabwe*. Johannesburg: Ravan Press.

Newspapers and other printed publications

Amani Trust, Zimbabwe.

Commercial Farmers' Union: Farm invasions and security reports, Zimbabwe.

Daily News Online, Zimbabwe.

Daily News, Zimbabwe.

Daily Telegraph Online, UK.

Farmer Magazine, Zimbabwe.

Financial Gazette, Zimbabwe.

Helen Suzman Foundation, South Africa.

Herald, Zimbabwe.

Mail and Guardian, South Africa.

Standard, Zimbabwe.

Sunday Times Online, UK.

Tobacco News, Zimbabwe.

Washington Post Online, USA.

Zimbabwe Independent, Zimbabwe.

Broadcast media
BBC World Television: News.

BBC World Television: Hardtalk.

BBC World Television: Simpson's World.

CNN Television.

SABC Africa Television: News.

SKY Television: News.

ZBC Television.